A Memoir of Felix Neff, Pastor of the High Alps
by William Stephen Gilly

Address:
HardPress
8345 NW 66TH ST #2561
MIAMI FL 33166-2626
USA
Email: info@hardpress.net

A

MEMOIR

OF

FELIX NEFF,

PASTOR OF THE HIGH ALPS;

AND OF

HIS LABOURS AMONG THE FRENCH PROTESTANTS

OF DAUPHINÉ,

A REMNANT OF THE PRIMITIVE CHRISTIANS OF GAUL.

BY

WILLIAM STEPHEN GILLY, D.D.

PREBENDARY OF DURHAM, AND VICAR OF NORHAM.

" There are very few habitations in Dormilleuse which are not liable to be swept away, for there is not a spot, in this narrow corner of the Valley of Fressinière, which can be considered absolutely safe.   But terrible as the situation of the natives is, they owe to it their religious, and perhaps their physical existence.   If their country had been more secure, and more accessible, they would have been exterminated, like the inhabitants of Val Louise."—NEFF's JOURNAL.

THIRD EDITION.

LONDON:

PRINTED FOR J. G. & F. RIVINGTON,

ST. PAUL'S CHURCH YARD,

AND WATERLOO PLACE, PALL MALL.

LONDON:
GILBERT & RIVINGTON, PRINTERS,
ST. JOHN'S SQUARE.

PREFACE

THE SECOND EDITION.

———

THE rapid circulation of the first edition of this Memoir has been such, as to confirm the opinion of those, who are persuaded that biography, and especially religious biography, is one of the most attractive departments in literature. It may also be rendered one of the most instructive, for example speaks louder than precept: and when history and truth are accompanied by familiar illustrations, and virtue and piety are delineated by the portraits of those who have moved amongst us, they produce a lasting effect upon the reader. Upon this principle, when a faithful picture is drawn of that which is holy and good in real life, it never fails to be interesting. And whenever the question is asked of an experienced adviser, what kind of book is likely to make an impression upon the youthful mind, which requires to be moulded to piety, or upon the hardened heart, which requires to be softened?—the most frequent answer is—Christian Biography.

After the perusal of the Ordination Service of the Church of England, or of such precious volumes as Baxter's Reformed Pastor, Burnet's Pastoral Care, and Bridge's Christian Ministry, who does not take delight in reading the memoir of some eminent clergyman, in whose life and conversation every precept of devotedness to the service of the Gospel, there inculcated, has been practically exemplified?

It was in expectation of a favourable reception of a narrative of this sort, and in humble reliance upon the blessing of God, which has been often vouchsafed to such works, that I first determined to make the labours of Felix Neff known to English readers, and to show that the Protestant Churches abroad are still adding to the Noble Army of Martyrs, who praise the Lord as much by their patient witness to his grace, as the confessors of old who suffered for his name's sake.

I was also assured in my own mind, that while many would be stirred up to emulation, by contemplating the character of a minister of the Church, contemporary with themselves, who in his faith and conduct, and meekness, and self-denial, has realized as lovely a picture of a servant of Christ, as any of the ancient examples handed down to notice, others would take an interest in tracing the footsteps of this Apostle of the nineteenth century, among the remains of the primitive Christians of the Alps. It was not my happiness to have a personal knowledge of Felix Neff, but I have been gratified by learning from those, who did enjoy this privilege, that his merits and labours of love have not been overstated by me.

In the new form under which the Memoir is now presented to the public, some additional anecdotes will be found, and a few alterations in the arrangement of the materials, such, as the transposition of the historical sketch of the Alpine congregations of France (and of their line of succession from the Primitive Churches of Gaul) from the Introduction to a chapter in the body of the work, where it will be in immediate connection with the course of the Narrative. The size and price of the volume have also been considerably diminished, to increase the prospect of its more extended circulation.

I have had many communications announcing that the publication has not been unproductive of good. Among the most valuable testimonies to this effect, are the following, received from clergymen who have already distinguished themselves as able ministers of the word, and diligent labourers in the vineyard. " Neff delights and humbles me, may he also stimulate and improve me." " The apostolic Neff makes me feel my grievous inferiority." " The work will probably

make many, as it has certainly made me, not a
little ashamed of their own ministerial defects."

These testimonies to the usefulness of the
Memoir, lead me to hope, that it will continue to
excite many of my brethren not only to greater
activity, but also to greater condescension to the
wants of the ignorant, and of the younger portion of their flocks.

May the great Head of the Church still be
pleased to bless this, and every similar record of
the labours of his faithful servants, to the honour
of his holy name, and the extension of his kingdom in Jesus Christ.

Norham,
January 9, 1833.

PREFACE

TO

THE THIRD EDITION.

A BOOK has recently been published under the title of " Memorials of Felix Neff, the Alpine Pastor, by T. S. Ellerby." In his preface Mr. Ellerby has stated, as his reason for the publication of his Volume, that my Memoir of Neff " appeared to him to be extremely defective, not merely with regard to some of the important occurrences in the Life of Neff, but more especially as to those views of Theology, to the influence of which, there can be no doubt, we owe much of that ardent zeal, and those various and incessant labours, by which the Pastor of the Higher Alps was so eminently distinguished."

With regard to the first objection, I have already expressed my regret, in the former editions, at not having been able to fill up those gaps in the narrative, which leave it incomplete; and I should be thankful for any information which would enable me to supply the deficiency. I have made many attempts to obtain additional materials, and in answer to a letter which I wrote to a friend of Neff's family, last month, " Je vous promets," says my correspondent, "que je ne retournerai point à la ville sans voir la mère de Neff, et sans faire en sorte qu'on vous envoye de nouveaux documens, s'il en est qui vaillent d'être publiés."

When I learnt that Mr. Ellerby's reasons for publishing his " Memorials" were, that my account was " defective" and " unsatisfactory," I naturally began to hope that I should find much in his pages, which would be new to me, and which would render the history of Neff more complete.   But I was presently disappointed, by casting my eye over the following sentence in Mr. Ellerby's introductory remarks.   " It will be easily seen, that to both works the principal source of information has been the same, viz., ' Notice sur Felix Neff,' published at Geneva in 1831."   And here I must enter a protest.   The manuscript Journals of Neff entrusted to me in 1830, " these form the principal source from which the substance of my Memoir is drawn," as I have distinctly stated in p. 11. First Edition, and p. 13. Second Edition, and not the " Notice sur Felix Neff," printed at Geneva in 1831.

Had Mr. Ellerby enjoyed the same advantages with myself of having visited the scenes of Neff's labours, and of being acquainted with persons and places mentioned in the narrative, he would not have fallen into such mistakes as these.

" Amongst whom was Monsieur Antoine Blanc, *Vaudois Pastor*, from the valleys of Piedmont, who had been invited by Neff to preach the dedication sermon," p. 224. Monsieur Antoine Blanc could not have been invited to preach, because he is not a pastor. His brother Andrè Blanc, the French Pastor of Mens, was not present on the occasion alluded to.

" On leaving La Tour, Neff proceeded, accompanied by M. Blanc, *through several of the Vaudois communes*, until they reached St. Jean," p. 232. St. Jean is the commune which lies immediately contiguous to La Tour; there are no intervening communes.

Mr. Ellerby's second objection is, that my Memoir is especially defective as to " views of theology," and in the religious character of the work. Mr. Ellerby is a Dissenter, and I am a Churchman, therefore, as a matter of course, he may fairly advance this objection, and I am so far from disputing with him on this ground, that I will merely remind him, that however much we may differ on other topics, we agree in one main point,—in our admiration of Neff. If his work, as coming from a Dissenter, is likely to give an extended circulation to the reminiscences of this excellent Alpine pastor, to make his labours more generally known, and to render him an object of imitation among a denomination of Christians, with whom I can have no influence, then I owe a debt of thanks to Mr. Ellerby, which I most gladly acknowledge, and in return, he is welcome to all the information which he has gathered from my pages, in the compilation of his book.

Perhaps some of my readers will indulge in a good-humoured smile, if I farther endeavour to vindicate the religious character of my Memoir, by suggesting that it cannot be very far from the right mark, since the only critics who, to my knowledge, have been severe upon it, have examined the work somewhat in the spirit of *Ultras.* For example, a Reviewer, in a Roman Catholic Journal, has signified his displeasure at some of my Protestant opinions; and another, in an article in the British Critic, thinks I go too far, and calls my " Anecdotes of death-bed scenes and conversions a little highly coloured, and not in very sober taste," and quarrels with my " Scripture phraseology ;" while Mr. Ellerby, on the other hand, complains that I do not go far enough, and animadverts on what he considers my low estimate of the value of prayer-meetings [1].

It has been my earnest desire to exhibit Neff in the character of a labourer in Jesus Christ, whom all, who profess and call themselves

---

[1] I refer the reader to the whole of Chapter VII., and to page 264 of this Memoir, and there he will find the subject of prayer meetings fully discussed.

Christians, might rejoice to call their brother in the Lord. With this view, I do not think so much of contending to what class of Christians Neff belonged, as of showing that all classes may admire him, and regard him as an example. In this I hope to do the cause of religion a service, and I am encouraged by the assurances of many pious and judicious persons, that hitherto I have succeeded.

An intimate friend of Neff has expressed himself thus on this subject. " Certainement votre livre a fait beaucoup de bien. Dieu vous continue son secours, mon cher frère, et bénisse en toute chose l'œuvre de vos mains ! Il me semble, que ses heureux resultâts sont à la fois pour vous de la part du Seigneur un encouragement, et une sommation pour que vos travaux continuent à faire connoître l'Evangile, soit dans ses principes, soit dans ses actions."

Norham,
July 15, 1833.

CONTENTS.

CHAPTER I.

PAGE

Introductory Remarks—Vestiges of the Primitive Christians—The Author's first acquaintance with the Labours of Neff—Extract from a Letter of Neff—The Author's Journey to the Scene of Neff's Labours—Alpine Churches of France 1

CHAPTER II.

Neff's Birth and Education—His first Tastes and Occupation—His Military Career—Leaves the Army and becomes a Probationer for Holy Orders—Exercises the Functions of a Probationer in the Swiss Cantons . . . 15

CHAPTER III.

Neff goes to France to officiate at Grenoble and Mens—His Observations on National Churches—The Nature of his Charge at Mens—His laborious Duties—Remarks on the Effects produced by Sacred Music—Neff's Method with his Catechumens 23

CHAPTER IV.

PAGE

Neff's difficulties as to Ordination—His reasons for not being ordained by the Genevan Clergy—Goes to England for his Diploma—His return to France and reception at Mens—His nomination as Pastor of the High Alps—His first visits to the mountain hamlets of his parish 55

CHAPTER V.

Synoptical View of the Alpine Churches of France—I. Situation of this Region of the Alps—De Thou's Description of it—II. Evidence that the Alpine Protestant Congregations of Dauphiné, are the remains of the Primitive Christians of Gaul 78

CHAPTER VI.

Further Description of the Department of the High Alps—Restitution of Protestant rights—Organization of Reformed Churches of France—Nature and extent of Neff's pastoral charge—Henry Oberlin—Description of the Valleys of Fressinière and Queyras, and of Neff's parish—The pass of the Guil—Neff at Arvieux, and in his Presbytery at La Chalp—His progress through his parish—San Veran—Pierre Grosse—Fousillarde—The Pastor's manifold duties—Neff's winter journey to Val Fressinière — Palons — The Rimasse—Dormilleuse—Neff's description of Dormilleuse, and of the condition in which he found the remains of the primitive Christians there—His perilous labours there 106

CHAPTER VII.

Neff organizes Réunions, or Prayer-meetings—His opinion of the necessity of such meetings—Neff's last exhortation to his flock on the subject—His exhortations

PAGE

examined—An inquiry into the effects and utility of Prayer-meetings—The sentiments of Thomas Scott not in favour of them—Those of Bishop Heber the same—Observations on Family Worship 146

CHAPTER VIII.

Neff at Champsaur—His difficulties there—From Champsaur to Val Fressinière—His Employments from break of day to midnight—His account of the Consecration of the new Church of Violins—His discussion with a Vaudois Pastor—Wretched condition of the Natives of Val Fressinière—An affecting Incident—Neff institutes associations of the Bible and Missionary Societies among his Alpines—Passage of the Col d'Orsière—Progress of his Catechumens at Champsaur—Laments over the levity of some of his Flock—Prevents the appointment of an unworthy Pastor at Champsaur 157

CHAPTER IX.

Neff's method and good understanding with the Roman Catholics—His interview with a Romish Priest—A family sketch—The convert of Arvieux—A death-bed scene—The Mission—Controversies—Anecdote—The Curé—Palons—The shepherdess Mariette 185

CHAPTER X.

Neff's self-denial—Reminiscences in Val Fressinière and Val Queyras—The Alpine Pastor's duties and mode of life—Passion week in Dormilleuse and Val Fressinière—Captain Cotton's Account of an Excursion with Neff . . 214

CHAPTER XI.

Neff's extraordinary influence over his Flock—How obtained—His improvements introduced into the condition

PAGE

of the Alpines—Their wretched state previously to his arrival—Proposes to himself the example of Oberlin—The Aqueduct—The Christian Advocate—Neff a teacher of Agriculture—Neff at the Fair of St. Crepin—Observations 242

CHAPTER XII.

Neff's caution in the choice of his Catechists—Neff in his schools—Works at the building of a school-room in Dormilleuse—Establishes and conducts a Normal School for the training of catechists and schoolmasters—The difficulties of this undertaking—The farewell repast—Neff's remarks on the characters of the young men of his adult school, and on the effects produced by it—Observations on the state of public instruction in France 262

CHAPTER XIII.

Neff's strength fails—Winter horrors of Dormilleuse—Neff obliged to return to Switzerland—Parting Scenes—Neff goes to the baths of Plombières—His last address to his Alpine flock—His sufferings and patience—His last hours—His death at Geneva 297

CHAPTER XIV.

Review of Neff's character—Its value as an example—His practical wisdom and usefulness—His prudence and caution—His gentleness of spirit—His conciliating manners—Two remarkable traits—Neff compared with Bernard Gilpin, George Herbert, Oberlin, and Henry Martyn—Testimonies to Neff's services 326

Postscript, with additional Anecdotes of Neff 347

A

MEMOIR OF FELIX NEFF,

&c.

CHAPTER I.

INTRODUCTORY REMARKS—VESTIGES OF THE PRIMITIVE
CHRISTIANS—THE AUTHOR'S FIRST ACQUAINTANCE WITH
THE LABOURS OF NEFF—EXTRACT FROM A LETTER OF
NEFF—THE AUTHOR'S JOURNEY TO THE SCENE OF NEFF'S
LABOURS—ALPINE CHURCHES OF FRANCE.

WHEN a volume is sent from the press, containing memorials of persons and places unknown to the world, and the author claims the attention not only of those, who read for amusement principally, but also of the learned and the reflecting, he must expect some such questions as these to be asked: Upon what documents are these statements founded? From what original papers are these memoirs composed? How came the author acquainted with scenes and people, whose history he alleges to be of moment to society at large, but whose names are perfectly new to us? How has he had access to records, which we did

B

not know to be in existence? I hope to answer these inquiries satisfactorily, and to show that those, who have extended their rambles to some of the obscurest corners of civilized Europe, or who have been poring over the most neglected, dull, and wearisome pages of writers and chroniclers of days long since, may bring facts to light which had escaped notice, and may illustrate some of the most important subjects in history[1].

It has been my good fortune to have had op-

[1] I am greatly indebted to Mr. Faber, for a most interesting example of the important discoveries, which may be made by a patient investigation of the pages of ancient Christian writers. That profound theologian had been reading my observations, in the first edition of this Memoir, and in my Waldensian Researches, on the Antiquity of the Alpine Churches, and had been putting the justice of my remarks to the proof, by following up the inquiries which I suggested. In the course of his examination, he turned to Jerome's account of Vigilantius, a native of Aquitaine, in Gaul, and afterwards a presbyter of Barcelona, who in A.D. 397, had incurred the displeasure of those, who were beginning to introduce the corruptions into the Christian Church, which Rome has since sanctioned, by his censure of such errors. In this search, Mr. Faber found a passage, (Hieron. adv. Vigil. Epist. liii. Opera, vol. ii. p. 158.) in which Jerome states, that Vigilantius was then living in the vicinity of the Cottian Alps ; in a region, as the following page in Jerome shows, where religious opinions were entertained contrary to the prevailing dogmas of the day " Here, therefore," as Mr. Faber says, " only seventy years after the death of Pope Sylvester, we actually find a Church in the valleys of the Cottian Alps, the theological condition of which exactly corresponds with the accounts, handed down from generation to generation, among the Vallenses themselves : that is to say, we actually find a Church protesting

portunities of examining treasures of ecclesiastical history, in libraries rich in such stores; and the more I have read, the more I have felt convinced that the secluded glens of Piedmont are not the only retreats, where THE DESCENDANTS OF PRIMITIVE CHRISTIANS may be found. Under this term I mean to speak of persons who have inherited a Christianity, which the Church of Rome has not transmitted to them, and who, from father to son, have essentially preserved the mode of faith, and the form of discipline, which were received, when the Gospel was first planted in their land. I have discovered ample reason to believe, that there is scarcely a mountain region in our quarter of the globe, which is poor, and uninviting, and difficult of access, where the primitive faith, as it was preached by the earliest messengers of the truth, did not linger for many ages, after the Romish Hierarchy had established itself in the richer countries, and in the plains; and moreover, that there are still many mountain districts, where the population has continued Christian, from generation to generation, to the present hour; Christian, in non-conformity with the Church usurping the appellation, Catholic. It was the obscurity of these people and their

against the superstitions of the times, and openly differing from the bishops of Rome." This case of Vigilantius is the more extraordinary, considering that he was born in the region of the Albigenses, that he ministered in Spain, and also among the Vallenses of Italy.

non-intercourse with the world, during the period of almost general submission to the Romish yoke, which preserved them from corruption. Traces of such Churches in the Alps, in the Pyrenees, and in the Apennines, are clearly discernible in the Canons of Councils, and in the writings of most of the Romish annalists and controversialists of France, Spain, and Italy, up to the great epoch of Papal supremacy in the eleventh century; and the light, which modern researches are casting every year upon the history of nations, helps us to perceive, that the chain, which connects the Primitive and the Protestant Churches, is unbroken in various places, where it was supposed to have been dissevered.   There are very few readers, who do not imagine, that every vestige of the Albigensians was swept from the earth, during the crusades of Simon de Montford, and that the ancient Churches of Provence and Dauphiné, which formed the stock, on which the Reformed congregations[1] of the south of France were grafted in the sixteenth century, were utterly cut down, root and branch, after the revocation of the Edict of Nantes.   This, however, was not the case: some few remnants were spared; and families in the remote valleys of the Pyrenees, and of the

---

[1] Mr. Smedley *, in his " History of the Reformed Religion in France," does not seem to have been aware of the extent and influence of these branches of the primitive Church of Gaul.

* See note at the end of this Chapter.

Alps, have been permitted to experience the promise of the Redeemer, " where two or three are gathered together in my name, there am I in the midst of them." These have preserved the pure knowledge which their forefathers transmitted to them : and the Scriptural greeting, " Aquila and Priscilla salute you much in the Lord, with the Church, which is in their house," has oftentimes been passing from one secluded spot to another, when all were supposed to have been dragooned into the service of the Mass. And not only so, but in some few instances, whole communes, or parishes, have refused to submit, even outwardly, to the exactions of Romish usurpation.

The following pages record an example of this.

My belief, that the dreary wildernesses of the Alpine provinces of France might still be harbouring some of these descendants of the primitive Christians of Gaul, was confirmed by a letter which I received in the winter of 1826, from the Reverend Francis Cunningham, to whom the Protestant cause owes much. His frequent journeys, and correspondence, and his unlimited philanthropy, have put him in the way of knowing much of that which is going on among all that is truly Christian on the Continent. He was greatly instrumental in bringing the imperishable name of Oberlin under the notice of English readers, and to him my grateful thanks are due, for the first information I received of

Neff, and his Christian labours.   The letter, to
which I allude, contained the information that
Felix Neff, a young clergyman, was then toiling among a people, in Dauphiné, so poor, that
they had no means of providing salaries for ministers or schoolmasters : and so little favoured
by nature, that for seven months out of twelve,
their land lay buried in snow.   Two years afterwards Mr. Cunningham sent me a paper, drawn
up by Neff himself, describing the nature of his
charge, and some of the difficulties he had to
encounter.   I now present the substance of that
paper to the reader, as an explanatory preface
which will at once put him in possession of some
of the circumstances, which ought to render the
name of Neff himself, and of his Alpines, dear
to all who venerate heroic zeal, and devoted.be-
nevolence.

Extract from a Letter of Neff.

" In those dark times, when the Dragon, of
whom St. John speaks [1], made war with the
remnant of the seed, which kept the commandments of God, and have the testimony of Jesus
Christ, some of those, who escaped from the
edge of the sword, found a place of refuge
among the mountains.   It was then that the
most rugged valleys, of the French department
of the High Alps, were peopled by the remains

[1] Rev. xii. 17.

of those primitive Christians [1], who, after the example of Moses, when he preferred the reproach of Christ to the riches of Egypt, exchanged their fertile plains for a frightful wilderness. But fanaticism still pursued them, and neither their poverty, nor their innocence, nor the glaciers and precipices among which they dwelt, entirely protected them; and the caverns which served them for churches, were often washed with their blood. Previously to the Reformation, the Valley of Fressinière was the only place in France where they could maintain their ground, and even there, they were driven from the more productive lands, and were forced to retreat to the very foot of the glacier, where they built the village of Dormilleuse. This village, constructed like an eagle's nest, upon the side of a mountain, was the citadel where a small portion that was left established itself, and where the race has continued, without any intermixture with strangers, to the present day. Others took up their dwelling at the bottom of a deep glen, called La Combe, a rocky abyss, to which there is no exit, where the horizon is so bounded, that, for six months of the year, the rays of the sun never penetrate. These hamlets, exposed to avalanches and the falling of rocks, and buried under snow half the year, consist of hovels, of which some are without chimneys

[1] Les restes des Chrétiens Primitifs.

and glazed windows, and others have nothing but a miserable kitchen, and a stable, which is seldom cleaned out more than once a year, and where the inhabitants spend the greater part of the winter with their cattle, for the sake of the warmth.   The rocks, by which they are enclosed, are so barren, and the climate is so severe, that there is no knowing how these poor Alpines, with all their simplicity and temperance, contrive to subsist.   Their few sterile fields hang over precipices, and are covered, in places, with enormous blocks of granite, which have rolled from the cliffs above. Some seasons even rye will not ripen there. The pasturages are, many of them, inaccessible to cattle, and scarcely safe for sheep.   Such wretched soil cannot be expected to yield any thing more than what will barely sustain life, and pay the taxes, which, owing to the unfeeling negligence of the inspectors, are too often levied without proper consideration for the unproductiveness of the land.   The clothing of these poor creatures is made of coarse wool, which they dress and weave themselves.   Their principal food is unsifted rye; this they bake into cakes in the autumn, so as to last the whole year.

" The revocation of the Edict of Nantes, in 1686, deprived them of their ministers, and we may judge what their condition must have been for many years; but still there was not a total famine of the Word among them. They met together to read the Bible and to sing psalms; and although they had an ancient church in Dormilleuse, they were building a second in La Combe, which was not finished when I first arrived there. Such was their situation when Providence directed me to their valleys in 1823. They received me most gladly; they attended my preaching with eagerness, and gave themselves up to my guidance in all that I undertook for their improvement. The limits of this short notice will not permit me to enter into any detail of my proceedings, during the three years and a half that I remained with them. I will merely state that my instructions have not been unproductive of good : that many young men have been put in the way of opening schools during the winter; that the Sunday-schools have been frequented by adults, who could not profit by the lessons given in the day-schools open to younger persons. Up to this period the girls and the women had been almost entirely neglected. With the assistance of subscriptions from foreigners, one school-room has been built, and another is in preparation. Several of the inhabitants have shown a strong inclination to take advantage of the information, which I have given them in agriculture and architecture, and in the principles of some of the useful sciences, which hitherto were utterly unknown to them. I have distributed many Bibles, New Testa-

ments, and other books of piety among them,
which I have been pleased to find, were not only
received with gratitude, but such as were sold
were readily purchased at prime cost. In truth,
the religious knowledge communicated to them
has been so blessed, that you would not find in
any part of France more genuine piety or simplicity of manners. But still it can hardly be
expected that this improvement will be permanent, considering their physical, moral, and
religious condition, so long as they are without
the ministration of regular pastors. Up to the
present time the valley of Fressinière has not a
pastor of its own. It is served in connection
with the churches of Val Queyras, which are
ten leagues distant, on the other side of the
Durance, and are separated by a lofty range of
mountains, whose passes are not only very difficult, but absolutely dangerous in the winter.
The visits of the pastor are, therefore, necessarily few and at long intervals, and the people
are obliged to wait his convenience, until they
can have their children baptized, the nuptial
blessing pronounced, or any of the church services performed. Moved by the destitute condition of these mountaineers, who are endeared
to me, not only by their own amiable disposition,
but by their interesting origin, I would most
willingly continue to devote myself to their service, and submit to all manner of deprivation
and fatigue as their pastor; but the frequent

journeys from one church to another, in the Valleys of Fressinière and Queyras, have been too much for me : and total exhaustion, proceeding from this cause, and from a stomach complaint, brought on by living on unwholesome food, have so disabled me, that I am obliged to remove myself for the present, with very slight hopes of ever being so restored as to be able to return.

" At this juncture of time when respect for the adherents of the primitive doctrines and forms of Christianity has been manifested so conspicuously, in behalf of the Protestants of the Valleys of Piedmont, I have thought it my duty to give publicity to the fact, that their brethren of the French Alps are equally objects of interest, and are much more indigent, although they have hitherto remained unnoticed and unknown. It is therefore my intention to publish a history of this church, in which I shall not only give a detailed account of its present condition, but shall trace its origin up to the remotest antiquity."

There was enough in this modest allusion of Neff to his own labours, and in his generous expression of concern for the Alpines of Dauphiné, to make me anxious to know more both of this apostle of the Alps himself, and of his flock; and as I was about to make a journey to the Waldenses of Piedmont, I determined to visit the sublime and secluded scenery of the Val Fressinière, either on my way to Italy or on my return.   This resolution was carried into effect in 1829, and I had the gratification of traversing nearly the whole of the mountain region, which is now consecrated to the memory, not only of martyrs of former times, but of an eminent confessor of our own days, who, combining in his individual character the usefulness of the pastor Oberlin, and the devotedness of the missionary Martyn, did spend and was spent in the service of his Redeemer.   Neff had gone to his rest a few months only before my arrival at Dormilleuse; and from all that I saw and heard of the effects of his ministry, I judged that a memoir of his short, but extraordinary career, would not be an uninteresting addition to the Christian records of the age in which we live. Having explored the scenes where he prepared the children of the mountain for the coming of the Lord, and made myself acquainted with the locality of every hamlet within his extensive charge, I hope to be better able to elucidate the present and former history of this Alpine church, than any person who has not enjoyed the same opportunities of picking up information on the spot.   The notes of my journey contain many anecdotes of Neff, supplied by those who knew him, and some observations on the country and its peculiarities, while its grand scenery was before my eyes.   But still, with all these advantages, I could not have done justice to my subject, had I not been indebted to the great kindness of a lady, whose name I am not permitted to mention here, for the Journals of Neff himself.   These form the principal source from which the substance of the memoir is drawn; and if I had been put in possession of all the circumstances relating to those papers, I believe I should have had to state, that many of Neff's noble projects could not have been carried into effect, but for this benevolent friend in England, to whom his Journals were consigned.   I have further acknowledgments to make to the Rev. Richard Burgess, the well-known and highly respected British chaplain at Geneva, for the transmission of a small tract, lately published under the title of " Notice sur Felix Neff, Pasteur dans les Hautes Alpes."   From this I have enriched the narrative with recollections, that have been preserved of Neff's early life and of his dying moments ; but not having found any trace, either in this " Notice," or in the Journals, of his intended history and origin of the church of the French Alps, I conclude that Neff was disabled by long illness from carrying his design into effect, and I have therefore attempted to supply the defect, by giving the result of my own researches, in a succeeding chapter.   I have also, in the course of this Memoir, filled up the relation with such remarks as naturally occurred to one who had visited the scene under description, and conversed with the extraordinary race, of whom it may literally

be said, " strong is thy dwelling-place, and thou
puttest thy nest in a rock[1]."

---

[1] In the first edition, the Author's sketch, of the origin of
the Alpine churches of France, and of their succession from
the Primitive Christians of Gaul, was introduced here, but he
has now transferred it to Chapter V.

I am sorry that Mr. Smedley has taken such offence at my
note, p. 4, as to resent it by writing a sarcastic article at my
expense in the British Critic.   If the public voice, in favour
of this Memoir, had not been expressed by the demand of a
third Edition in less than a year from the publication of the
first, and by approving Reviews, in the Quarterly, Athenæum,
Christian Remembrancer, Protestant Journal, Christian Exa-
miner, Eclectic, and several other Journals, the intended blow
might have fallen less harmlessly. Upon reflection, I trust Mr.
Smedley will do me the justice to believe, that, although I may
prefer my own views to his, on the historical question, which we
have both examined, yet I did not mean to undervalue his labours,
by those unlucky observations which have brought down such
a storm of displeasure.   His literary reputation will not suffer
from my venturing to say that he is in error on a particular
point, and mine will survive an attack, which was probably
made upon me in one of those moments, when an author is
more sensitive than considerate.   If, however, Mr. Smedley
shall continue to sneer at me, because I have maintained, and
will persevere in maintaining, the Protestant opinion, that there
are existing Alpine Churches, which do not derive their Christianity from Rome, but have preserved the Primitive Faith, as
it was transmitted to them, when the Gospel was first planted
in their mountains, then I must bear the taunt, consoled by
the knowledge that critics and historians of profound inquiry,
like Usher and Allix, Faber and Southey, have not only expressed
the same opinion, but have supported it by the weight of un-
questionable authorities.

CHAPTER II.

FELIX NEFF, the subject of this Memoir, was
born in the year 1798, and was brought up in
a village near Geneva, under the care of his
widowed mother; and he has added one more
to the number of distinguished men, who have
owed their first strong impressions to the admirable effects produced by maternal vigilance,
and to lessons taught by female lips.   The pure
air of the delightful region, where he spent his
boyish days, and the long rambles which he was
permitted to take in the midst of splendid
mountain scenery, not only contributed to form
a robust constitution, but to inspire a taste for
the sublime and beautiful, which displayed itself
in his character, throughout the whole of his
very remarkable career.   Even when he was a
child, there was no amusement, which the town
of Geneva could offer, greater than the enjoyment which he derived from following his own

more rational and invigorating diversions, by the side of the torrent or the lake. When twelve years old he was invited by a companion to accompany him to some theatrical spectacle, which was in great favour at the time, and upon his declining to go, he was asked, " Do you think you will not be entertained ?"   " Perhaps," said he, " I should be too much entertained."

After his mother had laid the first foundation, the village pastor gave him instruction in Latin, botany, history, and geography.   The books which were within his reach were probably but few, and of these, the works of Plutarch, and some of the less objectionable volumes of J. J. Rousseau, are said to have had a large share of his attention : the former delighted him, because they made him acquainted with great men, and great achievements : and the latter, because they gave encouragement to his natural taste for scenery.   With one of these in his hand, he would scale the rock, or climb the mountain, and spend hours in imagining the useful actions which he might be destined to perform, and the regions which it might be his fate to explore. It would seem that military exploits and scientific research were the visions of his boyhood, and, in the course of this narrative, it will be found that those early predilections, and the employments of his youth, when he was obliged to pursue some occupation for his subsistence, proved an eminently beneficial training for the more sacred duties, to which he afterwards consecrated himself. The same ardent spirit and high courage, the same meditative disposition and inquiring genius, the same love of mountain life and scenery, accompanied him to the Alpine wilderness ; and the same burning desire, to be useful in his generation, found ample gratification, when he became the spiritual shepherd of a flock, who had none to guide them before he undertook the charge.

When it was time for Neff to select a profession, necessity or choice, or perhaps both combined, induced him to engage himself to the proprietor of a nursery-ground, or florist gardener, and at sixteen he published a little treatise on the culture of trees. The accuracy and arrangement of this juvenile work, and the proof of deep observation which it manifested, were subjects of no small praise at the time. But the quiet and humble walks of the florist's garden were soon exchanged for the bustle of a garrison, and at seventeen, Felix entered as a private into the military service of Geneva, in the memorable year 1815. Two years afterwards, he was promoted to the rank of serjeant of artillery, and having raised himself to notice by his theoretical and practical knowledge of mathematics, he continued to make this branch of science his study during his continuance in the army.

The wisdom of God, in the choice of his in-

struments, was singularly exhibited, when He
called Neff to be a minister of his word, and sent
him to preach the Gospel to the rugged and
half civilized mountaineers of Dauphiné.   The
work of a pastor in the Alps, as Neff expressed
it, when he came to have an experience of its
duties and its difficulties, resembles that of a
missionary among the savages.   He had to
teach them every thing.   He had to show them
how to build a school-room; how to use the line
and plummet; how to form levels and inclined
planes; how to irrigate their meadows, and to
cultivate their barren soil, so as to be the most
productive.

A mere scholar from the university, or even an
ardent preacher with the whole scheme of the
Gospel written in his heart, could not have accomplished what this extraordinary man did,
who, with his thorough knowledge of the Book
of Life, possessed also a stock of available information, which was brought from the nursery-
ground and the camp.

Neff was soon distinguished in the corps to
which he belonged, not only as an efficient sub-
officer, but as a devoted soldier of the cross.
The influence, however, which he hourly obtained over his comrades, excited a degree of
jealousy among the superior officers, which was
far from being honourable to them.   They
wished him out of the service; he was too religious for them, and after a few years the serious

turn of his mind became so marked, that he was advised to quit it, and to prepare himself for holy orders.

During the mental struggles, and the investigation of his own motives and spiritual condition, which occupied him previously to that important step, his frequent prayer for guidance and illumination was to this effect. "Oh, my God, whatever be thy nature, make me to know thy truth; and deign to manifest thyself in my heart."

After his supplications were heard, and he was fully settled in his resolution to dedicate himself to the work of the ministry, he quitted the army, and placed himself under pious instruction and superintendence, which gave a right direction to his studies and reflections. He read the Bible with earnest prayers to God, that he might so read as to understand the Divine will; and that he might render every passage in Scripture familiar to his mind, he made a concordance of his own, and filled the margins of several copies of the Old and New Testaments with remarks and memoranda. Some of these are still in possession of his friends, and are held in most affectionate estimation, and are consulted as the voice of one who, being dead, yet speaketh.

Those, who had opportunities of conversing with Neff during this season of solemn preparation, relate that his powers of acquirement, and aptitude for abstract study, were very extraordinary. The exercise of the memory gave him no trouble; he could repeat whole chapters from Scripture. His conversation, at the same time, was agreeable and easy; he expressed himself with great readiness, force, and accuracy; but though he spoke often, and always correctly and to the point, yet it was in short sentences, and in few words.

There is a practice in the Protestant churches of Switzerland and France, which is extremely beneficial to candidates for ordination. The theological student, after having passed certain examinations, is received as a *proposant* into the confidence of some of those, who exercise the pastoral office, and is employed as a lay-helper, or catechist, in their parishes. This custom is as old as the Christian Church; it was the usage of the primitive churches, and cannot but be of the greatest improvement to the probationer. He is acting under the eye of an experienced minister; he has an example and a teacher before him to regulate his actions and opinions; he is trying his own strength, and feeling his way, and assuring himself of his preference and fitness for the sacred work, before the irrevocable step is taken. It is not too late to retire, if he finds himself in any degree unequal to the arduous charge.

These probationers are not permitted to put their hands to the ark, and to perform services which are strictly sacerdotal, but they instruct the young, and visit the sick, and even preach from the pulpit, at the discretion of the pastor, in whose parish they are thus making their advance towards the ministry [1].

Neff seems to have put on his spiritual armour, and to have essayed to go in it, in the year 1819, in the neighbourhood of Geneva: and in the two following years in the cantons of Neufchatel, Berne, and the Pays de Vaud. It was at a very trying crisis, that he officiated in the character I have described, in the latter canton. Lausanne, and many of the towns and villages of the Pays de Vaud, were then divided by religious controversies, which were carried on with much indiscretion and bitterness on both sides, but Neff endeavoured to pursue a course which spoke well for his Christian temper and wisdom. " The Lord," said he, in one of his letters from Lausanne, " has opened a wide door for the preaching of the Gospel in this canton, which will not soon be shut, provided that the

---

[1] " A system of probationary exercise upon a spiritual basis, preparatory to ordination, would be a most desirable appendage to our own National Establishment. In defect of this advantage, an interval more or less protracted, according to circumstances, and spent in inspection, or initiation into the routine of the Christian ministry, under the superintendence of a judicious and experienced pastor, might prove a commencing era of ministerial usefulness. Opportunities would be afforded of learning, which is the best preparation for teaching."—Bridge's Christian Ministry, Part I. Ch. 7. Sec. 4.

preachers conduct themselves with prudence, and are cautious not to agitate any question, which is of secondary importance only, and which, without being directly necessary to salvation, may excite suspicion that some schism is intended."

CHAPTER III.

IT was in 1821, when Neff was in his twenty-fourth year, that he first exchanged his native Switzerland for those wilder scenes in France, where the rough places were made smooth to his fervent spirit, by the hope of being of some use to the Protestants there, who were very ill provided with clergy. He was not yet in orders, but in the dearth of regularly appointed ministers, he had been invited to the assistance of a pastor of Grenoble, in the same capacity as that which he had held in some of the Swiss cantons, and having remained at Grenoble about six months, his services were requested at Mens, in the department of the Isère, to supply, as far as might be done, the place of an absent pastor. Here he had many difficulties with which to contend. He was a stranger, and an object of suspicion to the local authorities.

His office and functions were but ill defined : the dialect of the country people was a patois, of which the French supplied but very few terms : the tone of his piety was too high for many of those whom it was his duty to instruct, and his sensitive mind was severely wounded in the conflict between his high sense of duty, and his belief that it might be expedient to make some allowances for the weak in faith, to give milk to babes, and not to put new wine into old bottles, but to relax in his demands upon the self-denial of those, who were unable to give full proof of religious sincerity. " I often retire to my chamber," he wrote to one of his friends, " ill at rest, and greatly dissatisfied with myself. I reproach myself on the one hand for having betrayed my sacred trust, and on the other hand for being a time-server, and afraid of pressing my opportunities."

In this letter he complained also of the cold and heartless Christianity which prevailed around him, in consequence of that rage for controversy, which made men think more of other people's spiritual condition than their own. One of the pastors, under whom he was to act, seldom held any religious conversation with his flock, unless it was to discuss the points of difference between Protestants and Roman Catholics. But this person soon afterwards began to enter most warmly into all Neff's views, subdued by the sincerity and earnestness which he could not fail to discern in him.

I shall now begin to draw largely from the letters and journals of Neff; and wherever he is found to express his sentiments with freedom, the language of his own private remarks, and of his confidential communications, will be the best illustration of his character and conduct. The following letter shows, that his sanguine temperament and burning zeal were under the constant control of prudence and discretion. The letter was written to one of his friends, who had scruples as to remaining in communion with the national Church of Geneva, at a time when many of its clergy had avowed Socinian principles, but before it was so deeply infected with error as it is at present.

" Mens, February 11, 1822.

" You ask my opinion as to the proposition which is made, or about to be made, of admitting members into your association without requiring them to separate from the national Church. You ought to know my sentiments on this subject. I am not aware of any passage in the Gospel, by which a Christian is obliged to recognise, as a Church, a congregation which has no discipline, and which does not even profess the essential doctrines of Christianity ; nor do I find that there is any authority given to exact that all the brethren should think alike, and surrender their right of private judgment. Consequently, I maintain, that the Christian is at liberty to separate, but that he is not obliged to do so, so long as the Church, to which he belongs, does not formally prevent his seeking edification wherever he is likely to find it, and that she does not openly profess opinions which are anti-christian. On this principle, if one awakened is anxious to form an union with the children of God, but is at the same time desirous of continuing his connexion with the national Church, either because he considers it an useful institution, which every body ought to agree in preserving, or because he thinks he should lose his influence with certain persons, whose improvement he is bent on promoting, and who would be so shocked at his separation, as to refuse to listen to him; in short, whatever be his reasons, if they be conscientious reasons, and founded on his concern for souls, I do not think he ought to be rejected. I will explain myself more in detail. I have said that national churches ought to be regarded as useful institutions; in fact, without them, how would the knowledge of God and of Jesus Christ have been preserved in many places, where there have been no true Christians for many ages, and where, according to the principle of your separatists, there has been no church? What would have become of the Protestants of France? What would have become of those many families, in different places, who have preserved the Bible, and who have had family worship, and who have been in the habit of meeting once a week, or not so often, to hear the word of God? To whom would the missionaries be able to address themselves, and the evangelical pastors? What would have become of the churches, and of the Sabbath? and where would have been the remembrance of the death and resurrection of Jesus Christ? and what would have become of the Bible, on the knowledge of which all our instructions depend? and what would have become of the elements, out of which you must now form and restore a spiritual and a living church, if the national churches had not subsisted for the ordination of ministers, and for the ministration of the Sacraments? And again, if all these churches had not subsisted, what would have become of those nominal Christians, whom you cannot admit into the churches which are really Christian? What instruction would their children have received? What recollection would have been preserved of the Gospel? Where would have been the Bible Society? In short, what would have become of those, who are susceptible of life, and who, though too often dead, have not ceased to be in the way of becoming pious, and of being prepared for the reception of the true Gospel? I am now stationed in a place, where I have better opportunities than most others of forming a judgment upon this subject. If, then, every true Christian in the visible

Churches had absolutely abandoned them, (on your principle), what would have become of them ? Who would have been left to contend against unbelief in the academies and in the consistories ? Who would have preached the true Gospel in the churches, where many go merely in compliance with custom, and for nothing else ? Would they not have fallen back again into Paganism, and would not every thing that savours of life and truth have been totally lost? It is necessary, then, in my opinion, at the same time that we recognise the right of a Christian to separate (and it is often absolutely expedient to do so), to admit also, that there are many strong reasons to induce a great number of the children of God to remain in connexion with the national Church, so long as it does not compel them to profess or to teach a lie, and that it does not reject them from its bosom, because they are in union with a more spiritual congregation. Such are my opinions, and I should wish that you would communicate them to our little flock, with the assurance, that I must always regard it as the duty of Christians to be in union with a true Church, that they may live under evangelical discipline. I think nothing ought to be insisted upon, as to name or form, but only as to the reality ; and I not only believe it to be essential, and enjoined by the Lord, but I regard it as an invaluable privilege to be in communion with such a flock, which alone has the means of observing that rigid discipline, in which true separation consists."

I gather from his Journals, that the system which Neff pursued at this period of his career, (that is to say, before he had consecrated himself to the ministry, according to any regular form of ordination,) while he had as yet no pastoral charge, was to collect as many young people as he could, for purposes of religious instruction. These he called catechumens. At the date of the above-mentioned letter, he had as many as eighty catechumens; these soon increased to ninety, the greatest part of whom spoke only the patois of the country, which was a dialect of the old Provençal language, and which he himself was obliged to learn, before he could make himself well understood [1]. There is no regular funeral service among the French Protestants. To supply this defect, when there was a death in a family, Neff used to go to the house, where the body lay, and deliver an exhortation, just before the assembled concourse was ready to bear it to the grave. He also vi-

[1] He assembled his catechumens four times a week at his own lodgings, the girls twice, and the boys twice. He directed them to come prepared with passages by heart, out of the New Testament, and after these had been repeated, he expounded them to his young hearers in a manner that made a lively impression upon their minds. Some were in the habit of attending these catechetical instructions from a distance of more than three miles.

sited the sick, and whenever it was known that
he was to be at the bed-side of the afflicted, many
of the neighbours begged to be admitted, that
they might have the benefit of his exhortations.
The pulpit was open to him very frequently.
At one time he would preach from a text, at
another time he would select a chapter, and enlarge upon it in the form of a lecture or paraphrase.
He found this latter mode of instruction to be particularly attractive and successful. The simple
peasants, who flocked into Mens from the neighbouring villages, were grateful to hear a familiar
exposition of God's word, and to have an application made to their own condition or wants, in
language which they had no difficulty in understanding.

Our indefatigable catechist did not confine his
labours to Mens, or to its immediate neighbourhood. Wherever his presence was required, there
he went, be the distance what it might. At this
time, and in this department, (that of the Isère,)
there were about 8000 Protestants, scattered over
a surface of about eighty miles square, with only
three regular pastors to look after them, one of
whom was now absent. When his visits were
paid in one direction, his services were required
in another, and nothing but a frame of iron could
have enabled a person of Neff's zeal to encounter
the toil, which his reputation soon imposed upon
him. One of the districts, which he visited with
the greatest personal satisfaction to himself, was

that of Vizille. Its situation, on the banks of the Romanche, one of the wildest mountain torrents in France, with lofty mountains encircling it on all sides, had great attractions for him. The place, too, where his little flock was folded, had charms of a peculiar nature for his turn of mind. It was a large hall in the Gothic castle of the family of Lesdiguières. The celebrated constable of France, of that name, was the champion of the Huguenot cause in his youth; but apostatized from it, in old age, when ambition and cold worldly calculation got the better of the more generous feelings of his earlier days. The present possessor of the castle, actuated by a better spirit, lent his fine baronial hall, as a place of worship, to the Protestants, and the congregations which gathered round Neff were so attentive to his lessons of piety, that he always spoke of Vizille as his "dear Vizille." But great as was his fatigue, being constantly on the move from one remote quarter to another, it was the sort of life that he preferred before any charge, which would have kept him in a comparative state of confinement. "A sedentary or a fixed life," said he, "has no pleasures for me. I should not like to be constantly labouring in one place: I would infinitely rather lead the wandering life of a missionary." Thus, among the diversities of gifts, and among the differences of administration, by which the manifestation of the Spirit is granted for men's profit withal, the

Almighty was pleased to raise up a teacher for the natives of the French Alps, whose habits and tastes exactly suited the wants of a people, who had not the benefit of a sufficient supply of resident pastors.

The following letters give an interesting description of one of his village tours, and of his usual employment.

" Mens, April 4, 1822.

" Yesterday, after the service, I went to Guichardière, a hamlet three miles from this place, and I returned delighted with my excursion. There are already many signs of the seed springing up among my catechumens. I was lately accosted by several peasant women, one of whom begged me to give her a copy of the prayer, which I had delivered on the previous Sunday, before my sermon. I asked her name and residence, and told her to come to me on the following Sunday. She kept to her appointment, and I then gave her the prayer, and with it a little tract containing the parable of the ten virgins. These interviews made me desirous of knowing more of her, and I proposed to accompany her some day to her own village. Yesterday Elizabeth and I set out together for her parents' cottage, and as we walked along, she told me that many of the young women of the neighbourhood met at appointed times to practise psalmsinging, and to read the Bible. Upon reaching the village where she lived, which is charmingly situated in the midst of trees, at the foot of a high mountain, and on the edge of a torrent, I was most kindly received by her parents. They said they could not themselves go to church, but that their daughter always repeated to them that which she had heard. The old man recounted a history of the persecutions, which his own parents and himself had suffered, and he added, ' In those times there was more zeal than there is now. My father and mother used to cross mountains and forests by night, in the worst weather, and at the risk of their lives, to be present at Divine service performed in secret, but now we are grown lazy. Religious freedom is the death blow to piety.' He afterwards talked to me of his unhappiness in having only one son left, a young man of eighteen, who was clever, and blessed with a good memory, and had read the Bible, and all the pious books in the house, but who did not believe in the word of God. I read some verses of the fifteenth of St. John, and explained them. These good people pressed me to stay with them, but I had an engagement to be present at a meeting at Mens, where my young people were to practise psalm-singing, and could only thank them for their kindness."

In another place, Neff has given this beautiful description of two villages where he had the satisfaction of seeing much fruit come to perfec-

D

tion.   " These two lovely villages, which are
at the foot of Mont Chatel, in a little dell
watered by a charming stream, tapestried with
rich verdure, and shaded by a grove of beech
trees, had often tempted me to extend my walks
from Mens in 1822.   They seemed to be the
peaceful retreat of true piety, and their humble,
moss-clad cottages, appeared to offer a natural
tabernacle for the good shepherd Jesus Christ."

Mens, May 15, 1822.

" Far from having time to write letters, I
sometimes can scarcely find time to take my
meals.   May I say, with our Lord, ' My meat
is to do the will of him that sent me, and to
finish his work.'   From before Easter I have
been visiting all the hamlets and villages of the
parish.   I have held meetings nearly in every
one, at each of which there was a good attendance after the labours of the day.   When I am
in Mens, of an evening I always give a catechetical lecture, or an exposition.   Besides this, I
have called on all my catechumens in their own
communes.   The sermons of an evening, and
particularly the paraphrastic explanations, are
constantly well attended.   Out of seventy-seven
catechumens whom I have at present, more than
thirty are seriously inclined.   Fifteen of those
seem to be more or less aware of their true condition, and four or five have found peace in
Jesus Christ.   Since I have been here, and es-

pecially of late, God has given me a facility of expressing myself, an energy, and a degree of boldness, at which I am myself astonished, and which they certainly would not endure in Switzerland. With respect to my health, it is much stronger since I have been constantly on the move and making long excursions, although many of these are very fatiguing, for it often happens that I go several leagues, and perform as many as four or five services in one day, especially on Sundays. I have not unfrequently been thus engaged, instructing or conversing, from five o'clock in the morning, till eleven at night, and all this without any cough or ailment of the stomach: I have recovered my appetite, and can drink wine at my meals without any inconvenience."

Neff's Journals contain frequent mention of evening hours spent in the exercise of sacred music with his catechumens, and other young persons, whom he could persuade to attend his instruction in this branch of knowledge. It will appear extraordinary to those who have been accustomed to think of France as the land of the dance and song, and whose ideas of mountain amusements have been formed by hearing airs, which go under the name of Savoyard and Provençal, to find our catechist complaining, that the common people of Mens, and the mountaineers of the neighbourhood, had not the least notion of music. "They do not sing at all, neither well, nor ill, no, not even songs." This was his remark in one of his letters, and with that intuitive knowledge of human nature, and of the chords by which it is moved, which so eminently distinguished him, he soon employed himself in giving lessons in psalmody, which added very substantially both to his own influence, and to the numbers of those, who expressed a desire to enrol themselves in his little company of hearers and learners. I annex his own description of the successful effects of this device, to combine innocent and rational entertainment with his more grave instructions, and of the manner in which the time thus spent was made to pass agreeably, by diversifying the employment, and alternating the singing lesson, and the scriptural lesson.

"Our sacred music meetings, both on Sundays, and on other evenings, are always numerously attended; sometimes we count above a hundred, and there would be more if we had room for them. On these occasions we have a great deal of singing, both to practise them in the psalm and hymn tunes, and to preserve the inviting name of sacred music meeting. We do it also to prolong the assembly till a late hour in the evening, that they may not be able to go to the dances [1]. The singing is frequently in-

[1] One of Neff's most anxious objects was to put an end to the Sunday games and dances which then prevailed, even

terrupted either by M. Blanc (one of the pastors of Mens,) or myself. M. Blanc explains some verses of the Bible, which bear upon the verses of the hymn, or enlarges upon any subject which he thinks applicable. There is a simplicity in his addresses, and often a cast of humour, which is extremely engaging. Last Sunday evening, perceiving some symptoms of inattention and drowsiness in the party, while he was expounding very seriously, he suddenly exclaimed, ' I see you are tired of this, but before we conclude, I will teach you something new.' Every body was immediately all attention. 'I will relate a fable to you,' he continued, ' a fable of La Fontaine. There were an ant and a grasshopper living near each other. The ant worked hard all the summer to provide against the wants of the winter; but the grasshopper did nothing but enjoy herself during the whole of the fine weather. When winter came the idler found herself in very great distress, and applied to her neighbour, the ant, for some food.——What were you doing all the summer? asked the ant.——I sung and danced, answered the grasshopper.——Well then, sing and dance now, said the ant.' When they heard this, a smile ran through the room. ' Yes,' said M. Blanc, ' you may laugh now, but this fable is

among the Protestants, in all parts of France, and he happily succeeded in opening the eyes of many of his young catechumens to the profaneness of the practice.

like the parable of the ten virgins : and since the parables of Christ send you to sleep, I thought it necessary to disguise them under a more attractive form. The ant represents the wise virgins, and the grasshopper represents the foolish virgins. Like the grasshopper, the foolish virgins beg oil of the wise virgins, but they refuse to give it, for fear of wanting it themselves. Then comes the bridegroom and shuts the door, and when the foolish virgins wish to enter, he says unto them, Verily I say unto you, I know you not. Watch, therefore, for ye know not, neither the day, nor the hour, when the Son of man cometh.' The tone, with which M. Blanc delivered this, produced an irresistible effect."

In remarking upon Neff's anxiety to promote psalmody, I would observe, that the effect produced by the words, or by the music, or by the combination of the two, is such, that the cultivation of psalmody has ever been earnestly recommended by those who are anxious to excite true piety. Tradition, history, revelation, and experience, bear witness to the truth, that there is nothing to which the natural feelings of man respond more readily. Every nation, whose literary remains have come down to us, appears to have consecrated the first efforts of its muse to religion, or rather all the first compositions in verse seem to have grown out of devotional effusions. We know that the book of Job, and others, the most ancient of the Old Testament, contain rythmical addresses to the Supreme Being. Many of the Psalms were composed centuries before the time of king David, and it is not extravagant to imagine, that some of them may have been sung even to Jubal's lyre, and were handed down from patriarch to patriarch by oral tradition. Nor did the fancy of Milton take too bold a flight, when it pleased itself with the idea that our first parents, taught by the carols of the birds in the garden of Eden, raised their voices in tuneful notes of praise to the Creator of all, when they walked forth in the cool of the day to meet their God before the fall. But this is certain, that one of our Lord's last acts of social worship on earth was to sing a hymn with his disciples. Few, therefore, can be slow to understand, that if Christ and his disciples broke forth in holy song, immediately after the solemnities of the Last Supper, and just before the Shepherd was smitten, and the sheep were scattered; and if Paul and Silas sung praises unto God in their prison-house, congregational worship may always be the better for such helps. Add to these examples, the apostolical exhortation to the merry-hearted to sing psalms, and the apostolical descriptions of the choral strains which resound in the courts of heaven, and we cannot but feel certain, that the services of the Christian church were cheered from the earliest times by hymns and psalms. " Those

Nazarines sing hymns to Christ," said Pliny, in contempt. We thank him for recording the fact. The words of the Te Deum were composed by a native of Gaul, (for the use probably of one of the churches on the Rhone, or of the Alps) about the third century; and at the same period, men, women, youths of both sexes, and even children, joined in the psalmody of the sanctuaries, in such cordial and harmonious unison, that a father of the church has well compared the sound to the loud, but not discordant, noise of many waves beating against the sea shore.

At the time of the reformation, sacred music, which had begun to run wild, was brought back to its first principles. The melodies of religious worship were rendered more heart-touching, by being set to words in the vernacular tongues, which every body could understand. Luther's hymn, " Great God, what do I hear and see," led the way. Henry VIII. hated the German reformer, and all that he did, but he burned to rival him in every thing, and he gave a stimulus to the public taste, by composing words and music for the service of the English church. In France, soon after the middle of the sixteenth century, when it was doubtful whether the nation would become Protestant or remain Roman Catholic, the pathetic tunes and devotional stanzas of the reformers obtained so great an influence over the minds of men, that the music of the temples, as the Protestant sanctuaries were called, to distinguish them from the Roman Catholic churches, became the fashionable melodies of the day. This taste found its way even to the court, and to the great alarm of the Romish party, some of the sweetest and most stirring of the psalms, which had been translated into French metre by Clement Marot, were set to music by Louis Guadimel, and were constantly in the mouths not only of the Protestant families of the provinces, but of the ornaments of the saloons of Paris, and even of the palace of the Louvre. It is said to have been quite astonishing how much this pious and simple device found favour for the Protestant cause, and induced people, who had never read Scripture before, to search the holy volume out of which those treasures were drawn, which so charmed their ears and their imagination. It is still the practice, in most of the mountain churches, to make sacred music a part of family devotion, and many of the tunes, which Guadimel composed with such success, are still sung to the praise of God. I can bear witness to the forcible manner in which these strains, rising to heaven from the lips of parents, children, and domestics, quicken piety, and stir up the best affections of the heart towards God and man. I have seen and felt the effect produced by them in the humble dwelling of the village pastor, where none but human voices swelled the notes; and in the chateau,

9

where the harp and the organ have mingled their fine sounds with the well-modulated tones of an accomplished family of sons and daughters. My thoughts, at the moment that I am writing this, are at Chateâu Blonay, but most of the voices, which I heard there, are now silent in death! I am thoroughly convinced that family worship, and congregational worship lose a great auxiliary to piety, when there is not the power or the inclination to join in psalmody.

Neff knew the human heart, when he determined to cultivate a taste for sacred music among his flock; he felt assured, both from experience and observation, that when impressive words are set to expressive music, the effects produced must be both delightful and beneficial to those who take part in them [1].

The return of the pastor to Mens, whose place Neff was appointed to supply in part, was not favourable to the progress of improvement in that neighbourhood. Having absented himself for a longer period than the circumstances of his case could justify, a question arose as to his re-instatement. This produced some party feeling, and the clergyman himself, jealous of Neff's influence, and angry with the consistory for not permitting him to resume his functions at once, raised a cabal against the man, whose

---

[1] The reader would be highly gratified by a perusal of Archdeacon Bayley's observations on Psalmody, in his admirable Charge, delivered May, 1826.

anxious object had been to feed and to watch the flock during the shepherd's absence. The effect of his ungenerous misrepresentations, and of the levity with which he spoke of the catechist's rigid sentiments, was more visible in the town of Mens than in the neighbouring villages, and it wrung from Neff's wounded spirit a melancholy expression of regret at the falling off of many, of whom he had entertained better hopes.

But it is gratifying to be able to report of the people generally, to whose instruction Neff devoted so much of his time and anxiety, that they were not insensible of his merits. The day of his departure was a day of mourning to them, and the testimony which M. Blanc, the other pastor of Mens, bore to his character after his death, and to the success of his labours, is highly honourable to all parties.

Extract of a Letter from M. Blanc, pastor of Mens, dated 1st. Dec. 1829.

" About five months after the arrival of M. Neff at Mens, more than a hundred persons, principally the heads of families, lamenting that he was not appointed to the station of assistant pastor, petitioned the consistory to retain him under the designation of pastor-catechist, and offered to provide a stipend for him, as long as they should have a farthing left. The consistory nominated M. Felix Neff pastor-catechist

on the 1st of June 1822. Every where, in
Mens and its environs, the name of our friend
was never pronounced but with respect : and
there were few who did not regard him as a
saint, almost exempt from sin.   This was a subject of deep affliction to him, because he saw
that they attached themselves too much to him
personally, and too little to the Saviour whose
servant he was.   He said to me one day with
deep feeling, ' They love me too much; they
receive me with too much pleasure ; they eulo-
gise me too much ; indeed they do not know
me.'   During the space of nearly two years,
which he spent among us, he did a prodigious
quantity of good.   Zeal for religion revived ; a
great number of persons began to think seriously
of the condition of their souls.   The Word of
God was more sought after, and more carefully
read, the catechumens were better instructed in
their Christian duties, and gave proofs of it in
their conduct : family worship was established in
many houses : the love of luxury, and personal
vanity decreased : almsgiving was more generally practised, and the poor were not so numerous.   Schools were opened in different places,
and both in Mens, and in our neighbouring
villages, every body remarks a sensible improvement in the manners and industrious habits of
the Protestants.   In short, the numberless labours of Neff, his indefatigable activity, and his

instructions, will long be remembered at Mens, and his sojournment among us will be recorded as a signal blessing."

Amiable and Christian-minded must be the man, who thus bears witness to the labours of his humble brother. Without any unworthy derogation, without the least shadow of envy, the pastor of Mens attributes all the improvement produced in his flock to the labours of a stranger; of a coadjutor, whose office was nothing more than that of a catechist! Great reason had Neff, in his Journals to speak of the singleness of heart, of the pure religious motives which actuated M. Blanc. But before we dismiss this part of Neff's history, when he was acquitting himself so well as a proposant, or probationer, in the ample field, to which he returned after a short absence, in the character of a regular pastor, it will more fully illustrate the resources of his mind, and explain the mode of treatment which he adopted with his catechumens, if I select one of the many sketches which his Journal contains.

" You will, perhaps, remember," said he, in a letter to one of his friends, " that in the notice of my first lecture at Mens, I spoke of a daughter of my host, named Emily, one of my catechumens, as being very intelligent, but at the same time extremely devoted to the pleasures of the world. She used to be at every frivolous amusement. Upon one occasion, having understood that she meant to perform a part in a comedy, I signified my displeasure so plainly, that she gave up her design ; but I perceived that it was sorely against her real inclination.   While she regularly attended all our private and public services, and particularly our evening meetings, her whole heart was with the world.   Her lips only gave confession of the truth.   Things were in this state with her when she heard my sermon on Good Friday.   She was struck by these words, which I repeated more than once : ' Go to Golgotha, and there you will see how odious sin is to God ?'   For the first time she understood, in the sufferings of our Lord, the terrible demands of the holy law of God.   In the bitterness and anguish of her soul, she shed many tears during the service, and her heart was on fire when she left the church.   During the whole of the day her uneasiness increased, though she did all she could to give another turn to her thoughts. She cursed the hour when she had asked God to give her a knowledge of her heart.   She continued in this state without disclosing her feelings to any body till the Tuesday morning afterwards.   It was in vain that I endeavoured to find an opportunity of speaking to her.   She avoided me.   Her parents and friends tortured themselves to divine the cause of her disquietude. At last, on the Tuesday morning, I made her search for some passages in my Testament, and in turning over the leaves she found the text on which I had preached, Mat. v. 20. ' It is too true,' said she, ' that our righteousness does not surpass that of the Scribes and Pharisees: it is even less than theirs.'

" ' And St. Paul says,' I rejoined, ' that no flesh shall be justified by the works of the law.'

" Upon this she made many objections to the doctrine, not being able to understand how we are excited to good works by it.

" I then read to her the passage in St. Paul's Epistle to Titus, and I reminded her of the example of true Christians who are rich in good works, although they do not attribute any merit to them. I explained to her the motives of love and gratitude, which incline them to obedience, and to a renouncement of the world.

" ' Do you think,' added I, ' that they, who have such sentiments as these, can find any pleasure in the things of the world?'

" ' No,' said she, ' but I do.'

" I then endeavoured to make her perceive how the consideration of the truths of the Gospel ought to make us serious.

" ' It does not make me serious !' she exclaimed, bursting into tears.

" ' I return thanks to God for the disposition in which I now find you, for those who weep shall be comforted. Be of good cheer, there is a Comforter. He, whom Jesus Christ promised to his disciples, will be sent to you also.'

" ' His disciples did his will, but as for me, I do it not, and I have never done it.'

" ' His disciples did not only do his will, they believed.'

" ' Yes, and I do not believe.'

" ' They did not believe as much as they ought, for Jesus reproached them with not having faith as big as a grain of mustard seed. But they did as you ought to do : they asked the Lord to increase their faith.'

" ' But they, at that time, had a little, and I have none at all.'

" Here her tears burst forth again, and all that I said appeared to have no effect upon her. She continued all day in such a melancholy mood as to alarm her parents. She could scarcely utter a word; she avoided company, and ate scarcely any thing.

" The next morning she told me that she was in the same frame of mind, and when I urged her to tell me what it was which so afflicted her, she exclaimed, sobbing, ' I am too proud, I never can be saved.' I assured her that I was rejoiced to find that she had attained this knowledge of her own heart, and then I opened before her all the treasures of the mercy of God in Jesus Christ. But she persevered in objecting the excess of her pride and vanity. She could not believe in the glad tidings, she could not believe that her prayers would be heard.

" ' Poor Emily, you are very unhappy at present, but your sadness shall be turned into joy. The Lord will comfort you.'

" ' But if I should die in this condition?'

" ' Be not afraid; I am as sure as I am of my own existence, that God does not light the candle and take the broom, to leave the piece of silver in the dust. He will finish the work which he has begun in you. He will call you to himself, after he has purified you.'

" It was in vain that I endeavoured to console her by such discourse as this; I could not succeed, and I left her with these words: ' My dear Emily, I am very sorry to have to quit you at this moment, but I leave you in the hands of the Lord, who will comfort you better than I can. Go to him with perfect confidence. I recommend you to acquaint your mother with the cause of your distress, in order to remove any unpleasant suspicion.' I then parted from her, and went to La Mure, where I preached at one o'clock, and in the evening I slept at La Baume, near the Drac, where I held a numerous meeting in the house of the mayor of the commune. All the inhabitants of this little village are Protestants; and not one of them stayed at home, even mothers attended with children at the breast, for in the memory of man, there had never been any preaching performed in this place, which is very remote from any road, and has no church near it. The next morning I set out at a very early

E

hour : the mayor accompanied me as far as the
Drac, and I ascended the mountain towards St.
Jean d'Héran, to visit a sick person.   He was a
wicked old man, who had all his life boasted of
his irreligion, but the fear of death had softened
him.   I found him in full possession of his intellect, although he was very near his end.   I
read to him, and I explained to him the parable
of the labourers in the vineyard, and dwelt upon
those who were hired at the eleventh hour.   He
listened, and then made some objections.   He
did not appear to be persuaded.   I prayed with
him, and then took my leave, after having addressed him with great earnestness, and I hope
with affection.   I do not know, whether the
Lord, who came five or six hours afterwards,
found him clothed with the white garment, or
naked.   I also visited another sick person, whom
I found much better disposed, and then returned
to Mens, to receive my catechumens.   In the
course of my excursion I did not forget Emily.
At one time I felt rejoiced, and blessed God for
his dispensation of mercy to her.   At another
time, I was afraid lest this sudden awakening
should produce bad effects, especially if her anguish of mind should continue, and affect her
health, which is but feeble even now.

" In the midst of these reflections I arrived
at home, fearing to find Emily in her bed, and
her parents miserable, but I found her full of
joy.   ' Oh how happy I am,' she exclaimed, the

moment she saw me. ' You have not left me in the hands of a severe judge. How gracious the Lord has been ! Oh ! he is rightly called the Saviour :—but what agony ! what sufferings ! Oh ! what he must have suffered ! He who drank the cup of bitterness even to the dregs. Now I understand what he meant to say, when he exclaimed, ' My soul is full of heaviness, even unto death.' I should never have done, if I were to endeavour to transcribe all the expressions of gratitude and admiration, which poured from her mouth : from that mouth, which heretofore had been full of the attractions of the world. Not only was her language new, but her air and aspect were changed. The vain and self-important deportment had now given way to modesty and sweetness. It was no longer the same Emily. My first movement was naturally to bless the Father of Mercies and the Saviour of Sinners."

The reader will be glad to know that the improvement, which had been now going on for a week, and which had been assisted so judiciously, and with so much tenderness and supplication by her pious instructor, continued until she began to bring forth the fruits of a holy life, and that she remained a faithful servant of her God and Redeemer.

As an accompaniment to the method used by Neff of gently leading on those, who were slow to approach the Lord, I subjoin his account of the language he was wont to hold with those, who appeared to be declining from their devout resolutions. "After having been awakened, D—— seemed to be on the point of relapsing into her former state. I asked her, what will become of the soul which neglects the means of grace, after having received them? 'It will fall into condemnation,' said she, in a faint voice. 'You ought,' said I to her, 'to know something of this by experience;' and then I spoke to her of her defection, and of the fate which awaits the branch which does not abide in the vine. Yesterday, at the evening catechising, I pursued a similar course with L——. She had repeated the verse containing those words of Jesus,—— 'Even the Spirit of Truth, which the world cannot receive, because it seeth him not, neither knoweth him, for he dwelleth with you, and shall be with you [1].' After she had explained what is meant by the habitation of the Spirit, I asked her if that Spirit was given for a time only?

" 'No,' said she, 'He is to abide with us for ever [2].'

" 'But if this Spirit will not depart of himself, may we not lose him?'

"She had great difficulty in making any reply. At length she answered in a low voice, and with tears in her eyes, 'Yes.'

[1] John xiv. 17.   [2] Ver. 16.

" ' Yes,' replied I calmly, but with considerable emphasis, ' and you are a proof of it. The Lord has enlightened you with his Spirit. You have been made sensible of the weight of your sins; and the time was, when you found rest at the feet of the Redeemer. You have known him. You had his seal set upon you, and now you have fallen back again into a state of spiritual death. You have only preserved the form of Christianity, by which you may more easily deceive the children of God! But beware! Woe unto him by whom the Son of man is betrayed!'—This apostrophe had a striking effect upon L——, and all who listened to it."

One of Neff's Journals contains these interesting remarks upon the village of La Baume, " For nine months I have made frequent visits to this place, but I have been heard without opposition, and without producing any positive good. The mayor has received me with perfect frankness, and the whole population have listened to me attentively. Lately, however, I have perceived something like signs of life in three or four young persons. At my last visit, when I had finished my exposition and my prayer, instead of going away, as they had hitherto done, at the termination of the service, all the people kept their seats, and remained silent. Full of real concern for these poor creatures, I rested my head upon my hands, and offered up a secret prayer to God in their behalf. They

thought I was taken ill, and many anxious inquiries were put to me. I lifted up my head,
and said, "I am not ill, my friends, but I am
distressed on your account. I am thinking that
most of you have already forgotten that which
you have just heard, and it is this which grieves
me.'"

CHAPTER IV.

NEFF'S DIFFICULTIES AS TO ORDINATION—HIS REASONS FOR
NOT BEING ORDAINED BY THE GENEVAN CLERGY—GOES TO
ENGLAND FOR HIS DIPLOMA—HIS RETURN TO FRANCE AND
RECEPTION AT MENS—HIS NOMINATION AS PASTOR OF THE
HIGH ALPS—HIS FIRST VISITS TO THE MOUNTAIN HAMLETS
OF HIS PARISH.

NEFF had now made sufficient proof of his inclination and powers. He had discharged the duties of a probationer and catechist for more than
four years, and in the course of this ministry,
first in his native country, and next in one of the
provinces of France, he found, by happy experience, that God had given him both strength
and willingness to do his work. He, therefore,
took his departure from Mens, in April 1823,
with the intention of seeking for the imposition
of hands, and of devoting himself to the service
of the Church by a solemn act of consecration.
He believed himself to be called, and tried, and
he humbly hoped, that he possessed such qualities as were requisite for the responsible station,
which he was desirous to fill.

The great difficulty, however, was this. By
whom should he be ordained? By the authori-

13

ties of the National Church of Geneva, the land
of his birth [1]? But these had avowed principles
from which his soul shrunk : and he felt a strong
reluctance to derive authority to preach the
Gospel from those who, in his opinion, had betrayed the Gospel, by ceasing to uphold the
divinity of Jesus Christ, and the essential doctrines of the Book of Life. Should he present
himself before those seceding pastors of Geneva,
who had separated from the national church, and
who declared themselves the members of a new
church ? A reference to Neff's letter, on the
subject of national establishments, will show that
he was likely to have scruples here, and that he
was unwilling to take any step, which could be
regarded as inconsistent with his declared opinions on the subject of disorganisation. He
could not wish, by any act of his, to be impair-
ing the maintenance of the church in which he
himself had been baptized, which had once been
the instrument of much good, and might again,
by a reformation within itself, become as illustrious for its orthodoxy, as it then was for its
learning.

[1] A friend, who read this observation in the first edition,
has objected that Neff could not have obtained orders in the
National Church of Geneva, for want of having pursued a regular course of academical studies. Neff had offers of assistance to enable him to pass through the "academy," but he
was unwilling to attend the theological lectures of a professor
of doubtful principles.

In further explanation of Neff's unwillingness to be ordained by the hands of ministers of the established Church of his native country, I must here offer a few statements, touching the departure of that Church from its ancient principles. For several years past, a spirit, hostile to the fundamental doctrines settled at the period of the Reformation, and sanctioned by the subscription of names illustrious in the ecclesiastical history of Geneva, such as Farel, Calvin, Viret, and Beza, has been openly avowed by many of the national pastors. Even the cardinal article of the Christian creed, the divinity of Jesus Christ, which the most distinguished confessors of every branch of the universal Church have agreed in receiving, from the apostolic times to our own, has been disputed, and the belief of Wicliff, Huss, Luther, and Fenelon, has been publicly controverted from the theological chair of the academy of Geneva. In 1817, the venerable company of pastors took upon themselves to declare, that the following subjects were not to be discussed in the pulpits, viz.

"The Divinity of Jesus Christ."
"Original Sin."
"The Operation of Grace."
"Predestination."

From this period the departure from apostolical Christianity has been so undisguised, that out of twenty-two recent elections to pastoral charges, there has been but one minister elected, who has ventured to preach the divinity of Christ. Under such circumstances, it is not to be wondered that Neff felt scruples of conscience, and could not consent to receive ordination in a church, in which it was prohibited to enlarge upon the great mystery of godliness, God manifest in the flesh. Within a few months, some of the brightest ornaments of the establishment, who have all along refused to be silent upon the prohibited topics, have been deprived of their functions, because they formed the committee of an association, which determined at last to take measures for the revival of the ancient principles of their Church, and to institute a school of theology, in which those principles shall be taught. The association has declared its strict adherence to the doctrines, which the Protestant Churches of Holland, England, Scotland, France, Germany, and Italy, profess with one accord, in their respective articles of faith.

I subjoin the contents of a paper lately circulated by the Rev. Richard Burgess, the English chaplain at Geneva, in which the lamentable falling off of the Geneva Church and academy, and the views of the association are ably stated.

" The decline of the orthodox faith in the ' National Church' of Geneva, and the consequent deterioration in the religious instruction of youth, have, for several years, been subjects of painful interest to the friends of the Protestant cause in Europe. Hitherto, however, they have

remained almost passive spectators of the conflict, which has been carried on between the
Unitarian principles of the great body of the
clergy and a few individuals among them, who
' have earnestly contended for the faith once
delivered to the saints :' for the principles of the
' National Church,' although evidently to be
traced in every act of its constituent body, were
not openly avowed, and the formal abolition of
all creeds kept many persons in doubt as to the
real doctrines of the majority of the clergy.   At
length, a series of publications, emanating from
the professor of divinity and other influential
members of the ecclesiastical body, have placed
the doctrines of that majority in a graduated
scale of heterodoxy between Arianism and So-
cinianism.   It then became imperative for such
of the clerical and lay members of the ' National
Church' as retained and cherished the true doctrines, and who conscientiously felt, that to be
silent any longer were to betray the sacred
cause of the Gospel, to form a religious union
for their edification, whilst they might maintain
their principles and disseminate them amongst
their fellow-citizens.   A society called the Société Evangélique, was accordingly formed, and
in a very short time received an accession of
more than two hundred members.   The committee of the society is composed of three ministers of distinguished zeal and piety, and several laymen of rank and consideration as citi-

zens and as Christians, 'strong in the grace that is in Christ Jesus.' The great object of the *Société Evangélique* is to restore the true and orthodox doctrines of the Gospel (which, through a vain philosophy, have been so long lost) to the Genevan Church, and one of the most effectual means for accomplishing this end is the establishment of a theological academy, to train up young men for the ministry in sound and orthodox principles. This institution has already been set on foot; the professors engaged are men of distinguished talent, expressing their firm adherence to the doctrines contained in the articles of the Church of England and the Helvetic confession of faith."

The three members, to whom Mr. Burgess alludes, Messrs. Gaussen [1], Merle d'Aubigny, and Galland, were ejected from the Church of Geneva, by an act of consistory, dated 11th October, 1831, and confirmed by the council of state. The alleged offence was the following passage in their circular.

" We have said that THIS SCHOOL WAS INDISPENSABLE; and it is but too easy to prove the fact. If the youths who go to the academies of France and Geneva to qualify themselves for the ministry of the Word of Life, are there

---

[1] Mr. Gaussen first incurred the displeasure of the Venerable Company of Pastors, by refusing to use new editions of catechisms in his schools, in which the fundamental doctrines of the Gospel were omitted or disguised.

taught Unitarian doctrines :—if the very truths, for the sake of which our professorships were founded, our schools opened, and our institutions formed, are there condemned :—if the studies in those schools are not free, that is to say, if the pupils attached to the faith of the apostles and reformers are not at liberty to follow the instructions, which correspond with their faith and satisfy their consciences :—if pious parents, desirous of devoting their sons to the ministry of the Gospel, are compelled to condemn them to consume the four best years of their youth in studies, which subvert the foundations of our faith:—in a word, if it be true that Arianism saps the very foundations of the Gospel,—then assuredly the establishment of a new school of theology was indispensable.

" In thus saying, we are but stating a fact well known to the Church of Christ. Indeed, those who teach the new doctrines in the theological chairs, have themselves proclaimed it in recent publications ; and, while we appreciate the candour which has at length brought to light such an evil, we consider it to be obligatory on all Christians, not only to desire, but to labour assiduously to provide a remedy.

" If then, we have presumed to propose a remedy, it is because it behoved some one to offer it: and if we entertain the persuasion that God will take this work into his all-powerful hands, it is because it is his own cause, and not ours."

Neff's eyes, in his reluctance to be ordained by clergy holding doubtful opinions, would next be turned to the Protestant Church of France, and as he had been a humble Levite in her temples, and hoped yet to serve before her altars, it must have been his devout wish, to receive orders under her sanction. But he was a foreigner, and without the process of naturalization, it was not then easy, perhaps not practicable to be admitted into her bosom.

One door only seemed to be open to him. To go to England, where his name and merits had been made known through the means originally, of the Continental Society I believe, and of Mr. Cook, and Mr. Wilks, two eminent dissenting ministers; and to ask for a public recognition as a devoted servant of God, in one of those independent congregations, whose ministers are received in the Protestant Churches of France, as duly authorized to preach the word of God, and to fulfil all the duties of the pastoral office.

Neff had no other mode of satisfying his conscience, and of assuming the functions of a minister "lawfully called," according to the regulations of the country, where he looked forward to pursue his professional career. He therefore proceeded to London in the beginning of May, and without being acquainted with a single word of the English language, we find the catechist of the mountains embarking on board a steam-boat at Calais, landing at Dover half dead with sea-sickness, consigning himself to the chances of a night-coach, and arriving in the metropolis on a Sunday morning, with no other aid to help him through the mazes of a city, (which is more embarrassing to a stranger than any other capital in Europe,) than a direction to the house of Mr. Wilks. After puzzling out his way to his friend's abode, judge what must have been his forlorn feeling upon learning that Mr. Wilks was not at home, and that nobody in the house could speak French. Somehow or other the intelligent stranger after many questions put to such passengers, as, he hoped, might be able to reply to him in a language he could understand, got a clue through the labyrinth of streets and lanes, to a French Chapel, where he considered, that, as it was Sunday, he should find somebody who could hold intercourse with him, and put him in the train of profiting by his letters of introduction. The excellent Mr. Scholl was the preacher at the chapel upon this occasion, and to him Neff addressed himself after the service with the modest request, that he would direct him to an hotel where French was spoken. The wanderer's delight must have been excessive, when Mr. Scholl kindly accosted him by name, and told him that he was aware of the errand upon which he had come, and that every thing should be done to promote his views.   He was placed in comfortable lodgings, and on the return of Mr. Wilks he was introduced by that gentleman to the ministers who were to receive him into their body.   But though he received every attention from his new friends, during the interval that elapsed before the public ceremony which brought him to England, yet one or two only could hold conversation with him, and his time hung heavily on his hands.   " My visits," said he in one of his letters, " are very insipid, I cannot talk English, nor they French, and the sooner I can get away, the happier I shall be; but I will remain as long as I can be forming connections, which may prove useful in promoting the reign of Christ in France."

It was on the 19th of May, 1823, that Neff, to use his own terms, " received a diploma in Latin, signed by nine ministers, of whom three were doctors in Theology, and one was a master of arts, and was ordained in a chapel in the Poultry in London."

The questions proposed to him, in examination, were :—

How do you know that you have been called by God ?

What is it which has induced you to devote yourself to the ministry ?

What are the doctrines which you regard as essentials ?

To the two first he gave answers, of which the following is the substance. "I have embraced the vocation of a minister of the Gospel, because the Sovereign Bishop of Souls has implanted an ardent desire in me to preach the Gospel, and because, whenever I have directed my thoughts to other professions, I have felt my conscience burthened, and a secret voice has commanded me to announce the kingdom of God. Because God has been pleased to bless my labours, and many souls have already been brought to a knowledge of the Word, which he has permitted me to declare in his name: because he has graciously opened many doors to me, and in the course of the last two years I have been invited many times, by consistories and churches, so that I shall not enter the vineyard of myself, and without a lawful calling."

To the third question, he replied:—"I do not pretend to penetrate into the secrets of God, nor to explain how or why evil entered into the world: but I know that it exists, and that it dwells in our hearts; that we carry it with us from our birth, and that, excited by the example of the world, and the influence of Satan, it reigns in our souls, and makes us bring forth evil fruits to our condemnation. I believe that in this state man is neither capable nor worthy of having any part in the kingdom of God, but that he deserves the Divine wrath, according to the justice of the Most High. I believe that there does not exist in ourselves, or in any created being, the means of escaping from this state of perdition, but that God, loving us when we were his enemies, has sent into the world the Eternal Word, by which he made all things, and that this Word dwelt among us, under the name of Jesus, which signifies the Saviour. I believe that this Saviour is our righteousness and redemption, and that his death and atonement have appeased the wrath of God. I believe that the true faith consists in being thoroughly convinced of, and deeply affected by, our state of corruption, and of the justice of our condemnation—in putting our whole trust in the sufferings of Jesus Christ,—and in the righteousness which is through Him and of Him. I believe that we are not saved because we love God, but that we may love him, and that if we are saved by faith without the works of the law, we are created again in Jesus Christ to do the good works for which God has prepared us. I believe that, in order to answer this object of our Saviour, it is absolutely necessary that he should write his laws in our hearts. I believe that a change of hearts is the result of true faith.

" After these principal points, I believe that we ought, in the course of our instructions, 1. To convince men of their guilt by all scriptural and reasonable means : 2. To conduct them to Jesus : 3. To engage them to read and meditate on the word of God, and to pray for them that know not the truth. I believe that we ought to announce Jesus Christ and him crucified, without entering into unedifying discussions on points of doctrine contested among Christians. I believe that it is the duty of a good steward to give to each the nourishment which he requires, milk to babes, and strong meat to men. Finally, I subscribe, both in matter of faith and practice, to the confessions of faith of the reformed Churches of France and Switzerland, in the which I was born, and to which I desire to dedicate the services of my ministry."

Neff lost no time in returning to France, and to the scene of his first labours in that country: but his journey to England had nearly been the means of defeating all his hopes and plans. He was represented to the French government as an agent of England, and when he presented himself before the prefect of the department of the Isère at Grenoble, to meet any charge that might be made against him, that functionary candidly told him, that the minister of the interior had received information, that all the preachers not French, and more especially those who had religious connections out of the kingdom, were in the pay of England, and were charged with some political mission. The prefect was at the same time polite and kind in his manner, and strongly advised Neff to take up letters of naturalization, as the best answer to the calumny, and the only way of securing his object in regard to a pastoral appointment.

The reception which the Protestants of Mens gave to their former catechist, on his reappearing among them, would have been felt like a triumphal entrance to any but a person of his gentle and unassuming spirit. They left their shops and their husbandry work to meet him. They crowded round him, some half-stifled him in their embraces, others kissed his hand, others wept with joy, and all signified the sincerity of their affection and respect. When he called upon his acquaintances in the villages, similar testimonies of veneration were displayed.

At St. Jean d'Héran, he was obliged to repress the out-bursting of delight with which he was welcomed. His approach had been announced by somebody who ran before to give the joyful intelligence, "he is coming," and on drawing near the village, he saw the bottom of the little hill, on which it stands, full of people, who were waiting to greet him. With his usual prudence and good sense, he foresaw that an unfavourable construction might be put upon these public indications of esteem, and he begged one of his friends to go forward, and to request that the honest villagers would return to their houses, where he would visit them successively, and receive their cordial assurances of affection. For eight days, previously to his arrival, the inhabit-

13

ants of St. Jean d'Héran had been anxiously expecting him, and its population had turned out more than once to hail his approach.

But the cabals, of which some mention has been made in a preceding page, rendered it unadvisable for Neff to remain either in Mens or its immediate neighbourhood. The principal inhabitants of St. Sebastian presented a requisition, in which they urged him to accept the office of pastor in that commune, and undertook to raise his salary among themselves, but he declined their generous offers, for the same reasons that induced him to remove himself from Mens. Perhaps it was no great act of self-denial to make up his mind to quit the department of the Isère, for though his affections were strongly fixed there, yet his anxious desire to be at the post, where he could most effectually be of use, made him frequently turn a longing eye towards the section of the High Alps. " I am always dreaming of the High Alps," said he in a letter of the 8th Sept. 1823, " and I would rather be stationed there than in the places, which are under the beautiful sky of Languedoc. In the higher Alpine region I shall be the only pastor, and therefore more at liberty. In the south, I should be embarrassed by the presence and conflicting opinions of other pastors. With respect to the description which B—— has given of those mountains, it may be correct as to some places, but still the country bears a strong resemblance to the Alps of Switzerland. It has its advantages and even its beauties. If there are wolves and chamois, there are also cattle and pasturages, and glaciers, and picturesque spots, and above all an energetic race of people, intelligent, active, hardy, and patient under fatigue, who offer a better soil for the Gospel, than the wealthy and corrupt inhabitants of the plains of the south."

At length his ardent wishes were gratified, and while he was staying at Grenoble, in October, 1823, he received intelligence that the elders of the Protestant churches of Val Queyras and Val Fressinière had made application to the Consistory in his behalf, and that he might shortly expect to receive his appointment from the president. " To-morrow," says the last sentence of one of his journals, " with the blessing of God, I mean to push for the Alps by the sombre and picturesque valley of Loysan." Within a few days after the first news of his intended destination, the impatient minister was on the scene of his future labours, exploring hamlet after hamlet, and forming plans for his conduct in that sacred office, which had so long been the subject of his hopes, and prayers, and hourly contemplation. To Fressinière he first directed his steps, next to Guillestre, where he met the elders of Val Queyras, and was hailed as their pastor elect. From Guillestre he lost no time in traversing the formidable pass that leads to Arvieux. Here all his enthusiasm was called into action by officiating in a church, which had recently been constructed on the ruins of that, which was destroyed at the revocation of the edict of Nantes. At La Chalp, a hamlet of Arvieux, they showed him a new cottage, which was just finished for the residence of the expected minister, and four leagues further to the east, he found himself at San Veran, on the frontiers of France and Italy, and at the foot of a snowy ridge, which is the boundary line between the French Alpine valleys, and those of Piedmont; but here he shall speak for himself, in a letter dated Guillestre, Oct. 31, 1823.

" I have only had a transient view of the churches of Queyras and Fressinière, but they seem to be extremely interesting. I do not think that all the Protestants together, in this section, would amount to more than 600 or 700, and they are divided into six groups, and are at a great distance from each other. In summer these distances are less, because you can cross the mountains ; but in the winter you are obliged to follow the valleys, which greatly lengthen the journey. The country nearer to Briançon is cold, and Queyras much more so, but there are some agreeable situations. La Chalp, in particular, where the pastor is to reside, faces the south, and is within a vast amphitheatre of mountains, where there is good milk, and excellent meat. The bread and the wine are brought from

Briançon, or Guillestre.   Besides his habitation,
they supply their pastor with fuel."

But before our candidate, for the most arduous
piece of ecclesiastical preferment in Christendom,
could be established in his mountain parish,
there were many preliminary steps which he had
to take.   He must receive his diploma from the
consistory of Orpierre, and his naturalization
from the office of the minister in Paris; and these
doubts frequently crossed his anxious mind.
Would the president of the consistory sanction
the election of the elders of the parish? Would
the minister of the interior confirm it? Would
the keeper of the seals grant him letters of naturalization?   Would he not be obliged to make
many an excursion to Orpierre, and even to
undertake an expensive and weary journey to
Paris, to press his suit, and perhaps to repeat
this more than once? Still he travelled on in
hope, and resolved, until all the formalities could
be settled, to take charge of these churches provisionally, and to run the risk of receiving the
government stipend or not, as it might happen.
In fact, some of the necessary forms never were
regularly obtained; but the consistory, and the
elders, and the inhabitants of the communes
were so well satisfied that the churches could
not be better served, than by this active and
right-minded foreigner, that by some management which the higher authorities winked at, he

remained in undisturbed possession of his cure of souls ; but I have not been able to ascertain, whether or not he received the government stipend, or whether he drew from the funds of the Continental Society only for his subsistence [1].

A letter to his mother, written on the 10th of December, 1823, gives a lovely picture of the cheerful and energetic state of his mind, at this period, and contains some touches in it, which remind us both of patriarchal times, and of the apostolical era of Christianity, when the messengers of the Gospel sallied forth with their scrips and their staves, preaching, as they went, that the kingdom of heaven was at hand ; and when they were received into the houses of the faithful as angels of God, and were ministered unto with all the hospitality and attention of primitive simplicity.

" Since my last letter, I have been constantly on foot to the present hour.   After having made several visits to my Alpine hamlets, I received a note from Blanc, which urged me to take the letters of the elders of Queyras and Fressinière to Orpierre, and to lay them before the president of the consistory.   I crossed the Col d'Orsière (probably from Gap) on the 27th of November,

---

[1] Since the above was written I have been informed, that Neff did not receive the government stipend, but that his salary from the Continental Society, of about 50*l.* a year, was his principal, if not his sole maintenance.

and went to our friend Eloi Cordier, who gave me an introduction to the president. On Saturday, the 29th, I was at Fressinière, when the elders added their signatures to those of the principal people of Queyras, and M. Barridon fortified my testimonials with the letter, which Professor Bonnard had written to him concerning me. On Sunday, the 30th, I preached at Dormilleuse, the remotest village in the valley, and on Monday morning, at day-break, I set out to pass the Col d'Orsière again, which separates Fressinière from Champsaur, a valley through which the Drac flows. I took two guides with me, to assist in the passage of the mountain, which is one of the highest in France, and very seldom practicable at this time of the year. After leaving the village of Dormilleuse, we walked three hours through snow, some of which had lately fallen, at the foot of a glacier, and incessantly on the ascent. The sky was clear, and the cold not excessive, although the elevation was so great. In many places the snow was hard, but in some we sunk above our knees. The peasants had protected my feet with slips of woollen cloth tied round my shoes, and we were well provided with provisions and good wine for the journey. Since the first fall of snow this season, which took place in September, only two men had effected the passage of the mountain. We could occasionally track their path, which also showed the foot-marks of wolves and chamois, and of some marmot-catchers. When we reached the summit of the Col, we had two hours of rapid descent before we arrived at the foot of the snow-line, where we entered the first hamlet of the Val d'Orsière, near the source of the Drac. Here we dined, and my guides took their leave. I continued my route along the Drac until nightfall, when I fortunately came upon the high road between Gap and Grenoble. The next morning, at the dawn of light, I resumed my journey, and where do you think I turned my steps? Can you guess? Towards Mens! (This was in the direction the very reverse of Orpierre, but Neff's affectionate yearnings after his beloved catechumens in that quarter were irresistible.) It was my wish to induce Blanc to fulfil his promise, and to accompany me to Orpierre. I walked for five or six hours on the high road, and then having crossed the Drac, I took to the bye-paths, and towards sunset I arrived at Peyre, at the foot of Mont Chatel, about three quarters of a league from Mens. Paul, the uncle of Peter Baulme, was working near the village, and as soon as he perceived me, he left his cart, and ran to meet me. Nothing could exceed his surprise or joy. I then went to Baulme's house. Peter's father and mother, and several of his neighbours were in the garden; they did not perceive me till I was in the midst of them. Their astonishment was as great as that of Paul. The wife of the elder

9

Girard, who happened to be there, ran to call her husband—another person went in search of Peter Baulme, who was looking after the sheep. After supper, a party of the neighbours assembled at Baulme's house, and I discoursed for a long time on the kingdom of God. Our conversation was in the patois. At ten o'clock at night, I proceeded on to Mens, accompanied by Peter Baulme and the elder Desloix. I did not wish to arrive during the day, for fear of the eclat. The door of Pelissier's house was closed for the night. The next day I had visitors in abundance. Never did the arrival of a beloved father, who had been long absent from his family and long expected, produce greater joy. For myself, although I am not easily affected, yet I could not suppress certain strong emotions, on finding myself once more among these dear friends and dear children. Poor Madame Bonnet, my former hostess, on hearing of my arrival, was seized with her old complaint, and was confined to her bed till my departure. Her temperament would never allow her to bear any great excitement. It was determined that Blanc and I should go to Orpierre next day, Thursday; but in the morning I found myself unwell. These frequent and long journeys had knocked me up. I took a warm bath, and found myself the better for it. Notwithstanding this delay, we meant to have set out the same day, but so much was said to Blanc, that he agreed to stop till the following morning. I, therefore, performed the Thursday service. A large congregation was present, although the country people had not been apprized of my arrival. In the evening I held a meeting of our brethren at the house of Louis Pagen, and at a later hour I held a meeting of our sisters at that of Madame Duseigneur. I meant to have proceeded on foot, but the kind family of Pelissier insisted on finding a pony for me; and at sunrise, with Blanc by my side, mounted on a large grey horse, we were on the road for Orpierre."

The interviews with the prefect and with M. D'Aldebert, the president of the consistory of Orpierre, were satisfactory, and we have now to contemplate Neff in a new character, as an authorized[1] pastor of the department of the High Alps.

[1] Mr. Smedley, in his bitter review of this Memoir in the British Critic, has said that Neff " vaulted into the fold,"— " unsanctioned by the approval of the Presiding Consistory of Orpierre."

CHAPTER V.

SYNOPTICAL VIEW OF THE ALPINE CHURCHES OF FRANCE—
I. SITUATION OF THIS REGION OF THE ALPS—DE THOU'S
DESCRIPTION OF IT—II. EVIDENCE THAT THE ALPINE
PROTESTANT CONGREGATIONS OF DAUPHINE, ARE THE RE-
MAINS OF THE PRIMITIVE CHRISTIANS OF GAUL.

BEFORE I enter upon the relation of Neff's personal exertions on the new scene of his labours,
I must clear the way, by describing the situation
of the country, where he was the hard-working
pastor; and by explaining the nature of the evidence, which may be adduced in support of the
hypothesis, that his mountain flock are the descendants of the primitive Christians of Gaul.
This exposition will, in fact, give a synoptical
view of the Alpine Churches of France from the
earliest times.

I.—*Situation of the country.*

The scene of Neff's principal labours is to be
found in the most elevated region of France: in
the heart of that mountain territory which lies
between the Rhone and the barrier Alps, which
separate France from Italy, and in the same degree of latitude, and within a hundred miles of

the Protestant Valleys of Piedmont. It is necessary to be minute in describing the exact situation of the country, and to give it both its ancient and its modern designation, because, without this, the reader may fall into the inveterate error, that all Alpine Protestants must be Swiss [1]. For notwithstanding all that has been

[1] So little is known of the Protestants of Dauphiné and Provence, and their origin, that the following is part of the account given of the massacres at Cabriéres and Merindol, in the sixteenth century, by the author of the life of Francis the First: "The inhabitants of Cabriéres and Merindol [*] had then a great inclination for the doctrines which Luther had so successfully promulgated, and which their neighbourhood to Germany and Switzerland had made these people more intimately acquainted with, than those of the surrounding French district. From being tolerated as they were at first, they began to indulge in that jealous insolence, which is common to heretics of all descriptions, and not content with pursuing their own system of worship, they attacked that of the professors of the Church of Rome."

The People here mentioned were not *Lutherans*, they were descendants of the primitive Christians of Gaul. Merindol and Cabriéres are not in the neighbourhood of Germany or Switzer-

[*] Mr. Smedley, in his "History of the Reformed Religion in France," has fallen into the error of describing the inhabitants of Cabriéres and Merindol, as colonists from the Valleys of Piedmont. They were remnants of the primitive Christians of Provence.

The Author of the "History of the Reformed Religion in France," has replied to the above note by the production of passages from the more modern authorities *Garnier, Honoré Bouche, Jacques Aubery*, and of documents of the 16th Century. My authorities are older by several centuries, authorities of the years 1144, 1134, 1119, and 1050, (See pages 95, 96,) which prove all that Mr. Smedley is disposed to question.—*Note to 3d Edition.*

written lately about those Italian Protestants, the Vaudois or Waldenses of the Valleys of Piedmont, there is scarcely one person in ten, to whom their history is otherwise well known, who does not yet run into the mistake, that they are natives of Switzerland and not of Italy.   Lest any confusion should arise as to the locality of Neff's flock, it must be borne in mind, that they are inhabitants of that province, which is delineated in the maps of ancient Gaul under the name of Gallia Narbonensis.   Alpes Maritimæ, and Caturiges, are subdivisions of Gallia Narbonensis, within the limits of which, we shall find the city Embrodunum (the modern Embrun), and the river Druentia, (now the Durance.)   These give the exact bearings of the deep glens, in which the ancestors of the objects of our interest took refuge.   In the maps of modern France, Embrun and the Durance, will be found in the province called Dauphiné, or the Delphinate, and in the department styled " Les Hautes Alpes," or the high Alps, a name which well describes the nature of the country, and its formidable aspect.   Ancient historians did not magnify the difficulties of traversing it, when they spoke of the region of the Durance as presenting more

land, they are villages on the Durance in Provence, in the south of France.   That the victims were not fanatics, that they had indulged in no insolence, and had not assailed the Roman Catholics first, may be learnt from the Roman Catholic historian De Thou.

impediments to the passage of an army, than any other region in Gaul [1]. A writer, of the present day [2], has represented the march of an army through this district to be utterly impossible, unless it be provided with the means of blasting the rocks, of throwing bridges over the terrible abysses that yawn on every side, and of cutting galleries on the edge of precipices. In one of the latest geographical delineations [3], the department is represented as being walled in and intersected by high mountains, whose tops are covered with snow, having a soil and climate so variable, that if you are making a journey of two short days, you will be in the midst of smiling villages, enjoying a bright sky and a warm sun, and delicious productions of the earth to-day, and to-morrow you will be shivering with cold, and chilled with the sight of black rocks, or frozen snows, and despairing of obtaining a morsel of food to your taste. The author of a well written little book, entitled " Hannibal's Passage of the Alps, by a member of the University of Cambridge," considers this to have been the region (and De Thou, the historian, was of the same opinion) where Hannibal found the greatest obstacles in forcing his way through the rugged depths, and over the lofty summits, which lay in his line of march. " The

[1] Livy, lib. xxi. Silv. Ital. lib. xxxviii.   [2] Sismondi.
[3] " Tableau Géographique et Statistique du Département des Hautes Alpes."

G

appearance of the Alps (altitudo montium, nivesque cœlo prope immistæ,) and the savage and dreary aspect of every thing, animate and inanimate, around them, absolutely terrified the Carthaginians." That, which will be thought as much to our purpose as the face of the country, is the character of the people there. The indomitable spirit imputed to their ancestors by ancient historians, has been inherited, from generation to generation, by the mountaineers of more recent times; and the compiler of the " Atlas of Gaul" enumerates them among the most resolute defenders of their liberties[1]. But the most extraordinary description of all is that, which is recorded in the pages of De Thou, and for this reason: what De Thou represented the mountaineers of this territory to have been in the sixteenth century, Neff found them, with very little difference, in the nineteenth; and I myself saw them in 1829, under circumstances which recalled the French historian's account strongly to my mind.

" Of all these regions the Val Fressinière is the most repulsive and wild; its soil is sterile and unproductive, and its inhabitants are most lamentably poor. They are clothed in sheepskins, and they have no linen in use, either for their garments or their beds. They sleep in

[1] Atlas Novus Galliæ. Amstelodami, 1649. " Incolæ magni sunt libertatis suæ assertatores et æstimatores.—Militia contra hostem feroces."

the clothes which they wear during the day.
They inhabit seven villages, and their houses
are made of stone, with flat roofs, and mud ce-
ment. In these hovels the people and their
cattle live together, and they often take refuge
in caves, when they expect an attack from their
enemies, in one corner of which they themselves
lie concealed, and, in the other, their sheep and
kine. They subsist principally on milk and
venison, and their occupation is tending their
cattle. They are skilful marksmen, and seldom
miss either the chamois or the bear; but from
the filthy manner in which they devour the flesh
of these animals, they become so offensive to
the smell, that strangers can scarcely bear to be
within scent of them. Happy in these their
scanty resources, they are all equally poor alike;
but they have no mendicants among them, and,
contented among themselves, they very seldom
form either friendships or connexions with others.
In this state of squalidness, which causes them
to present a most uncouth appearance, it is surprising that they are very far from being uncul-
tivated in their morals. They almost all understand Latin, and are able to write fairly enough.
They understand also as much of French as will
enable them to read the Bible, and to sing
psalms; nor would you easily find a boy among
them, who, if he were questioned as to the religious opinions, which they hold in common with
the Waldenses, would not be able to give, from

memory, a reasonable account of them. They pay taxes most scrupulously, and the duty of doing this forms an article of their confession of faith. If they are prevented from making payment by civil wars, they lay apart the proper sum, and on the return of peace, they take care to settle with the royal tax gatherers[1]."

De Thou gives the locality of these Alpines with equal precision. " As you proceed towards the east, from Embrun, the capital of the maritime Alps, when you have travelled about five leagues, the Valley of Queyras branches off towards the right, and that of Fressinière towards the left hand. Between the two the ruins of the ancient city of Rama are still conspicuous. From thence, on the other side of the mountain ridge, a narrow pass is hewn out of the rock, by dint of human labour, and opens a way across some difficult and rugged country, which is still called, by the natives, Hannibal's road. In the direction towards Briançon, there is another valley, opening to the left, called Louise, from Louis XII. who gave it his own name, in a moment of compunction for the injuries, which he was well nigh about to inflict upon it, instead of the contumelious appellation of Val Pute, which it had received in contempt for the false religion of its inhabitants[2]."

This is the Alpine desert where Neff sacri-

[1] Thuani Hist. lib. xxvii.   [2] Ibid. xxvii. 9.

ficed his life in the cause of pure religion, and its natives are the people, whom he considered to be the lineal and unmixed descendants of the first converts to Christianity, in the mountain province of Dauphiné, in other words, the remains of primitive Christians.

II.—*Evidence that the Alpine Protestant Congregations of Dauphiné are the remains of the Primitive Christians of Gaul.*

It was my original intention to prefix, or to append to this work, a regular historical detail, and to transcribe such records as I have, in proof of the reality of the descent of our Alpines from a line of ancestors, who never worshipped God as they do at Rome, that is, after a manner which Protestants believe that God has forbidden. But when I came to commit my materials to paper, I found they were so voluminous, that it was necessary to recast my plan, and to give an outline only of the argument. My inquiries had led me through divers literary records of every century, contained in the sheets of Ecclesiastical History, or of Polemical Theology ; and in every century up to the second, tracing the vestiges retrogressively in the line of antiquity, I found myself in the footsteps of Christians, dwelling in the Alpine Valleys of Dauphiné, who might claim fellowship with the primitive Christians of antiquity, and with the Protestants of modern times, in two characteris-

tic points of resemblance : first, in their reject-
ing unscriptural helps to devotion, such as image
worship, and the intercession of any but the one
Mediator between God and man ; and secondly,
in their steady resistance of the unscriptural authority usurped by the bishops of Rome.

Between the revocation of the Edict of Nantes
in 1686, and the Edict of Toleration by Louis
XVI, in 1786, it was forbidden to exercise any
form of religion in France, except the Roman
Catholic ; but I have conversed with aged natives of Dormilleuse, Neff's principal village,
who remember the tales, which were told them
by their fathers and grandfathers, concerning
Vaudois pastors, harboured in their houses, at
the risk of their lives, who had crossed the Alps
in disguise to administer the services of their
Church to families, to whom the presence of those
devoted men was like angels' visits—strengthening the weak, and confirming the strong.   I
have also seen Bibles, printed in the seventeenth
century, which have been handed down from
father to son, "the big hall Bible once their
father's pride," and had been concealed from inquisitorial search by being buried in the earth.
For the Christianity, not Romish, which prevailed in an unbroken line in this part of Dauphiné, during a hundred years before the revocation of the Edict of Nantes, the reader may
consult the general and ecclesiastical historians
of France, who will place before him articles of

synod and confessions of faith, which sufficiently identify the principles of the primitive and those of the reformed churches. These authorities will also tell him, that this province had, at one period, as many as ninety-four Protestant pastors, and a Protestant University at Die, with an array of Hebrew, Greek, and Divinity professors, and a respectable body of teachers in the different branches of science and literature [1].

The great Protestant muster in France, and the gathering of those, who determined to vindicate their religious rights, took place between the years 1550 and 1572. The first national synod of Protestants was held in 1559, and in the twelve years that followed, there were no less than seven synods. The places, where some of these councils were held, bear witness, that from the centre of the kingdom, to its farthest extremities, east, west, north, and south, the standard of religious independence had been displayed. At Paris, Poictiers, Orleans, Rochelle, Lyons, and Nismes, delegates assembled in council, and there represented Churches, which declared themselves Reformed and Protestant. But some of these, particularly the delegates from parts of Dauphiné and Provence, announced, " We consent to merge in the common cause, but we require no reformation, for our forefathers and ourselves have ever disclaimed the corruptions of the Churches in communion with Rome."

[1] Gallia Reformata, vol. i.

I have not been able to ascertain the exact number of the remains of the primitive Christians in Dauphiné and Provence, between the years 1550 and 1572: the first being the date when the mountain Churches of France began to have rest, and the second the epoch when they were frightfully wasted by the persecutions, subsequent upon the massacre of St. Bartholomew; but in the beginning of the sixteenth century, we know that they amounted to 50,000. This enumeration is made in the report of an inquisitorial process issued against them in 1501. The destruction of most of their own manuscripts relating to their history, at different periods of persecution, was so complete, that we should have had but few memorials to produce, had not the documents of their enemies furnished us with indisputable evidence. When the palace of the archbishop of Embrun was taken by the duke de Lesdiguieres in 1585 [1], there was found, among the archiepiscopal archives, a collection of papers, (which are now in the public library at Cambridge) containing an account of processes from time to time against the non-conformists of Dauphiné, and these are our authority for many of the statements that have been made. "Not being fully extirpated," is the language of the process, "they betook them-

---

[1] Histoire du Connetable de Lesdiguieres par Louis Videl. liv. ii. chap. 7.   Perrin, liv. ii. chap. 3.

selves to the utmost parts of Dauphiné, among the Alps, and in the caves of the mountains, places exceedingly difficult to approach, where more than 50,000 of them did inhabit [1]." The same inquisitorial report, from which this extract is taken, makes mention of previous proceedings against our mountaineers for the same alleged crimes, viz. that " they considered the Roman Church to be the Babylon of the Book of Revelations, and they believed it to be as efficacious to pray to God in a stable as in a church. For this cause the most reverend prelates of Embrun, and the inquisitors, have taken great pains to root them out [2]."

A Papal Bull of this period is another clue to guide us through the labyrinth. This instrument was dated 26 June, 1487 [3], and promised the apostolic benediction to all who should distinguish themselves in the work of extermination, against those " *inveterate* heretics of the dioceses of Lyons, Vienne, and Embrun." It consecrated the war that was to be waged against them, under the high and holy name of a crusade, and invited all the faithful " to tread them under foot as venomous adders, and to destroy them." This humane recommendation was followed up with zeal corresponding with the wishes of the holy Father at Rome.

[1] Origo Waldensium, cited by Morland, p. 215.
[2] See vol. H. of the Waldensian MSS. in the Cambridge Library.
[3] See Morland's Churches of Piedmont, p. 196.

" The secular power was employed," said the report, " under that valiant soldier the Lord Hugo de Palide, Count of Varax, and Lieutenant of Dauphiné, who proceeded against them, on which they left their houses and betook them to the holes and secret places of the mountains, and the cliffs of the rocks, for their fortresses."

Perrin gives a most lamentable account of the extirpation of the Protestants of Val Louise in 1488. " When the king's lieutenant arrived with his troops in the valley, none of the inhabitants were found, for they had all retired into the caverns on the highest mountains, having carried with them their little ones, and all that they could transport there for nourishment. The lieutenant commanded a great quantity of wood to be laid at the entrance of those caverns, to burn or smoke them out. Some were slain in attempting to escape, others threw themselves headlong on the rocks below, others were smothered; there were afterwards found within the caverns 400 infants stifled in the arms of their dead mothers. It is believed, as a certain fact, that 3000 persons perished on that occasion in the valley. In a word, the religionists there were wholly exterminated, so that from that time forward it was peopled with new inhabitants, and none of the ancient race ever established themselves there again [1]."

[1] Perrin, liv. ii. chap. 3.

A horrible crusade had been carried on previously to this, in the year 1478, when even the ruthless Louis XI. was so disgusted by the cruelties of the inquisitors, and by the confiscations in the valleys of Fressinière and Argentière, that he issued an edict to check them. This was dated Arras, May 18, 1478[1].

Advancing still higher up, into those gloomy ages when it was guilt, for which there was no pardon, to hold religious opinions different from the papal clergy, I find that Perrin, the Waldensian historian just quoted, had but very limited information, when he spoke of the persecution of 1380 as the first against the non-conformists of Dauphiné. The annals of the prelates of Embrun[2] acquaint us, that in 1360 Gulielmus de Bardis distinguished his episcopate, by directing fierce warfare against the non-conformists of his diocese. Bertrand d'Eux is represented as covering himself with glory in 1337 after the same manner. A hundred years before this, I find Aumarus staining his crozier in the blood of those, who would not acknowledge the supremacy of the Roman pontiff. His immediate predecessor, Bernard Chabert, first carried fire and sword into the plains of Languedoc, by the side of Simon de Montfort, and then pursued the Albigensian fugitives, when they thought to take refuge in the fastnesses of the Durance, among brethren of the same faith. Raimond de

[1] Perrin, liv. ii. chap. 3.　　　[2] Gall. Christiana, tom. i.

Salvagris, archbishop of Embrun in 1210 [1], was equally on the alert against the impugners of papal infallibility. These two last mentioned prelates achieved so much against the mountaineers, who would not prove false to the creed of their forefathers, that it was a saying of the times, that a sufficient quantity of lime and stone could not be procured, to build prisons for those who were convicted of hostility to the religion of Rome.

I have thus traced in this Alpine region the prevalence of the same religious principles, at the beginning of the thirteenth century, which attracted Neff's notice in the nineteenth. The Romanists allow that this may be done, but they say that such principles were then new to the Christian world, and that the spirit of enmity against their Church, which has since spread over great part of Europe, and which gave birth, as they pretend, to the Waldensian separatists of Spain, France, and Italy, and to the Protestant communities of Great Britain, Switzerland, Germany, and other countries, was first cherished in the bosom of the followers of Waldo, when they were chased from Lyons in 1172, and fled into the valleys of Dauphiné and Piedmont. The Waldenses, or members of the mountain Churches, whether of Spain, Italy, or France [2], (for the

[1] Gall. Christiana, tom. i.
[2] The more the remote valleys of the Alps and Pyrenees are visited, and the history of their natives is developed, this truth

term Waldenses means nothing more than natives of mountain valleys,) were not sects : they
were true component parts of the body of Christ,
and faithful asserters of the truth as it is in Jesus,
when others declined from it.

But I am not going now into the theological
question, or into the wide field of the general
inquiry; my present business is to connect the
Christians of Dauphiné with the Christians of
primitive times, and to fix the attention of my
readers upon the broad partition wall, which,
through the whole of the dark and middle ages,
divided certain religionists of this province from
those, who consented to receive spiritual law
from Rome.

" *A sect which took its rise from Peter Waldo,
in* 1172." This is the calumny which has been
so long perpetuated against the churches of the
mountains on each side of the Alps. What can
we adduce in refutation of it, with regard to the
non-conforming Churches of Dauphiné? Were
there no determined confessors in this province,
who opposed themselves to the phalanx of the
Vatican, and declared Rome to be Babylon, and
her canons and articles of faith and discipline to
be unscriptural, before the year 1172? It is the

will emerge into clear and bright light—that the Italian Waldenses, the Albigenses, the Subalpines of Dauphiné and Provence, and the Pyrenean Waldenses, were all independent of
each other, and remains or branches of the primitive churches
in those parts.

highest satisfaction to fathom among the archives
of an adversary, and to draw, from the depositories of his documents, evidence to establish our
own case.   From the same Romish Chronicles [1],
which tell us that the hierarchy of Embrun was
persecuting the congregations of Val Fressinière,
at a period when Perrin (who could find no
mention of it in Protestant annals) meekly hoped
that his brethren of the mountains were unmolested, from these we learn that the bishops of
Vaison, a diocese in the province of Dauphiné,
were nominated and received their investiture,
not from the pope, but from their native and
petty sovereigns, the lords of the territory.   We
are even informed by what right they exercised
this patronage, namely, in virtue of their descent
from Faida, heiress of Gilbert, Count of Provence.
The sovereign pontiff fulminated his protests,
his interdicts, and his excommunications, whenever a new bishop was made : as all the popes
had been taught to do by Gregory VII., who
denounced anathemas against every one, who
should venture to have any opinion of his own
on matters of religion.   But the maledictions of
Heaven were especially proclaimed against all,
who should take any part in the distribution of
church dignities without papal permission.   There
was to be no election, no investiture, no con-
ferring even temporalities upon bishops or
clergy, but in the name and under the authority

[1] Gall. Christiana.

of the pontifical seal. Nevertheless in the middle of the twelfth century, thirty years before the alleged origin of the Waldenses of France, we find distinct mention of a series of episcopal elections at Vaison, without any authority from the pope, in spite of the anathemas which were issued to prevent such proceedings. This, however, is only one example—we are directed by other Romish documents to still more convincing witnesses, that the " new sect of 1172 " was a venerable branch of the apostolical stem. There is a large collection of ancient epistles and documents, published by two Benedictine Monks, Marten and Durand [1], which the editors state to have been preserved in the manuscript libraries of certain cathedrals and monasteries. In the first volume of this curious publication, there is the copy of a letter addressed to Pope Lucius II. in 1144, in which the writer describes to his holiness the great influence of a religious community of Dauphiné, which had " its divers degrees, its neophytes, its priests, and even its bishops, as we have. It maintains that sins are not remitted by the sprinkling of water only in baptism—that the eucharist, and the imposition of hands administered by our clergy, avail nothing." " Every part of France," such is the concluding sentence of the letter, " is polluted by the poison issuing from this region."

[1] " Veterum Scriptorum et Monumentorum Amplissima Collectio."   Paris, 1724.

Other letters, addressed by the celebrated Peter, Abbot of Clugny, to the Bishops of Embrun, Gap, and Die, all in Dauphiné, between the years 1120 and 1134, contain pressing exhortations to those prelates to check opinions, which had taken fast hold in their dioceses, and had spread from thence into Gascony and Languedoc.

" You must still persevere," said the pious Abbot, " you must root out the mischief from its hiding places [1], by preaching against it; but if that will not do, and if necessary, by an armed force."

The third canon of the council of Thoulouse, held A. D. 1119, bears witness to the activity of Christians in the same quarter, who were then " busily agitating the questions of the real presence, infant baptism, and validity of sacerdotal orders."

These are some of the essential questions of controversy between all Protestant Churches, (especially those of the Alps,) and the Romish Church, and the records of the eleventh century prove, that even then they were not new to France, and more particularly, that they were not new to the Alpine regions of Dauphiné. In 1050, a Romish controversialist complained to the king of France, that Berengarius was re-introducing there that *OLD* [2] matter of differ-

[1] " Latibula."   Gall. Christiana, tom. i.
[2] Labbæi Con. tom. ix. p. 1061.

ence, the eucharistic discussion; and in 1025, when some recusants were accused, before a public tribunal at Arras, of holding sentiments such as Neff's Churches of Vals Fressinière and Queyras, and other Protestant Churches now hold, it came out, in evidence, that they had acquired their opinions of certain strangers from the Alpine borders of Italy [1]!

What then becomes of the Romish fable, that the mountain congregation of Dauphiné was a new sect in 1172, when we can thus distinctly trace the existence of Alpine Churches, opposed to Rome, in the same province, one hundred and fifty years before? And what lights were there at that dark period, which would enable poor illiterate shepherds and herdsmen to see their way out of the gloom, into which the ignorance and wickedness of the age had cast men of all ranks and stations? If in 1025 Christian communities could be found, in remote glens and forests, who worshipped God and his Christ without the aid of images, and without any of those adjuncts and helps, to which the Roman Churches then had recourse, the probability is, *not* that they had learnt a new lesson, but that they were practising a very old one, which had been handed down to them from their fathers. Well, then, what do we discover in the ecclesiastical or general history of this Alpine province,

[1] Dacherii Spicilegium, vol. xiii. p. 2.

H

previously to the period which we have just been examining, which leads us to suppose that religious opinions or practices were then cherished there, which were not in accordance with the Romish Churches?

It was about the middle of the ninth century, that the bishops of Rome established their pretensions in France : before that epoch a certain degree of deference was paid to their decisions, while their jurisdiction was by no means acknowledged.   But at the very time when they were making rapid advances towards the object of their ambition, the prelates of the sees, which lie between the Rhone and the Alps, resisted their encroachments on some very material points.   For example, there is a rescript of pope John VIII. complaining, in 877, that the archbishop of Embrun had consecrated a bishop of Vienne, according to the ancient formulary of the Gallic Churches, and not in conformity with the ritual prescribed at Rome.   And just at the crisis, when the prelates of Dauphiné began to be more obedient to their foreign master, the Saracens invaded the province, the bishops of Embrun fled, and the see was left many years without its head.   This was after the year 916, and thus the remains of the primitive Christians, in the valleys of the Durance, were left many years without the presence of an oppressive and proselytising hierarchy, at the very time when Romish influence was on the alert elsewhere.

When the foreign invaders were expelled, troubles of a different kind proved favourable to the independent spirit of the mountaineers. The feudal lords of the territory carried their exactions so far, as to exasperate the citizens of walled towns, who shut their gates against their former masters. To obtain partizans, the barons granted extraordinary privileges to the occupiers of lands, and brought the rural population into a state of hostility with the inhabitants of the towns. The Romish bishops and clergy sided with the latter; so that while they were bringing over to their interests the dwellers in cities, they were making less progress among the people of the field and the hill-country.

It has been already observed, that the great distinguishing marks of the Primitive and Protestant Churches, is the rejection of all helps to devotion, which have not the sanction of Scripture. The prominent feature of the Romish Church is the adoption of such helps. Image worship is one of these. To show that image worship was a matter of abhorrence throughout the region of our inquiry, in the centuries through which we desire to trace the existence of a community protesting, from age to age, against the dogmas of Rome, is a great step towards the accomplishment of our object. In the ninth, eighth, and seventh centuries, (still tracking the vestiges of the primitive Christians of the Alpine regions of France upwards, from more recent periods, to the earliest times of their conversion,) there were signal testimonies given, in the Churches of this quarter, of adherence to forms of worship unadulterated by the introduction of external representations.   In the eighth century, Agobard, archbishop of Lyons, wrote a work, which he called " a Treatise on Pictures and Images," and in which he pronounced image worship to be idolatry.   A more able refutation of the errors on this subject has never been written either before or since.   One passage I cannot but transcribe.   After citing Deuteronomy iv. 12—15, Agobard makes this remark on the sacred text :—" On which words it is to be observed, that if the works of God's hands are not to be adored and worshipped, no, not even in honour of God himself, much less are the works of men's hands to be adored and worshipped, in honour of those whom they are said to represent [1]."   Protestants will smile to learn, that against this remark of Agobard, the popish editors of the publication which contains the Treatise, have put this admonitory note :— " Caute lege." i. e. Read this cautiously.

I must not dismiss Agobard without relating another service which he did to the Christian Church universal, against the corruptions and arrogance of the bishop of Rome.   He strongly maintained the independence of the Gallic

---

[1] Bib. Patr. ix. 590.

Churches, and in two of his works, still extant, he entered into an argument to prove, that the councils of Gaul had full authority to make canons and regulations for the Churches of Gaul, and that their synods were legitimate, and in possession of plenary powers, although there were no papal legates at the session [1].

In 794, the Gallic bishops at the council of Frankfort, and among the rest the bishops of Grenoble, Gap, and Embrun, entered their solemn protest against that article of the second council of Nice, which was meant to make image worship the law of the Christian Churches, and which was sanctioned by all the authority the popes could give it. But the most memorable effort, in defence of images, was resisted by an equally memorable rejection of them about the year 600. Pope Gregory the First signalized his pontificate by a correspondence with Serenus, bishop of Marseilles, which forms a most curious link in the chain of our evidence, as proving, first, that the popes had no jurisdiction beyond their own Italian see ; secondly, that Rome had not then gone all those lengths in the error of image worship, to which she has since run ; and thirdly, that the superstitions, which were thickening elsewhere, were held in check by the wisdom and piety of Christians in this part of the world. Serenus had given orders for the

[1] Bib. Patr. ix. 548. Justel. Bib. Can. Juris. Pref. p. 23.

destruction of some images which had been set
up in churches of his diocese. This gave offence
to his brother of the Seven Hills, who addressed
a letter to him, not however of command, but of
expostulation, begging him to think better of
the matter, and not to destroy that which should
be preserved for expediency sake. " You ought,
at the same time," said Gregory, " to caution
the people against adoring the images." Images
and pictures, then, according to the opinion of
papal casuists of that day, were to be introduced
into churches as memorials, but not as objects of
worship.   Very different is the language of the
councils of Nice and Trent, and therefore not
altogether illustrative of the unities and un-
changeableness of the Romish faith.   Serenus
would not tolerate images even in Gregory's
sense of their usefulness. He paid no attention
to the pontiff's admonition, and for three years
Gregory bore his disrespect in silence. He then
wrote another epistle to Serenus, still remonstrating only with him, and repeating his former
advice : " For it is one thing," said the holy
father, " to adore an image, and another thing
to learn from it what ought to be adored."   But
Serenus was not to be moved from his righteous
purpose : he destroyed all he could find.

As the tone of pope Gregory's letters [1] to
Serenus proves, that Rome exercised no spiritual

[1] Sismondi Concilia Galliæ, ii. 431. 449.

authority over the Gallic provinces in the seventh century, so does an epistle of pope Innocent to a prelate of the same country, in the year 404, attest, that papal domination was not then established in the transalpine provinces [1]. Innocent, in this epistle, appears to be exhorting, advising, and persuading his correspondent to adopt the regulations of the Church of Rome; a clear proof that such regulations had not then been adopted, and that the documents of antiquity are against the pretensions of Rome to universal obedience, and to prescriptive sway from the earliest ages.

The records of these more remote ages testify equally to the existence of pure Christianity, and of independent church government, in the mountain provinces of France. The canons of the council of Orange in 529, at which the delegates of the Churches of Dauphiné were present, differ very little from the Thirty-nine Articles of the Church of England, and are at utter variance with those of modern Rome. The council of Arles, in 314, which represented all the Churches of Europe, put forth nothing which a Protestant of the present day could not sign; and the thirteen bishops of Gallia Narbonensis, (the country between the Rhone and the Alps,) who held a synod, at which Irenæus, bishop of Lyons, presided, towards the end of the second century, may fairly be supposed to have subscribed to the

[1] Sismondi Concilia Galliæ, i. 30.

same opinions with Irenæus himself. What those sentiments were, is collected from his works.   It is enough for our present purpose to state, that those works have rendered it a matter of certainty, that Irenæus held it to be a mark of decline from the pure Gospel to embrace any doctrines, that might want the sanction of Scripture, or to maintain that the Scriptures were unintelligible without the help of tradition, or to assert that Scripture does not form an infallible rule of faith.   This apostolical father also denounced the use of images, as a heathen abomination, rejected the invocation of saints, spoke of the profession of celibacy as violence done to nature, and lifted up his voice against the rash attempt of Victor, bishop of Rome, to dictate to foreign Churches on the paschal controversy.

It is most probable that the Alpine Churches of Dauphiné were planted while Irenæus was bishop of Lyons.   The vicinity of this mountain region to the cities of Lyons and Vienne—the asylum which it was likely to offer to the Christian fugitives from the banks of the Rhone, during the persecution of Marcus Aurelian : the fact related by Irenæus himself, that he learned the dialect of the country [1], to enable him to preach to the natives (the language spoken at Lyons and Vienne was Latin) : the journey which Irenæus took to Rome, and which must have

---

[1] Neff did the same.

been undertaken by the great military road, which passed through the very heart of the territory described in these pages; all these concur in persuading us, that the Gospel was first preached there towards the end of the second century. The evidences, which have been here pointed out to notice, are intended to prove, that as the Gospel was delivered to the mountaineers of Dauphiné by the missionaries of that period, so it has been professed by some of their descendants ever since, and that Neff's flock have a just claim to the venerable appellation which he gave to them, " The remains of the primitive Christians of the French Alps."

In the words of Allix, " May such evidence be of use to strengthen the faith of Protestants, who will perceive from thence, that God never left them without witness, as having preserved in the bosom of these Churches most illustrious professors of the Christian religion, which they held in the same purity, with which their predecessors had received this precious pledge from the hands of apostolical men, who at first planted their Churches among the Alps and Pyrenæan mountains, that they might be exposed to the view of four or five kingdoms all at once."

CHAPTER VI.

FURTHER DESCRIPTION OF THE DEPARTMENT OF THE HIGH ALPS—RESTITUTION OF PROTESTANT RIGHTS—ORGANIZATION OF REFORMED CHURCHES OF FRANCE—NATURE AND EXTENT OF NEFF'S PASTORAL CHARGE—HENRY OBERLIN—DESCRIPTION OF THE VALLEYS OF FRESSINIÈRE AND QUEYRAS, AND OF NEFF'S PARISH—THE PASS OF THE GUIL—NEFF AT ARVIEUX, AND IN HIS PRESBYTERY AT LA CHALP—HIS PROGRESS THROUGH HIS PARISH—SAN VERAN—PIERRE GROSSE—FOUSILLARDE—THE PASTORS MANIFOLD DUTIES—NEFF'S WINTER JOURNEY TO VAL FRESSINIÈRE—PALONS—THE RIMASSE—DORMILLEUSE—NEFF'S DESCRIPTION OF DORMILLEUSE AND OF THE CONDITION IN WHICH HE FOUND THE REMAINS OF THE PRIMITIVE CHRISTIANS THERE—HIS PERILOUS LABOURS.

HAVING brought Neff to his land of promise, and placed him in that sphere of action so suitable to his character, it is necessary to fill up the outline which I have sketched in the preceding chapter, and to delineate the locality and condition of the group of Protestant villages, which constituted his pastoral charge.

The department of the High Alps is so called, from its being within the region of that branch of the Alps, which separates France from Italy. The two loftiest mountains, on this part of the chain, are Mont Genevre and Mont Viso. The latter is one of the most conspicuous in Europe, from its elevation and bright snowy aspect and conical form. It rises as high as 13,000 feet above the level of the sea, and there being no gigantic pinnacle in the neighbourhood, which rears his head to the same height as Mont Viso, it appears to be exalted to the very sky, and to leave all the other summits in the plains below. As the eye is directed towards Mont Genevre on the left, and towards Mont Viso on the right hand, looking from Gap, which is nearly the centre of the department, it ranges over a succession of jagged peaks and icy ridges, which seem to be utterly inaccessible to the foot of man. But in the gorges of these mountains, there are spots which the necessities of man have rendered habitable. These, as I have already shown, have been the asylum of families, who have suffered oppression for conscience sake at all periods of persecution: from the persecutions of Marcus Aurelian in the second century, to those of Louis XIV. and Louis XV. In the year 1786, the successor of these monarchs published an act of toleration, and for the first time since the revocation of the edict of Nantes, (a century before), Christians, who were not Roman Catholics, were permitted to worship God in public without molestation. But so little intercourse did the inhabitants of this remote and secluded quarter hold with the rest of the world, that I was assured by an aged Protestant of San

Veran, a French village, at the foot of Mont Viso, that he and his family did not hear of it till four years after. And many years subsequently to this, the Protestants of the department had no other opportunity of receiving the consolations of religion, according to Church ordinances, than that which was afforded them by the precarious visits of the Vaudois ministers from the Italian side of the Alps. During the hundred years of persecution from 1686 to 1786, and up to the period of the establishment of a native ministry, these services had been cheerfully rendered by the pastors of the valleys of Piedmont, as often as they could; but the distance and the danger (while it was at the risk of the heaviest personal penalty to perform these duties,) rendered them necessarily few and far between. At length the consular government of France, in the year 1802 [1], conferred privileges on the members of the reformed religion,

[1] The French reformed Church, therefore, after the year 1802, became a national, legalized, established Church, governed by its own laws, and at liberty to follow its own movements. Its ministers were recognised, protected, and paid by government, but still in a certain degree the regulations, according to which it was to entitle itself to its privileges, fettered it. After the restoration of the Bourbons, a jealous court took care to have it tied fast to rule, and, by the technical obstacles which were thrown in the way of organization and church building, retarded the progress of Protantism. The note at the end of this chapter will show, that the number of Protestant churches and pastors in France is still very small.

which proved a new era for Protestantism. The Protestant Churches were so far put on a level with the Roman Catholic Churches, that they were permitted to have an organization sanctioned by the state, and their pastors were to receive stipends from the public treasury. But at the same time, it was enacted, that these privileges could be enjoyed under certain regulations only. The principal of these were:——

That none but Frenchmen should exercise the ministerial functions.

That no pastoral appointment should take place, except under the seal of a local consistory, and with the sanction of the government.

That a consistory should consist of not less than 6000 souls of the same communion, and might be divided into sections.

That each consistory might have a certain number of pastors——(six, the greatest number,) but that this number should not be augmented without the express permission of government.

That where a consistory had not been established, and there were Protestants enough to constitute one, the heads of twenty-five of the principal families might proceed to carry their wishes into effect, by a requisition to the prefect or sub-prefect.

That the discipline of the Churches, thus organized, should be the same as that of the reformed Churches of France previously to the revocation of the edict of Nantes, and that there should be no change in the discipline, without the authority of government.

That the amount of stipend to be allotted to each pastor should depend upon the population of the commune, wherein the pastor should officiate : and that 3000 francs should be the highest, and 1200 francs the lowest amount of stipend.

That a house, or presbytery, and garden, might be provided for the pastor, at the expense of the commune, in addition to his stipend.

That the expense of building, and repairing churches and presbyteries, should be defrayed by the commune, according to a fixed assessment.

That all persons born in foreign countries, who are descended from Frenchmen or Frenchwomen, exiles on account of their religion, may obtain the rights of French subjects, on fixing their residence in France, and taking the oath of allegiance.

The Protestants of the department of the High Alps were not able to establish a consistory till the year 1805, and though the department is eighty-four miles in length, and fifty-seven in breadth, it has never had but two ecclesiastical sections, or divisions, since the restitution of Protestant rights, to which pastors have been appointed, *viz.* those of Orpierre and Arvieux. The section of Arvieux (so called because the Presbytery is in the commune of

Arvieux,) is nearest to the frontier of Italy, and spreads over two civil divisions or arrondissements,—the arrondissement of Embrun, and the arrondissement of Briançon. This constituted the *parish* of Neff: it consisted of seventeen or eighteen villages, occupying an extent of sixty miles, taken in a straight geographical line from east to west, but nearly eighty miles must be traversed through the winding of the mountains, in the journey from one extreme point to the other. Up to the time when Neff took charge of this laborious parish, there had been no regularly appointed and resident minister for any length of time together. It had been occasionally served by the pastor of Orpierre, and at one period a son of Oberlin had taken charge of it for a few months. Every thing connected with the name of Oberlin, the celebrated pastor of the Ban de la Roche, is so precious that it will be a matter of painful interest to the reader to know, that this son of his, Henry, of whom mention is here made, fell a sacrifice to his exertions among the Protestants in the south of France. His dying moments form a beautiful episode in the Memoirs of Oberlin, which I gratefully transfer to these pages.

" The immediate occasion of Henry's death was supposed to arise from a cold, which he took while assisting to extinguish a fire, that had broke out in the night in a town on his route, as he was making, in 1816, a circuit of

1800 miles in the south of France, with a view to inspect the state of the Protestant Churches, and to ascertain the means of supplying them with the Holy Scriptures. The fatigue attending the remainder of the journey, added to the seeds of incipient disease, so shattered his constitution, that soon after arriving in his native valley, he was induced to remove to Rothau, instead of remaining at Waldbach, in order to receive the benefit of his brother Charles's advice, who, in addition to his clerical functions, was a medical practitioner. On perceiving, however, that the complaint rapidly gained ground, he desired, with the greatest resignation and composure, to be conveyed home again to his father's house, that he might die there. So universally was Oberlin beloved, that his parishioners seized every opportunity of proving their attachment to him and his family, and on this occasion a truly affecting scene presented itself. No sooner was Henry's request made known in the village, than twelve peasants immediately presented themselves at the parsonage-house, and offered to carry him upon a litter to Waldbach, which is about six miles distant from Rothau. He could not, however, bear exposure to the open air, and it was therefore found expedient to place him in a covered cart, but as it slowly proceeded through the valley, the faithful peasants walked before it, carefully removing every stone, that the beloved invalid might experience as little inconvenience as possible from jolting over the rough roads.

" A few weeks after his arrival under the paternal roof, his life, which had promised such extensive usefulness, drew near its close. Faith mingled with pious resignation to the will of his heavenly Father, who was thus early pleased to call him to himself, was strikingly exhibited in his last moments, and on the 16th of Nov. 1817, without a struggle or sigh, he sweetly slept in Jesus."

For want of a regular pastor, the people of Vals Fressinière and Queyras used to assemble on Sundays in the churches and oratories, of which there were six of the former, and two of the latter, and some one or other read the service. Such was the general situation and the condition of the parish, which Neff undertook to serve, and in which he first made trial of his strength in the winter season. But before I proceed with my narrative, I will run over the names and relative positions of the several villages, inhabited by Neff's scattered flock, reserving the description of them till I accompany him to those scenes of his arduous duties.

The valley of Queyras (which communicates directly with the Protestant valleys of Piedmont by the pass of the Col de la Croix), extending from the foot of Mont Viso to Mont Dauphin, along the whole course of the river Guil, and comprising the glens, which follow the direction of the mountain torrents which roll into the Guil, forms the eastern quarter of the section of Arvieux. The Protestant families dwell principally in the commune of Arvieux, and its hamlets La Chalp and Brunichard, and in the commune of Molines, and its hamlets San Veran, Pierre Grosse, and Fousillarde. They have a church at Arvieux, one at San Veran, and another at Fousillarde. The distance between the churches of Arvieux and San Veran is not less than twelve miles. The western quarter of the section consists of the valley of Fressinière, and its hamlets Chancelas, Palons, Violins, Minsas, and Dormilleuse, which occupy the banks of a torrent that pours its waters into the Durance, half way between Briançon and Embrun: and of the commune of Champsaur, separated from the valley of Fressinière by a mountain and glacier. In the valley of Fressinière, there are two Protestant churches, those of Violins and Dormilleuse; and in the commune of Champsaur, there is a church at St. Laurent. Sixty miles nearly of rugged road must be trodden, before the pastor, whose residence is at La Chalp, beyond Arvieux, can perform his duties at Champsaur. But besides these two principal groups of Protestant villages, there are two outlying branches of the section, that of Vars, which is eight miles south of Guillestre, or twenty from Arvieux, and that of La Grave, which is beyond Briançon, and twenty-one miles north of Guillestre, or thirty-three miles from the minister's presbytery. Suppose, then, that the pastor has fixed his abode at the house which is provided for him at La Chalp, in the commune of Arvieux, he has a journey of twelve miles before he can reach the scene of his labours in a western direction, and sixty before he can arrive at it in the opposite quarter. He has also a distance of twenty miles towards the south, and thirty-three towards the north, when his services are required by the little flocks at Vars and La Grave. A man of Neff's zeal could not but sink under the weight of such a burthen. And who does not glorify God on reflecting, that if the seeds of real piety could spring up in this rugged ground, it is only to the protecting culture of the Great Sower, that any production can be ascribed! There is a twofold lesson to be learnt in following the steps of a pastor through these wilds. It is well that we should see, how hard some of our brethren work, and how hard they live; and that we should discover, to our humiliation, that it is not always where there is the greatest company of preachers, that the word takes deepest root.

There is this difference between the valleys of Piedmont, and those of Fressinière and Queyras. The former are for the most part smiling with verdure and foliage, the latter are dark and sterile. In each, alp rises above alp, and piles of rock of appalling aspect block up many of the

defiles, and utterly forbid any further advance
to the boldest adventurer.   But the Italian valleys are so beautifully diversified by green meadows and rich corn fields, and thick foliage of
forest and fruit trees, that the eye is perpetually
relieved and delighted.   Add to these the herds
of cattle in the pasturages, and the innumerable
flocks of goats and sheep browsing upon the
mountain sides, and skipping from rock to rock,
and you have an animated picture of life and
enjoyment which cannot be surpassed.   The
Piedmontese valleys form a garden, with deserts
as it were in view: some of them indeed are
barren and repulsive, but these are exceptions.
On the contrary, in the Alpine retreats of the
French Protestants, fertility is the exception,
and barrenness the common aspect.   There the
tottering cliffs, the sombre and frowning rocks,
which, from their fatiguing continuity, look like
a mournful veil, which is never to be raised, and
the tremendous abysses, and the comfortless
cottages, and the ever present dangers, from
avalanches, and thick mists and clouds, proclaim
that this is a land which man never would have
chosen, even for his hiding-place, but from the
direst necessity.

Neff's Journal has noted the 16th of January,
1824, as the day on which he arrived at Arvieux,
to take possession of the habitation provided for
the pastor of the district.   I have stated in more
places than one, that a taste for magnificent

scenery formed a strong feature in his character, and it never could have been more gratified than on his journey from Gap, through Guillestre to his new abode. The road from the latter is by the pass of the Guil, and in the whole range of Alpine scenery, rich as it is in the wonders of nature, there is nothing more terribly sublime than this mountain path. A traveller would be amply repaid in visiting this region, for the sole purpose of exploring a defile, which in fact is one of the keys to France, on the Italian frontier, and is therefore guarded at one end by the strong works of Mont Dauphin, and at the other by the fortress of Château Queyras, whose guns sweep the entrance of the pass. For several miles the waters of the Guil occupy the whole breadth of the defile, which is more like a chasm, or a vast rent in the mountain, than a ravine : and the path, which in places will not admit more than two to walk side by side, is hewn out of the rocks. These rise to such a giddy height, that the soaring pinnacles, which crown them, look like the fine points of masonry-work on the summit of a cathedral : meantime the projecting masses, that overhang the wayfaring man's head, are more stupendous, and more menacing than the imagination can conceive. Many of these seem to be hanging by you know not what, and to be ready to fall at the least concussion.

> Quos super atra silex jamjam lapsura, cadentique
> Imminet assimilis.

Perhaps they have been so suspended for centuries, and will so continue for centuries to come; but be that as it may, enormous fragments are frequently rolling down, and as the wind roars through the gloomy defile, and threatens to sweep you into the torrent below, you wonder what it is which holds together the terrifying suspensions, and prevents your being crushed by their fall. Much has been related of the peril of traversing a pass on the summit of a mountain, with a precipice yawning beneath your feet; but in fact there is no danger equal to a journey through a defile like this, when you are at the bottom of the Alpine gulf, with hundreds of feet of crumbling rock above your head. But terribly magnificent as this pass is, and though it must at other times have made a powerful impression on Neff's mind, his journal does not contain a word either of its grandeur or its terrors. He forced his way through it in the middle of January, when it is notoriously unsafe to attempt the passage. Several travellers lose their lives here almost every year; but our pastor's anxiety to be at his post of duty was the strongest feeling that moved him, and he thought of nothing but the field of usefulness which was now before him.

On issuing out of the depths of the defile, the frowning battlements of Château Queyras, built on a lofty projecting cliff, on the edge of the torrent, and backed by the barrier wall of Alps, which at this season of the year towers like a bulwark of ice between the dominions of France, and the king of Sardinia, present a picture of the most striking magnificence. Every thing combines to give an interest to the scene. In the far distance are the snowy peaks of Mont Viso, of dazzling white, and, in the foreground, the rustic aqueducts, composed in the simplest manner of wooden troughs, supported on lofty scaffolding, and crossing and recrossing the narrow valley, which form a striking contrast between the durability of the works of God's hands, the everlasting mountains, and the perishable devices of men. About a mile and a half, on the Guillestre side, from Château Queyras, a rough road, on the left, conducts to Arvieux : and here a different prospect opens to the view. The signs of cultivation and of man's presence increase : some pretty vales, and snug looking cottages please the eye ; and in one spot a frail but picturesque foot-bridge of pines carelessly thrown across a chasm, invites the stranger to approach and inspect it. He is almost appalled to find himself on the brink of an abyss, many fathoms deep, at the bottom of which a body of water foams and chafes, which has forced itself a passage through the living rock. The narrowness and depth of this chasm, and the extraordinary manner in which it is concealed from observation, till you are close to it, form one

of the greatest natural curiosities in a province,
which abounds in objects of the same sort.

Neff followed the custom of those who directed him to his pastoral dwelling-place, and
called it Arvieux in his journals. It is not,
however, situated in the principal village of the
commune so called, but at La Chalp, a small
hamlet beyond. The church is at Arvieux, but
the minister's residence is, with the majority of
the Protestant population, higher up the valley;
for in this glen, as in all the others where the
remains of the primitive Christians still exist,
they are invariably found to have crept up to
the furthest habitable part of it. In the Valley
of Fressinière, the Protestants, in like manner.
have penetrated to the edge of the glacier, where
they were most likely to remain unmolested;
and again, in the commune of Molines, Grosse
Pierre and Fousillarde are at the very furthest
point of vegetation, and there is nothing fit for
mortal to take refuge in, between San Veran
and the eternal snows which mantle the pinnacles
of Mont Viso.

In the page which records his arrival at the
humble white cottage, which had been recently
prepared for the pastor, in La Chalp, Neff has
not inserted any observation about the comforts
or conveniences of the habitation, designed for
his future dwelling-place. It is a small low
building, without any thing to distinguish it but

its white front; such at least was its aspect when I saw it: but there was an air of cheerfulness in its situation, facing the south, and standing in a warm sunny spot, which contrasted strongly with the dismal hovels of Dormilleuse, where he afterwards spent most of the winter months. It is most probable that he found it totally devoid of every thing which administers to comfort, except its locality, for a memorandum, written a few days after his arrival, mentions his having made a journey to Guillestre, for the purchase of some household utensils. Once for all, therefore, I may remark, that the reader, whose notions of the happiness of a pastor's life have been formed in the smiling parsonage, or snug manse, or who has considered it as deriving its enjoyment from a state of blissful repose and peacefulness, has widely erred from the mark in Neff's case. His happiness was to be busily employed in bringing in souls to God; he seems not to have set the slightest value on any of the comforts of a home: or, if he valued them, to have sacrificed them cheerfully to his sense of duty. One of the principal charms in the recital of a good clergyman's life, is the character of the clergyman at home. But Neff had none of the comforts of this life to cheer him. No family endearments welcomed him to a peaceful fireside after the toils of the day: nothing of earthly softness smoothed his seat or his pillow. His was a career of anxiety, unmitigated and uncon-

soled by any thing but a sense of duties performed, and of acceptance with God. The commune of Arvieux, and the cheerful hamlets of
La Chalp and Brunichard, were the brightest
spots in his extensive parish; but they were not
the fairest to his eye, for he complains in several
of his letters, that the people there were spoilt
by the advantages of their situation, and were
by no means so well inclined to profit by his
instructions, as the inhabitants of less favoured
spots.

The natives of Arvieux itself are almost all
Roman Catholics, those of La Chalp and Brunichard are, for the most part, Protestants. There
were eight families in the former, and eighteen
in the latter, who waited on Neff's ministry; and
two families in a small hamlet between Arvieux
and Château Queyras, were converted from the
Romish to the Protestant faith, by the force of
his reasoning, and the consistency of his holy
life. His gentle spirit had no relish for that
kind of controversy, whose object is the mere
triumph over an adversary by the force of argument; and his success among the members of
the other church, which was far greater than was
ever known before in the different quarters
where he explained the word of God, proceeded,
in a great measure, from the mild and affectionate manner in which he directed their attention to the only name in whom, and through
whom, they might receive health and salvation.

The impression which he left behind him, even in this quarter, where he thought that he did not perceive the most abundant fruits of his ministry, continued to be discerned when I visited Arvieux in 1829, in the amicable relation which still subsisted between the Roman Catholics and Protestants of the commune. The kindest interchange of friendly and charitable office took place between them: the children of the two Churches went to the same schools, and read the Bible together, without interruption: and a young man, who would not quit my side for a whole day, when he found that I took an interest in his late venerated pastor, spoke of the Curé as a good-natured man, whom every body respected.

It was on Friday, the 16th of January, 1824, that Neff established himself at La Chalp, as the pastor of the section of Arvieux; on the Monday following we find him, a second time within four days, encountering the fearful pass of the Guil, and on the evening of the same day looking after his little flock at Vars, twenty miles from Arvieux. He remained at Vars on the Tuesday, and part of Wednesday, organizing little associations for mutual instruction during his absence. On Thursday and Friday in the same week, he was at his post again at Arvieux, La Chalp, and Brunichard, catechising the children, and making himself acquainted with his people; and on Saturday, in spite of a fall

of snow, and a storm of wind which swept the
valley, he directed his steps towards San Veran,
that he might take the earliest opportunity of
administering the public Sunday service in the
church, which was situated in the farthest western boundary of his parish, twelve miles from
his head-quarters.

" The snow," says his journal, " was from
seven to ten inches deep, and the wind, which
blew a hurricane, raised and tossed it about in
clouds.   Not a trace could be seen of the paths,
and I was six hours performing twelve miles.
But this was the only bad journey that I have
yet made in the Alps, and notwithstanding the
exposure, I arrived perfectly well at San Veran,
and held a meeting in the evening.   The next
day I preached in the church, catechised in the
afternoon, and assembled some willing hearers
around me in the evening, whom I addressed
on the one thing needful, so that I did not
lose a single hour in that commune, during
my stay there.   It is the highest and consequently [1] the most pious village in the Valley of
Queyras; in fact, it is said to be the most elevated in Europe, and it is a provincial saying,
relating to the mountain of San Veran, ' La piu
alta ou l'i mindgent pan,' i. e. it is the highest
spot where bread is eaten.   The air is sharp, but

[1] A similar observation was made to me by more than one
Vaudois pastor in Piedmont, on the relative degree of piety in
the lower and more elevated mountain hamlets.

though it was the 25th of January, the weather was so fine that the snow melted on the ground, as it does in April. There are about twenty-three Protestant families here. The men are intelligent, well read in Scripture, and very anxious to converse on spiritual subjects. Some of the women are the same, but for the most part the females are ignorant, and confined in their notions, through the whole of this country. I have been much gratified by my excursions to this place, which I have already visited four or five times."

The date of these observations was the 10th of February, so that from the 16th of January, in the course of twenty-five days, this indefatigable servant of God had paid four visits, at the least, to his flock at San Veran, having, during the same period, as I shall presently show, displayed an equal share of anxiety for his parishioners in quarters still more distant. It was by these means that he was so successful in winning souls, and having favour with the people: he was in constant intercourse with them, going from house to house; praying with the sick, discoursing with those in health on religious topics, and inspiring a relish for pious conversation, and instructing the young with all the tenderness and assiduity of a parent. The reception which he met at San Veran, was exactly what might be expected from the descendants of those men, who used to put their own lives in jeopardy by receiving the fugitive Vaudois pastors, when they were obliged to fly from persecution in [1] their own valleys, and when a day's journey by the pass of Mont Viso, or the Col de la Croix, brought them to this secluded village. It is so secluded, so fenced in by rock and mountain barriers, that up to this hour there is not a road approaching it, over which a wheel has ever passed. Thus situated, on the very outskirts of human society, and at a distance from its vices, refinements, and luxuries, its natives rarely quit their own haunts to settle elsewhere, and strangers have no attraction to guide them to a corner, where none of the comforts, and very few of the conveniences of life, have yet been introduced. I believe one Englishman only had found his way to San Veran before myself; and when I entered it in company with Mrs. Gilly, the sight of a female, dressed entirely in linen, was a phenomenon so new to those simple peasants, whose garments are never any thing but woollen, that Pizarro and his mail-clad companions were not greater objects of curiosity to the Peruvians, than we were to these mountaineers. The wo-

[1] The Protestants of the valleys of Piedmont and Dauphiné afforded each other mutual shelter, when they were pursued by their enemies. Gilles relates an affecting incident of the refugees from Italy throwing themselves on the protection of their poor brethren of Fressinière in 1566, who most kindly received and shared their scanty pittance with them, fearless of the double perils of starvation and the vengeance of their common foe.

men gathered round us, and examined first one part of Mrs. Gilly's dress and then another, with an inquisitiveness and admiration, which were sufficiently amusing. We saw no symptoms of want, but every thing indicated that the necessaries of life are far from abundant, either in San Veran or the contiguous hamlets of Pierre-Grosse and Fousillarde, and that great abstinence at times, and moderation always, are required to discipline them against the long winters, and the scanty supply of food, which result from the climate and soil of a region, much better adapted to the habits of the bird of prey, and the wild beast, than of man.

But San Veran is a garden, and a scene of delights, when compared with Dormilleuse, to which the pastor hastened, as soon as he had put things in order in this part of his parish. Here the houses are built like log-houses, of rough pine trees, laid one above another, and composed of several stories, which have a singularly picturesque look, not unlike the chalets in Switzerland, but loftier and much more picturesque. On the ground floor the family dwell, hay and unthrashed corn occupy the first story, and the second is given up to grain, and to stores of bread-cakes and cheeses ranged on framework suspended from the roof. But at Dormilleuse, the huts are wretched constructions of stone and mud, from which fresh air, comfort, and cleanliness seem to be utterly excluded.

Cleanliness, indeed, is not a virtue which distinguishes any of the people in these mountains; and with such a nice sense of moral perception as they display, and with such strict attention to the duties of religion, it is astonishing that they have not yet learnt to practise those ablutions in their persons or habitations, which are as necessary to comfort as to health. The same uncleanliness prevails even among the better provided, for they are all peasants alike, tillers of the earth, and small proprietors, the wealthiest of whom (if we can speak of wealth, even comparatively, on such poor soil,) puts his hand to the spade and hoe with the same alacrity as the poorest: their apartments are unswept, their woollen garments unwashed, and their hands and faces are as little accustomed to cold water, as if there was a perpetual drought in the land. I should fear that the excellent Neff, with all the improvements which he introduced into his parish, either omitted, or failed to convince the folks there, that cleanliness is not a forbidden luxury, but one of the necessary duties of life.

But though their habitations and their persons are, thus far, likely to leave some disagreeble impressions in those, whose sensations have been rendered quick and impatient by English habits, yet the simplicity, amiability, and good manners which prevail among these children of nature, are so winning; and the images and associations that rise up in the mind, in this retreat of Protestantism in France, supply such profuse enjoyment, and give such a grace, as well as a charm, to any intercourse with them, that it is impossible not to write down the time, that may be spent in San Veran and in its contiguous hamlets, among the most interesting of one's life. To those who understand the patois, or to whom it is accurately translated, as it was to us, the poetical and elegant turn which is given to conversation, by the constant use of figures and metaphors derived from mountain scenery, and from the accidents and exposures of Alpine life, enhance the pleasure, and send the traveller home well satisfied with his excursion. In short, it is the moral and intellectual refinement about these mountaineers, which renders their society interesting in a high degree, and furnishes matter for reflection long afterwards.

The pastor devoted the Monday and Tuesday, of his second week in the Valley of Queyras, to Pierre-Grosse and Fousillarde, which, like San Veran, are frontier villages; and there too, he organized little companies of the well-disposed, who were to meet at stated times to read the Bible, and to do such things for their mutual improvement, as he thought might profitably be done, when they had not the benefit of his presence. He was obliged to perform divine service in a barn or large stable, for want of a better place of worship. He saw that he could not render his ministrations efficient in such a widely

K

extended parish, unless he resorted to such measures as these, and therefore he began at once upon a system which he pursued as long as he remained. The good effects were soon manifest, for the inhabitants of Pierre-Grosse and Fousillarde, who were first collected together for public worship in a rude stable, were anxious to gather round their pastor in a more suitable place. They willingly taxed themselves, and out of their slender resources built a neat little church, twenty-seven feet long by twenty feet wide, and thus added one more to the Protestant sanctuaries of God in this department. The cost in money was 24*l.* or 600 francs. Materials, such as the country afforded, and labour, were easily supplied, but it was far from easy to provide the extraneous adjuncts and the money contribution ; and when I was there, the year Neff died, there was still a debt of 300 franks, or 12*l.* upon the building, which the twenty-five humble families of the two hamlets will probably be long before they liquidate[1]. Money is necessarily very scarce among a people, who can seldom raise more corn than will meet their own demands. The few cattle that they rear are driven far, before they can be sold, and the return in coin will barely pay the taxes, and purchase the indispensable household articles and implements of

[1] The sum necessary to discharge this debt has lately been raised by a lady and her friends.

husbandry, of which they stand in need. Oftentimes even the ordinary resources, scanty as they are, fail them, and for this reason, the poor Alpine is frequently obliged, like the swallow, to migrate during the long winter, and to leave his barren rocks in search of subsistence, where the climate is more favourable to the wants of human nature. This was the case in 1824. The unproductiveness of the soil, and the dearth, were so great, that many were obliged to sell their cattle at a very low price, because the forage failed, and they had not the means of getting them into a saleable condition; and Neff frequently met large parties, consisting of young men, and even of fathers of families, moving from their own hamlets, and going to seek work on any terms in distant provinces.

On the evening of Tuesday, the 27th of January, Neff returned to Arvieux; and after catechising his young people, and putting things in a satisfactory train there, he set out for the eastern division of his charge; and having again traversed the formidable pass of the Guil in safety, reached the Valley of Fressinière in time to preach at Violins, on Sunday the first of February.

After leaving Guillestre, which is not far from the junction of the Guil and Durance, at the foot of Mont Dauphin, the traveller, whose steps are directed towards the Valley of Fressinière, pursues his path for about five miles northwards, along the high road which leads from Embrun to Briançon. This is a cheerful route, enlivened by the impetuous waters of the Durance, and a view of ever-changing mountain scenery, and lofty and rugged summits assuming new forms at every turn of the road. There are also some remarkable pretty spots in the vale, through which the river flows with turbulent force, and among these, the village of La Roche, with its small lake, cannot fail to please the eye. After passing through La Roche, and crossing the Durance by a long timber bridge, the ascent to the Valley of Fressinière begins. A steep acclivity rises so abruptly from the river, that at first sight there is no appearance of any practicable mode of advancing, but the eye presently discerns a shepherd's path, which creeps up the mountain in an oblique direction. This leads over some very rugged ground to a defile, through which a rocky torrent rushes with the noise of thunder. On each side of these wild waters, which roar and fling their spray about in clouds, there are groups of cottages, and an alpine bridge with a cascade above it. These, with the background of rocks, form as complete a picture of mountain life, as the imagination can require. This hamlet is Palons, and the torrent, called the Rimasse, is the guide which conducts to the Valley of Fressinière; there is no mistaking the way. The next village, at the distance of a league, is Fressinière, which gives its name to the valley. Another league brings to Violins; two miles beyond is Minsas; and then comes the toilsome, rough, and clambering route of three miles to Dormilleuse; so that, in fact, from La Roche to Dormilleuse is one continued ascent of five hours, or, supposing that a league an hour is the pace, fifteen miles. Between Palons and Fressinière, there is a lovely fertile vale, enclosed on each side by steep mountains, and producing several kinds of grain and fruit-trees; but this cheerful prospect soon changes, and every step leads to scenes which are more and more dreary. After passing through Minsas, the face of the country is perfectly savage and appalling. Blocks of stone, detached from the overhanging rocks, strew the ground, and threaten to impede all further progress. The signs of productiveness are fewer and fewer. Here and there some thin patches of rye or oats bespeak the poor resources of the inhabitants, who have been driven up into this desert, and the occasional track of the wolf, and the heavy flap of the vulture's wing over head, tell who are its proper natives. If such is its summer welcome, what must have been its chilling aspect when Neff made his journey thither on the last day of January? But he had that within him which warmed his heart, and animated his spirits, as he penetrated through the pathless snows of the defile, and crossed the raw gusty summit that lay in his way. His was a work of love—he was going to preach that word, of which the ancestors of the Dormilleusians had been the depositories for centuries, when France rejected it : and to trim the lamp which had been left alight here, when the rest of the land was in darkness.

The rock on which Dormilleuse stands is almost inaccessible, even in the finest months in the year. There is but one approach to it, and this is always difficult, from the rapidity of the ascent, and the slipperiness of the path in its narrowest part, occasioned by a cascade, which throws itself over this path into the abyss below, forming a sheet of water between the face of the rock, and the edge of the precipice. In the winter season it must be doubly hazardous, because it then leaves an accumulation of ice. Perhaps, of all the habitable spots in Europe, this wretched village is the most repulsive. Nature is here stern and terrible, without offering any boon but that of personal security from the fury of the oppressor, to invite man to make it his resting-place. When the sun shines brightest, the side of the mountain opposite to Dormilleuse, and on the same level, is covered with snow, and the traveller, in search of new scenes to gratify his taste for the sublime or the beautiful, finds nothing to repay him for his pilgrimage, but the satisfaction of planting his foot on the soil, which has been hallowed as the asylum of Christians, of whom the world was not worthy. The spot, which they and their descendants have chosen for their last stronghold, is indeed a very citadel of strength.

But the eye wanders in vain for any one point of fascination. The village is not built on the summit, or on the shelf of a rock. It is not like Forsythe's description of Cortona, "a picture hung upon a wall." It does not stand forth in bold relief, and fling defiance upon the intruder as he approaches. It is not even seen, till the upper pass is cleared, and then it disappoints expectation by its mean disclosure of a few poor huts, detached from each other, without any one building as an object of attraction, or any strongly marked feature to give a character to the scene. Neither is there any view which it commands, to make amends for this defect in itself : all is cold, forlorn, and cheerless. Thus the eye has no enjoyment in gazing on this dark waste : but the imagination roves with holy transport over wilds, which have sheltered the brave and the good from the storm of man's oppression, a thousand times more to be dreaded than that of the elements. Hence the spell thrown over the mind, for it is a place of fearful and singular interest. But still, great must have been the love which filled the pastor's bosom, to make him prefer this worse than wilderness, this concentration of man's wretchedness, to all the other hamlets of his parish. He turned from the inviting Arvieux, and the affectionate hospitality of San Veran, and the magnificent grandeur of Vars, to make his chief residence in the black and gloomy Dormilleuse, because there his services appeared to be most required.   Because there he had every thing to teach, even to the planting of a potatoe.   But his whole life was a sacrifice; he lived for nothing else than to be useful to his fellow-creatures, and to be a labourer in the service of his Redeemer.

An extract from Neff's Journal shall make him speak for himself.

"*Sunday, Feb.* 1.   I preached at Violins.   In the afternoon I delivered a catechetical lecture, and in the evening I performed a service at which the inhabitants, who are all Protestants, attended; and so did those of Minsas, who are also Protestants.   We sung a psalm, and I expounded a chapter to them.   At ten o'clock most of them retired, those who came from the greatest distance having brought wisps of straw with them, which they lighted to guide them through the snow.   Some stopped till midnight; we then took a slight repast, and two of them, who had three quarters of a league to return home, set out with pine torches, indifferent to the ice and snow which lay on their path.

" The next day I followed the route to Dormilleuse, with a man belonging to that village, who had remained all night at Violins, to accompany me.   Dormilleuse is the highest village in the valley, and is celebrated for the resistance, which its inhabitants have opposed for more than 600 years to the Church of Rome. They are of the unmixed race of the ancient Waldenses [1], and never bowed their knee before an idol, even when all the Protestants of the valley of Queyras dissembled their faith. The ruins of the walls and forts still remain, which they built to protect them against surprise. They owe their preservation in part to the nature of the country, which is almost inaccessible. It is defended by a natural fortification of glaciers and arid rocks. The population of the village consists of 40 families : every one Protestant. The aspect of this desert, both terrible and sublime, which served as the asylum of truth, when almost all the world lay in darkness; the recollection of the faithful martyrs of old, the deep caverns into which they retired to read the Bible in secret, and to worship the Father of Light, in spirit and in truth, —every thing tends to elevate my soul, and to inspire it with sentiments difficult to describe. But with what grief do I reflect upon the present state of the unhappy descendants of those ancient witnesses to the crucified Redeemer ! A miserable and degenerate race, whose moral and physical aspect reminds the Christian, that sin and death are the only true inheritance of the children of Adam. Now, you can scarcely find one among them who has any true knowledge of the Saviour, although they almost all testify the

[1] The Waldenses of Dauphiné ; a distinct branch of the primitive Church of Gaul.

greatest veneration for the holy Scriptures. But though they are nothing in themselves, let us hope that they are well-beloved for their fathers' sakes, and that the Lord will once more permit the light of his countenance, and the rays of his grace, to shine upon these places, which he formerly chose for his sanctuary. Many of them have already become sensible of their sad condition, and have thanked God for sending me among them to stir up the expiring flame of their piety. It is some years since Henry Laget paid them some visits, and when, in his last address, he told them that they would see his face no more, ' It seemed,' said they to me, using one of those beautiful figures of speech in which their patois abounds, ' as if a gust of wind had extinguished the torch, which was to light us in our passage by night across the precipice.' It is strange that although they have been visited by several pastors of late years, yet there has been no preparation for receiving the young people at the Sacrament. I have therefore employed myself in giving the necessary instruction, and have taken down a list of all the young persons between the age of 15 and 30. The number of catechumens amounts already to 80. On Tuesday (Feb. 3d) I preached in the church of Dormilleuse, and some of the inhabitants from the lower part of the valley attended. The narrow path by which they climb to this village is inundated in the summer by magnificent cascades, and in the winter the mountain side is a sheet of ice. All the rocks also are tapestried with ice. In the morning, before the sermon, I took some young men with me, and we cut steps in the ice with our hatchets, to render the passage less dangerous, that our friends from the lower hamlets might mount to Dormilleuse with less fear of accident. There was a large congregation. In the afternoon I catechized in a stable. Several people from below remained all night, and therefore I took the opportunity of pursuing my instructions in the evening, and the next day (Wednesday) was spent like Tuesday. Thursday morning was devoted to similar exercises of instruction and devotion, and then I descended towards the lower valley, with about a dozen of my elder catechumens, who persisted in accompanying me to Minsas, that they might be present at the lecture there. At night I took up my quarters in Fressinière, at the house of M. Barridon, who is the Receiver of the Commune. His eldest son is the only person in my parish, whose education gives him a claim to the title of *monsieur*. In garb and exterior he differs nothing from the others, and is the very *antipodes* of a *petit-maître :* a young man of good sense ; a zealous Protestant, but, Frenchman-like, not yet serious enough to answer my views of a Christian. The inhabitants of the High Alps, like those of the other provinces of France, have very little gravity, and though they are more pious than others, they are gay and full of humour : so much so, that very often a sally of wit or a bon mot will burst out very unseasonably, and excite a laugh in the midst of the most serious conversation. It is necessary to be on one's guard (which naturally I am very little qualified to be), or to be in danger of being disconcerted every moment. On Friday I went to Palons, on my return to Val Queyras, the first hamlet of the valley, where there are only eight Protestant families, but I collected some catechumens, and others, as soon as I could, and gave them a sermon, and afterwards catechized them. Palons is more fertile than the rest of the valley, and even produces wine. The consequence is, that there is less piety here, therefore I addressed them very seriously upon their condition, from the eighth chapter of St. John, ver. 23, 24. In the evening we assembled together again, and I gave them another service. There are some young females here, who have an ear, and love music. It is always an advantage to a minister to find such aid, and experience has taught me, that we may hope for some degree of success, when we have this help. On Saturday, Feb. 7, I set out very early in the morning, to return to Arvieux, and arrived there in the course of the evening. Such is the history of one of my rounds. I shall have to make the same continually. It is an affair of twenty-one days. Arvieux, where I am expected to take my principal residence, is likely to yield a less return than other parts of my parish. The inhabitants have more traffic, and the mildness of the climate appears somehow or other not favourable to the growth of piety. They are zealous Protestants, and show me a thousand attentions, but they are, at present, absolutely impenetrable."

Such is the history, as Neff called it, of his first three weeks' labour in his mountain parish. We find him, not only preaching, and performing public service, in every village between Dormilleuse and the frontier Alps, where there was a church, but gathering the young people about him; classing them, and instructing them in the first elements of Christianity; making lists of those who had not yet appeared at the Lord's table, and preparing them for that solemn ordinance; visiting from house to house; putting families in a train to pursue devotional exercises by themselves; inspiring them with the love of pious conversation and reading; and performing all those little offices of kind attention, and pastoral duty, which have the sure effect of endearing a parochial clergyman to his flock, by proving that he takes a real and an affectionate concern in all that interests them. This earnestness in " seeking for Christ's sheep that were dispersed abroad," through the far scattered hamlets of his burthensome charge, and in " using both public and private monitions and exhortations, as well to the sick as to the whole, within his cure," was displayed in the winter season; and we may understand what a winter is in the Alps, from the pastor's description of his journey to San Veran, through the snow storm, and of his employing a party of village pioneers, himself working at their head, to cleave a passage through the ice for those who had to clamber up the rock of Dormilleuse. Four times too, in these twenty-one days, did Neff encounter the pass of the Guil, an undertaking more serious than braving the snow storm, or the icy slope of a mountain, and there was but one accessible quarter of the section which he did not visit,—La Grave. He was entirely cut off from Champsaur, for there is no means of crossing the mountain of Orcière in the winter months.

We shall see that Neff did not relax in his efforts, and that the remainder of his ministry was a repetition of, or an improvement upon his first exertions, in the great work of winning souls. And here I cannot but call to mind, and lay before my readers the expression of a prophetic hope, recorded a century and a half ago, and when all was dark and threatening, that the Almighty would be pleased to remove the cloud which then hung over this region.

" And it is my hope after all," said Allix, at the end of his remarks on the ancient Churches of the South of France, " that as God hath illustriously displayed the care of his providence in raising the Church of Piedmont from those ruins, under which the spirit of persecution thought for ever to have buried it, so he will be pleased to vouchsafe the same protection to those desolate flocks, whom the violence of the Romish party hath constrained to dissemble their faith, by making a show of embracing the Roman religion, to avoid the extremities of their persecution." This hope has been realized, and Dormilleuse has been made a pillar in the temple of our God, round which the scattered of the Lord have gathered. Those timid families, too, in Val Queyras, which have had a little strength, and have kept God's word in secret, have been blessed, by being kept from the hour of temptation.

Note.—State of the Protestant Churches in France, extracted from Soulier's last published Statistique.

DEPARTMENTS.	Consistories.	Pastors.	Sacred Edifices.	Sunday-Schools.	Elementary & Boarding Schools.
Aisne, Seine et Marne	1	5	17	7	7
Hautes-Alpes	1	2	9	..	..
Ardèche	5	18	17	1	9
Aveyron	1	4	7	3	5
Arriège	1	6	12	3	8
Bouches-du-Rhône	1	3	4	..	4
Calvados et Orne	1	3	5	..	..
Charente	1	2	3	1	1
Carried over	12	43	74	15	34

DEPARTMENTS.	Consistories.	Pastors.	Sacred Edifices.	Sunday-Schools.	Elementary & Boarding Schools.
Brought over	12	43	74	15	34
Charente Inférieure	3	10	28	3	9
Dordogne	2	6	13	3	4
Drôme	5	23	32	..	24
Gard	17	64	75	23	110
Haute-Garonne	1	4	4	2	4
Gironde	3	9	13	..	13
Hérault	4	12	16	1	15
Isère	1	3	7	1	15
Haute-Loire	1	3	4	..	1
Loire-Inférieur et Vendée	1	3	9	..	1
Lot-et-Garonne	5	11	21	4	16
Lozère	5	13	8	3	17
Basses Pyrénées	1	5	8	..	4
Bas-Rhin	2	15	23	4	23
Haut-Rhin	1	10	7	..	26
Rhône	1	2	2	1	3
Seine	1	4	3	3	6
Seine-Inférieure	2	7	17	2	7
Deux-Sèvres	5	9	7	..	15
Tarn	4	13	18	3	18
Tarn-et-Garonne	2	8	2	..	1
Vaucluse	1	3	7	3	6
Vienne	1	2	..	..	..
DEPARTEMENS RÉUNIS.					
Loiret, Cher, Loir-et-Ch. Eure-et-L. . . . . }	1	6	7	4	4
Nord, Pas de Calais	1	4	7	2	1
Moselle, Meurthe	1	4	7	..	6
Doubs	1	2	1	..	3
ORATOIRES ANCIENS.					
Ardennes	1	1	1	..	2
Gex	1	1	1	1	2
Somme	1	1	2	..	..
Ain	1	1	1	..	2
Carried over	89	302	425	78	392

DEPARTMENTS.	Consistories.	Pastors.	Sacred Edifices.	Sunday-Schools.	Elementary & Boarding Schools.
Brought over	89	302	425	78	392
ORATOIRES RÉCEMMENT ÉTABLIS.					
Bouches-du-Rhône	1	..	1	..	..
Oise	1	..	1	..	..
Gironde	1	..	1	..	..
Vosges	1	..	1	..	..
Puy-de-Dôme	1	..	1	..	..
Seine-et-Oise	1	..	1	..	..
Côte-d'Or	1	..	1	..	..
Total	96	302	432	78	392

It will be seen from this statement, that the number of pastors in the French Established Protestant Church, in 1828, was only 302, less by one half than the number in the very worst times, between the massacre of St. Bartholomew, and the Revocation of the Edict of Nantes.

A statistique of the number of Roman Catholic Clergy, published by authority in 1829, renders an account of more than 30,000 of that order.

CHAPTER VII.

NEFF ORGANIZES RÉUNIONS, OR PRAYER-MEETINGS—HIS
OPINION OF THE NECESSITY OF SUCH MEETINGS—NEFF'S
LAST EXHORTATION TO HIS FLOCK ON THE SUBJECT—HIS
EXHORTATIONS EXAMINED—AN INQUIRY INTO THE EFFECTS
AND UTILITY OF PRAYER-MEETINGS—THE SENTIMENTS
OF THOMAS SCOTT NOT IN FAVOUR OF THEM—THOSE OF
BISHOP HEBER THE SAME—OBSERVATIONS ON FAMILY
WORSHIP.

IN whatever part of his parish [1] Neff was plying
his ministerial work, whether it was in the commune of Arvieux, or in that of Molines and San
Veran, or in the cheerless vicinity of Dormilleuse, there was one object which he kept stea-
dily in view,—to promote associations, (réunions)
among his flock, for purposes of mutual improvement in devotional exercises, that is to say, in
reading the Bible, in the practice of sacred music, in pious conversation, in joint prayer, and in
all other things which answer to the apostolical

[1] I use the word *parish*, in the ancient ecclesiastical sense
of the term, signifying the particular charge of a minister of
God. I have already explained that Neff's charge extended
over many communes, or parishes, in the civil acceptation of
the word, and in each commune there were several villages
and hamlets.

admonition, " Wherefore comfort yourselves together, and edify one another, even as also ye do [1]."
He was so persuaded in his own mind, not only of
the expediency, but of the absolute necessity of
this practice, that I find him expressing himself
thus emphatically in one of his Journals. " I am
confirmed in the opinion, that whosoever, even
were he an angel, should neglect such meetings,
under any pretext whatever, is very little to be
depended on, and cannot be reckoned among the
sheep of Christ's fold. It is to be wished that
the faithful would never forget the 133d Psalm,
or that promise of our Saviour, ' Where two or
three are met together in my name, there I will
be in the midst of them.' "

It is impossible not to respect the opinions of
such a man as Neff, but here I think he has de-
parted from his usual discreet and cautious rules,
and has stretched the point much too far. That
there may be a considerable degree of good re-
sulting from such meetings, when they are prudently conducted, is a truth which will be readily
conceded, but it is doubtful whether meetings of
the kind are likely to be soberly directed in most
cases, and therefore to insist, that there can be
no firm and steady religious principle without
their aid, is an unguarded assumption. Many
sound and single-minded Christians have seen
reason to doubt, whether there be not some risk

---

[1] 1 Thess. v. 11.

in promoting such meetings as those which Neff
commended so highly, even when they are vigi-
lantly superintended by an experienced pastor,
and much more so when the pastor is not at hand
to direct them.   In the destitute regions where
Neff's own lot was cast, the want of regular spiritual instruction might render many expedients
absolutely necessary, which would be questionable in other parts; and of the two evils,—shall
the scattered members of a mountain church be
left without any provision to quicken their devotion, and increase their religious knowledge,
during the absence of their appointed guide,
or shall they be advised to have recourse to a
practice which may lead to error, or to extravagant transports of over-heated and ill-directed
piety;—perhaps that is the least, where the mischief is only contingent.   Without helps of some
kind, the piety of a flock, left without a shepherd, must decline ; but it is no more than con-
jectural that it will run wild under imperfect
guidance. Neff never found reason to make any
change in his own sentiments on this subject; on
the contrary, to the last hour of his life, he attached the greatest importance to the practice of
holding such assemblies.   When this world, and
all its hopes and fears, its prejudices and its predilections, were rapidly passing away from him,
and he felt that his end was drawing near, he addressed a farewell letter to his beloved Alpines,
in which he most solemnly recommended them

to persevere in the system. I transcribe the whole of the passage. It will explain his method and his reasons.

" I exhort you most particularly, not to neglect the assembling yourselves together. I do not mean by this to recommend those assemblies only, where one speaks, and all the others listen : these, doubtless, where the Gospel is faithfully preached, are so greatly blessed, and are such powerful means of awakening and confirming souls, that you ought not to require any admonition touching them. But this service is not enough for the Christian, nor is it that which is described and enjoined in those passages, 1 Cor. xii. 5—12, 22, 28; xiv. 23, 24, 26, 27, 31, &c. The assemblies, of which I now desire to speak, are those, where all may exhort, and where all are edified ; where each may communicate to his brethren his own sentiments, and the illumination and the grace which he has received from God; in a word, where each gives and takes, teaches and learns in turn. These are the only assemblies which can strictly be called mutual : it is here that there is a communion between brethren, and that God has promised to give his blessing, Psalm cxxxiii. I repeat to you, then, my dear friends, take care to encourage such assemblies among you : and let them consist severally, as far as they can, of every age and of each sex, that they may be more simple, more unreserved, and more confiding. He who goes to an assembly only when a stranger, or one of more than common eloquence makes his appearance there, and who neglects the duty, when none but the humble and the simple attend, cannot be said to be spiritually-minded. You would then, indeed, be an assembly where the Lord would be in the midst of you, if each of you would bring with you a spirit of prayer and meditation, and your assembly would be as abundantly blessed as that of the first disciples was, when they met together in an upper room on that day of the outpouring of the Holy Spirit, and on that other day, when the Apostles returned from the council, rejoicing that they had been permitted to suffer for the name of Jesus Christ. Acts iv."

I have not introduced many discussions in interruption of a narrative, which is meant to be a simple relation of the practical good done by a good man; nor would I willingly pass censure upon any of Neff's proceedings, or opinions, because the general tenor of his ministerial career was so unexceptionable, and so wonderfully beneficial, that I should be inclined to doubt my own judgment when opposed to his. But in the case now before us, I have no hesitation in saying, after much reflection, that his reasoning is defective. The quotations, which he adduced in the passage above cited, are by no means happily chosen.   Those from the second and fourth chapters of Acts do not apply to the case in point, and the others, from the twelfth and fourteenth of the 1st of Corinthians, admit of a construction very little to his purpose.   The gifts of God, and the manifestations of the Spirit, there mentioned, were distinct from the ordinary operations of grace, and they were enumerated by the apostle as such : that is to say, not as spiritual gifts to be commonly expected in religious assemblies, by means of which the possessors of them may be mutually benefited, but as miraculous endowments, conferred on a few pre-eminently, that the Church at large might be edified, as occasion should require.   The working of miracles, and the powers of healing, and the talent of speaking in an unknown tongue, and of interpreting unknown tongues, and of discerning spirits, are not gifts which Christians are taught to look for in the ordinary dispensations of grace. Nor can the passage 1 Cor. xii. 28. where it is said, that God first set apostles in the Church, secondarily prophets, thirdly teachers, after that miracles, then gifts of healings, helps, governments, diversities of tongues, be fairly represented as giving encouragement to assemblies, where there can be no exercise of authority, and where no manifestation of extraordinary powers is likely to be displayed.   The reproof at the end of this chapter, and more particularly the general tone of rebuke, which pervades the fourteenth chapter of the same Epistle, would seem to enjoin the greatest caution upon the very subject, which Neff approached by far too confidently.

The practice of holding prayer-meetings, or assemblies of Christians for mutual edification, has been frequently put to the proof, but I have heard of very few instances (and those only where the organization and proceedings were under the most sage control), in which they have not proved a temptation and a snare to some of those, who have been engaged in them, for want of being kept under proper and competent management.   There is a seductive tendency, in them, which ministers to vanity and fond conceits, and while the humble and the diffident may be rendered uneasy and distrustful of their condition, because they cannot take a ready part in the conversation, or act of supplication in behalf of the rest, the forward may be puffed up, and indulge in lofty opinions of their own attainments.   I remember well, that in my visit to Dormilleuse, my companions and myself brought away an unfavourable opinion of a young man, who represented himself as leader in one of these assemblies, and who certainly held himself in high estimation above his companions, because of the fluency which he had acquired.   Whether it was simplicity, or forwardness, he made no hesitation in telling us, that the prayer-meetings could not be maintained without him.

A clergyman of our own Church, whose name, in many places, is one of no small authority, the late Thomas Scott, was once the curate of a parish where the system had been tried, under the most cautious and prudent superintendence, but he found himself constrained to refuse giving his countenance to it. For modest reasons of his own, he did not oppose himself to the practice, in that parish, but he watched its effects, and pronounced decidedly upon its inutility. He afterwards went so far as to declare, that he thought it very unlikely, that prayer-meetings, even under any regulations, " could be conducted in such a manner that the aggregate good would not be counterbalanced, or even overbalanced, by positive evil." His opinion is of the greater value, because of the diffidence with which he offered, and of the reasons he assigned for it. " But I am, I fear, prejudiced," said he, " as the evils which arose from those meetings at Olney induced such an association of ideas in my mind, as probably never can be dissolved. Two or three effects were undeniable. 1. They proved hot-beds, on which superficial and discreditable preachers were hastily raised up, who going forth on the Lord's day to neighbouring parishes, intercepted those who used to attend Mr. Newton. 2. Men were called upon to pray in public, whose conduct afterwards brought a deep disgrace on the Gospel. 3. They produced a captious, criticising, self-wise spirit, so that even Mr. Newton himself could seldom please them. These things had no small effect in leading him to leave Olney. 4. They rendered the people so contemptuously indifferent to the worship of God at the church, and indeed many of them to any public worship in which they did not take a part, that I never before or since witnessed any thing like it, and this was one of my secret reasons for leaving Olney [1]."

The necessities of his mountain parish, and its deprivation of ministers and regular services, may in some degree justify Neff for proposing an expedient of so doubtful a nature : but one, who, like himself, went forth into a region where the harvest was ready, and the labourers few, has left his testimony on record, that even in extreme cases, we must not resort to measures which are liable to abuse. " The effect of them," said Bishop Heber, when consulted upon this subject, " is not only often confusion, but what is worse than confusion, self-conceit and rivalry : each labouring to excel his brother in the choice of expressions, and the earnestness of his address : and the bad effects of emulation mixing with actions in which, of all others, humility and forgetfulness of self are necessary. Such too is that warmth of feeling and language, derived rather from imitation than conviction, which,

---

[1] Life of Scott, seventh edition, p. 518.

under circumstances which I have mentioned, are apt to degenerate into enthusiastic excitement, or irreverent familiarity."

But whatever may be the doubts of the pious and the reflecting, as to the effect produced by prayer-meetings, or by other religious associations for mutual edification, composed of persons brought together from different families, and subject to the emulations of which Heber was apprehensive, or to the discreditable admixture and self-conceited forwardness of which Scott complained, there is one kind of re-union, or of assembling ourselves together, which will admit of no objection, and which of all others is most likely to be blessed in its consequence; that of the family circle. This may admit within its bosom a few familiar friends, or near and intimate neighbours, whose sentiments are congenial, and whose character, knowledge, and religious progress are mutually understood. In such there is always some respect and veneration attached to one or more particular individuals, some opinion prevailing as to the superior piety, and intellectual superiority of one of the party, which has at the same time a controlling and stimulating influence extremely beneficial to all present.

A domestic association, such as I am supposing, which combines the advantage of family prayer, and edifying reading and conversation, is one of the most efficacious means, not only of awakening [1] and establishing religious feeling, but of increasing religious knowledge. It gives, with the Divine assistance, force and permanency to holy impressions; it draws out a spirit of self-examination, and quickens and directs it: it produces habits of religious vigilance: it inspires a taste and a preference for devout conversation and reflection. It leads to a communication of thought, and to an explanation of doubts, emotions, and opinions, and to an interchange of knowledge and acquirement, which enriches the whole circle. The individuals, composing a family meeting of this kind, are too well acquainted with each other's foibles and weakness, and virtues, and talents, to venture beyond the bounds of good sense, or to indulge in emulous or exciting transports, which are the bane of prayer-meetings composed of persons not well known to each other: and the mutual confessions which the former make, and the encouragements which they dispense, are all within the limits of sober and serious piety.

[1] I lately heard of three young clergymen, (and I trust there are many such) who are residing in adjoining parishes near London, and who meet at regular times, to read together, and to improve each other, according to the various modes of mutual edification, which open out upon such occasions. These, and the like, are meetings together of two or three, to which the Lord has promised his presence.

CHAPTER VIII.

NEFF AT CHAMPSAUR—HIS DIFFICULTIES THERE—FROM CHAMPSAUR TO VAL FRESSINIÈRE—HIS EMPLOYMENTS FROM BREAK OF DAY TO MIDNIGHT—HIS ACCOUNT OF THE CONSECRATION OF THE NEW CHURCH OF VIOLINS—HIS DISCUSSION WITH A VAUDOIS PASTOR—WRETCHED CONDITION OF THE NATIVES OF VAL FRESSINIÈRE—AN AFFECTING INCIDENT—NEFF INSTITUTES ASSOCIATIONS OF THE BIBLE AND MISSIONARY SOCIETIES AMONG HIS ALPINES—PASSAGE OF THE COL D'ORSIÈRE—PROGRESS OF HIS CATECHUMENS AT CHAMPSAUR—LAMENTS OVER THE LEVITY OF SOME OF HIS FLOCK—PREVENTS THE APPOINTMENT OF AN UNWORTHY PASTOR AT CHAMPSAUR.

IT has been stated in a former chapter, that Neff was not able to include Champsaur, the most western quarter of his parish, in his first parochial circuit. The direct path to that commune would have been over the Cold d'Orsière from Dormilleuse: but the state of the mountain would not permit it; he therefore returned to the valley of Queyras, and there remained, for a few weeks, performing the regular services of his vocation. But in the middle of March, 1824, his stirring spirit would not permit him to remain stationary in one quarter of his charge any longer. He required constant action, and the excitement of locomotion, and we find him making his way to Champsaur, by the circuitous route of Embrun and Gap. The whole country was still covered with snow, and a keen north wind rendered the pastor's journey an enterprise of no common difficulty, although he followed the high road from Mont Dauphin : for there was no avoiding the pass of the Guil, and avalanches continually menace the traveller in that gloomy defile during the snowy season. But to Neff's ardent mind every thing was resolvable into good. " Although the winter is prolonged," said he to one of his correspondents, " and its severity is very disagreeable, yet it is favourable to my work. The peasants are at leisure to attend my instructions." At Champsaur, as at other places, his invariable practice was to have morning service and a sermon, afternoon catechizing, and a familiar evening lecture or exposition, every Sunday and Thursday in the week, and catechizings or expositions every other day. Here he found his flock so intelligent, that they made as much progress in eight days as some did, elsewhere, in two or three months ; but it was the march of the understanding, and not the movement of the softened heart ; " for alas," said the pastor, making use of one of those beautiful images of Scripture, which give a peculiar character to the style of his Journals, " my words are not those of the Spirit, which can change stones into children of Abraham."

In another place, after remarking that they

7

were for the most part more Protestants in name than in spirit, he added; "An elder asked me the other day, 'how do the affairs of our religion go on at present?' 'Very badly,' said I, 'in France.' 'How so?' he rejoined. 'Because one finds nothing but lukewarmness and indifference.' 'Oh that is not what I mean.' 'I know very well what you mean, but my estimate of what is going on well or ill is very different from your's.'"

He thought that the fertility of the commune of Champsaur, and its proximity to the high road, and to Gap, were great stumbling-blocks; but whenever he was constrained, by the love of the truth, to remark upon the defects of any of his flock, his gentle and affectionate disposition always shone forth in some such apologetic note as this. "But, notwithstanding their levity and worldly-mindedness, they are always attentive hearers; they testify the greatest kindness towards me, and press me to repeat my visits as often as I can."

From Champsaur, proceeding ever and anon in his endless round, Neff went to the valley of Fressinière, and there remained a fortnight. It was during this visit to that secluded district, where the inhabitants are centuries behind in all the useful arts, as well as in the refinements of life, that his hands, which were so often spread forth to give the apostolical benediction, were now employed in the mechanical work of giving the last finish to the new church at Violins.

When the building was completed externally, not a soul there, either workmen, or others, knew how to give the interior the proper air and character of a house of worship. To fashion and place the pulpit, to plan and arrange the seats, and not only to direct and to superintend, but to labour with the smiths and carpenters, so called, was the pastor's occupation, when he could spare time from his preaching, and his catechizing, and his visiting from hamlet to hamlet, and from house to house. Nothing was too much, too great, or too little for this citizen of two worlds; this man of God, and servant of servants. From break of day to midnight he was toiling in one way or other, with unyielding perseverance, and as the season had now permitted some of his catechumens to return to their labours, the young men to their fields, or their slate quarries, and the young women to their flocks, in the few sunny corners, where a thaw had taken place, his evening expositions began later, and were extended far into the night. The ardour of the teacher and his scholars seemed to be equal: both stole time from their hours of rest: and the long glare of blazing pine-wood torches, and the shouting of voices, directing the footsteps of the timid, or of the tottering, often broke the silence and the darkness of the night in those wild glens, and announced that the pastor's catechumens were finding their way home from one hamlet to another, after the sacred lessons that followed upon the manual labours of the day.

Even the return of summer, which was very late, for there was a heavy fall of snow in the beginning of June, brought no intermission of toil to this indefatigable man. If his journeys were less painful, they were more frequent; and the perpetual variation in the date of his Journals, from Pierre-Grosse to Dormilleuse and Champsaur, and from La Grave to Vars, shows that he was perpetually on the move, looking after one part of his flock, and then another, and never resting satisfied unless he was assured, by his own observation, that his system was working with regularity. The climate meantime was so variable, that when the flowers were blooming at Guillestre and Palons, not a green bud or a blade of corn was to be seen at San Veran or Dormilleuse. One day's walk, however, would frequently bring him from the drifting snows of the mountain side, to the enjoyment of rich foliage and verdure in the vale of the Durance, and he would then exclaim in the cheerfulness of his heart, " the winter is past, the flowers appear on the earth, the fig tree putteth forth her green figs, and the vines, with the tender grape, give a good smell."

In August 1824, an event took place, which I will relate in the pastor's own words, because matters are mixed up with it which cannot be introduced by any body so well as by himself;

M

and because his simple narrative will carry us up to the mountains, and into the midst of Alpine life. This was the consecration of the new church of Violins, in the valley of Fressinière—the building whose internal arrangement owed all its propriety to his taste and judgment, when he acted the part of master-workman, and gave it the finishing hand.

Guillestre, 24th September, 1824.

" I must have mentioned to you, in one of my former letters, the intended dedication of the new temple [1] of Violins, in the valley of Fressinière. A dedication is no common solemnity in France. After having had all their temples demolished, and being obliged to assemble in secret, and at the peril of their lives, in forests, and in caverns, and on mountains, and now to behold their sanctuaries rebuilt under the sanction, and with the pecuniary assistance of the government, is it not natural that the Protestants should testify their sense of the mercies of Almighty God, and their gratitude to the king, in the best manner that they are able? We expected upon this occasion, that M. Blanc, pastor of Mens, M. Bonifas, pastor of Grenoble, M. Bert, pastor of La Tour, and moderator of the Waldensian Churches of Piedmont, with some

---

[1] The term *temple* is used by the Protestants to distinguish their consecrated buildings from the *church* of the Roman Catholics.

7

of his colleagues, and M. d'Aldebert, president of our consistory, would be present to do honour to the festival. The sub-prefect of Embrun, although a Roman Catholic, had promised to assist at the ceremony. But of all those who had engaged to come, the sub-prefect, and an aged Vaudois pastor, were the only personages there; all the rest, under some pretext or other, were absent. Had it not been for this good old man, who, at seventy-three years of age, had not hesitated to pass the Alps, and to make a journey of two days to be with us, I should have been the only officiating pastor, and the members of the church of Fressinière would have felt themselves sorely neglected. The solemnity took place on Sunday, the 29th of August. On the previous evening I had begun to make the necessary preparations. A bower of oak branches, in full foliage, decorated and shaded the front of the building, and protected those who could not find room inside, from the heat of the sun. Many strangers had arrived on the morning of the day before, and among the rest our friend Ferdinand Martin, of Champsaur, with his uncle and several others of that commune. Late in the evening came the venerable Vaudois pastor, accompanied by the two brothers and uncle of our friend Blanc, and other laymen from the valleys of Piedmont. My flock were sadly disappointed at not seeing the Moderator Bert, and the President D'Aldebert, for whom we waited a long time in vain.   Early on Sunday the temple was filled with people from all the neighbouring valleys, Roman Catholics as well as Protestants.   I ascended the pulpit at nine o'clock, and began with a preparatory service or form of prayer.   I then expounded some verses of the eighth chapter of the Epistle to the Hebrews, and drew a parallel between the two covenants, the old and the new.   After this service the sub-prefect arrived, and as there was no appearance of the president, I requested the Vaudois pastor to perform the ceremony of dedication.   It was a compliment due to his age. He ascended the pulpit, and preached from Jeremiah vii. 4—7.   'Trust ye not in lying words, saying, The temple of the Lord, the temple of the Lord, the temple of the Lord, are these. For if ye thoroughly amend your ways and your doings; if ye thoroughly execute judgment between a man and his neighbour; if ye oppress not the stranger, the fatherless, and the widow, and shed not innocent blood in this place, neither walk after other gods to your hurt; then will I cause you to dwell in this place, in the land that I gave to your fathers, for ever and ever.'   Old as he is, the Waldensian minister preached with all the ease and force of a young man.   After the sermon, I delivered the prayer of benediction, and the Lord assisted me therein,—and I felt that I was asking for those things for which we ought to ask.   This ended, the Vaudois pastor read some verses of his own composition to the congregation, which were exceedingly touching, by the recollections which they called up.   The service concluded with a psalm, and the apostolic benediction.   We then left the temple, and took our dinner in company with the sub-prefect, who was anxious to return to Embrun that evening.   This magistrate is very amiable and frank in his manners, and has thereby acquired great popularity.   He shook hands with all, even with the humblest mountaineer; talked patois, and replied with great good-humour and wit, to the compliments which were paid him.   He is an excellent botanist, and he takes great interest in the commune of Fressinière, which he frequently visits to inspect a flock of Thibet goats which belong to the king, and are kept here.   Perhaps it will be useful to me to have made his acquaintance upon this occasion.

" After dinner, which was soon dispatched, the prefect took his leave, and we returned to the temple, where Ferdinand Martin had been conducting some psalmody.   I learnt afterwards, that while we were at dinner, he had addressed those who were in the tent, near the door of the temple, on the salvation which is through Jesus Christ, and he did this in the hearing of so many, that it was mentioned to me afterwards by several persons in the different valleys.   Having expected, like every body else, that we should

have three presidents of consistory, I never supposed that I should have to preach at all this day,
much less twice, and therefore I was by no means
prepared, although I have been in the habit of
preaching extempore.   But no doubt it was the
will of God that this large assembly should hear
the Gospel of Truth delivered with simplicity,
and without any turning aside from it. I preached
therefore from Hebrews viii. 2. ' A minister of
the sanctuary, and of the true tabernacle, which
the Lord pitched, and not man.' In my exordium
I defined the material Church made with hands,
both according to the old and the new covenant,
and I anticipated that which I did not wish to
dwell upon in the body of my discourse.   After
this, I divided my sermon into three heads :—
1. Christ is the minister of the heavenly sanctuary, into which he has entered, as the priest
and the victim.   2. The Church militant and
triumphant is called a temple holy unto the Lord.
3. Our hearts are called the temples of the Holy
Spirit.   In discussing the second head, the Lord
put into my mouth some happy and important
expressions, as to what is the Church ; and at
the end of each division, particularly of the last,
I took the opportunity of addressing a pressing
invitation to my hearers to receive the proffered
grace of Christ, and to go to him.

" After the third and last service, there was
an ample repast for the principal members of the
Church, and for the strangers who came from a

distance.   I sat down to table with the rest, and then we went down the valley to Fressinière, with M. Marchand, and all the Vaudois, to the house of M. Barridon, the receiver.   Our friends from Champsaur, with some others, remained at Violins, and in the evening they returned to the temple, with the people of the village, to sing psalms.   Ferdinand offered up a prayer, and they remained in the performance of their devotional exercises till ten o'clock at night.   The next day the Champsaur people returned home by the Col d'Orsière.

" Here I must not omit to tell you of a discussion, which arose between the Vaudois pastor and myself, on the Saturday evening before the dedication of the temple.   He was praising Protestants most lavishly, and especially the Vaudois, whom he exalted to the very skies in comparison with the Roman Catholics.   I ventured to make some observations on the danger of flattering people, and the little good which arises from elevating them above their adversaries ; and I reminded him of the admonition of our Lord, ' that we had better first cast the beam out of our own eye.'   Mr. —— retorted, and displayed at once the fallacy of his principles.   I felt myself awkwardly situated: on the one hand, it was scarcely decent to enter into a controversy publicly, (for a great many persons were present,) with a respectable old man, who had been so kind as to come from a great distance for our sakes; and on the other hand, I could not suffer error to prevail, and to withhold my testimony from the truth. I therefore tried to express myself with mildness and frankness at the same time, and, in fact, the old man was the only one who put himself in a passion.—(I decline inserting the particulars of the controversy, because they are not entirely creditable to the aged pastor, who is still alive, and whose sentiments may have been misunderstood by Neff.) After the discussion had lasted a long time, he rose up in anger and left the room. But as I was unwilling that this dispute should become a subject of scandal to the weak, and throw a cloud over the festival, I followed him to the door of the apartment, and wished him good night. Touched by those advances of mine, and perceiving that he was wrong to manifest any signs of displeasure, he embraced me affectionately, and exclaimed, ' my dear friend, I admire your principles, but pray entertain a better opinion of ———— [1].' I laughed, and promised to do so, on condition that he would say no more about them. We then separated for the evening, without any ill-humour, to the great satisfaction of all who were present. From that time to his departure, no other altercation took place between us. I endeavoured to treat him with

---

[1] Two French authors, whose names were frequently mentioned during the discussion.

every mark of respect, and, on taking his leave, he pressed me, with great sincerity, to pay him a visit in his native valleys [1]."

After the dedication of the new temple at Violins, on the 29th of August, Neff spent the whole of September in visiting first one hamlet and then another, going from house to house, in the faithful discharge of his functions. There was no one corner of his parish which he did not inspect, in the course of this month, from San Veran to Champsaur, and from La Grave to Vars. Several of the villages were visited twice during this interval. But September, which is so delicious a month in most countries under the same latitude, wore the garb of premature winter in many of the hamlets, whither this good shepherd directed his steps, in search of the scattered sheep of his flock. It was not in Val Fressinière, as in more favoured lands, that autumn gave to the declining year a rich and mellow glory. Few of the balmy airs of the south of France breathe there at any time. Either a fierce and a suffocating heat prevails, which makes the narrow glens feel like a fiery oven, or a rushing blast, that shivers the rocks, and uproots the fir, and threatens to make the fugitives' last retreat still more desolate and comfortless. Even in the height of summer, when vegetation is most rich and fresh, there is so

[1] See note at the end of this chapter.

little of it here, that the arid rock, and the grim and blackening sides of the mountain, rivet the eye, and give a sombre sadness, not to say, deadness, to the landscape, which makes one even prefer the season of frost and snow, as being more congenial to the region.

On the 9th of September Neff crossed the Col d'Orsière, under a fall of snow, such, he remarked in his Diary, as is never known in his native land, (Geneva,) but in the depth of winter.   At Dormilleuse, the peasants were driven from their field works by the severity of the weather, and when he descended to Minsas, the dreary aspect of that hamlet, lying deep in snow, wrung from him many sympathetic expressions of compassion, which are recorded in the pages of his Journal.   It was the wretchedness of these poor mountaineers, in the three highest villages of Val Fressinière, which induced him to devote more of his time to them, than to any other quarter of his parish : seeing them deprived of almost every temporal enjoyment, he determined to give them all the spiritual comfort that he could impart.   "Their village, (speaking of one of these three, Minsas,) is squeezed up in the very narrowest gorge of the valley, and is now buried in snow, without the hope of seeing the sun during the rest of the winter.   The houses are low, dark, and dirty : and the people themselves seem to be stupified with the utter misery of their condition."   And yet it was in this forlorn place that one of the two brothers, Besson, whom he describes, as having displayed great anxiety to know more of the way of salvation, but whose understanding and attainments were of an ordinary scale, and who stammered in his speech, addressed the following mournful confession to him, in the rich patois of his valley. " You have come among us, like a woman who attempts to kindle a fire with green wood. She exhausts her breath in blowing it, to keep alive the little flame, but the moment she quits it, it is instantly extinguished."

In another place, he writes thus of the temporal and spiritual condition of Dormilleuse and Minsas. " ' The wilderness and the solitary place shall be glad, and the desert shall rejoice and blossom as the rose.' This dreary and savage valley seems to have realized an accomplishment of the prophecy. Desiring to have the inhabitants supplied with some good sermons for their use, on those Sundays when I could not perform the public service in their valley, I sent to Paris for some copies of Nardin's Sermons, but when they arrived, I was afraid that the price, fifteen francs the four volumes, would stand in the way of their sale. At first they were received coldly, but when I had read a few of the sermons, every body was anxious to know more of them. I proposed that four families should join in the purchase of one set, and offered to wait their own time for the payment. This was caught at with avidity, and the books were soon disposed of, and a fresh packet ordered. At Minsas, the Bessons having bought two volumes, were anxious to purchase the other two, but though they are the wealthiest in the hamlet, they had no more spare money left. ‘ Have we not laid by some francs to buy a pig?’ said one of the sons ; ‘ Let us give up the pig, and get the books.’ All the rest acquiesced, and they completed their set. At Dormilleuse I witnessed similar instances of self-denial. One young man said, ‘ I will devote all my earnings in the slate quarries to the purchase of Nardin.’ Another said, ‘ In the spring I will go into Provence, in search of work. I shall raise twenty-four francs, and will apply part of the money to the acquisition of the books.’ Others determined to go without salt, and to devote the purchase money to the sermons. The services, both public and private, are attended better and better. Their neighbours observe a manifest change in their manners. At Minsas in particular, the least civilized and most wretched hamlet in the valley, the improvement is so striking, that it may literally be said of them, ‘ The last shall be first.’ ”

During my rambles in the valley of Fressinière, I saw some of the identical copies of Nardin’s Sermons, which were thus purchased at the cost of personal comforts, and the reader may judge with what feelings I turned over their pages, and fixed my eyes upon their owners.

An affecting incident which took place one Sunday, displays the character of these simple people to the greatest advantage. Neff had been performing three services in the church of Dormilleuse, to a congregation which filled the little sanctuary, and he was afterwards proceeding towards Romas, the upper part of this mountain village, followed by many of the inhabitants of that quarter, who had been among his hearers. Suddenly they were alarmed by some loud cries behind them. These were occasioned by the sudden illness of a young woman of the party, who was stretched upon the ground, without any signs of life. In fact, the vital spark had fled, and thus a young person of twenty-six years of age, of a robust frame, who had been present at the three services in the course of the day, and who had been joining in the psalmody, with great animation but a few minutes before, was now carried home a breathless corpse. The consternation of her parents was extreme, for she had been the only strong and healthy member of the family, and the principal support of it; but they bore their loss without a murmur, and what they most lamented, was the suddenness of her death, without having had time to commend her soul to God. The poor mother, in particular, testified the utmost submission to the blow, although she had three children nearly blind, and her husband was feeble and in bad health. During the two nights that the corpse remained unburied, the house was filled with people, who came to offer their condolence, and especially with young women. Neff embraced the opportunity of reading appropriate passages of Scripture, and of pouring in such consolations and admonitions, as were most applicable, and exhorted them to watch and pray, and to keep themselves in readiness against the coming of the Lord. When the time came for placing the corpse on the bier, the unhappy mother repeated aloud a prayer, in French, for the dying, and then all of a sudden she burst out in patois— " Alas ! my poor child had not time to utter these words. Death has seized her, as the eagle snatches up the lamb, as the rock falls and crushes the timid kid of the chamois ; oh ! my dear Mary, the Lord has taken thee at the very gate of his temple. Thy last thoughts were therefore, we hope, directed towards him. Oh ! may he have made thy peace before the throne of God, and received thee in paradise !" All the inhabitants of Dormilleuse attended the melancholy procession to the grave, and their pastor read the nine-tieth Psalm, as the earth closed upon the coffin, and then delivered an address, which the mourn-ers are not likely to forget.

In several of his Journals, Neff speaks of the extreme poverty of the people, but poor as the district was, the pastor was successful in raising some small contributions in aid of religious societies. His good sense, and right feeling would not allow him to squeeze out the widow's mite, or weekly or monthly penny from the father of a family, in cases where it could ill be spared: but he understood the value of sympathetic concern in the religious condition of others, and therefore encouraged, where he could consistently, the interest which any of his flock might be inclined to take in the spiritual wants of their countrymen, and of others, who stood in need of that Gospel, whose light warmed their own hearts. The sum raised was very small, but Neff had the gratification to inform the committees of the Bible Society, and of the Missionary Society, that such feeble support as they could render to the cause, was cheerfully proffered by the shepherds and goat-herds of the High Alps.

The following account, transcribed from one of the reports of the Continental Society, of which Neff was an agent, is his own relation of the manner in which he established an association of the Bible Society; and annexed to this account, is a detail of some of his proceedings at Champsaur, which may very properly be introduced in this place.

"I left off in my last, I believe, at the joyful epoch of the revival here; but I think I have not spoken of the Bible Society, which was formed at the same time. In concert with Mr. B. jun. we called together ten of the principal inhabitants of the different Protestant hamlets.   I explained to them, in a few words, the design and progress of the Bible Society, and finding them well-disposed to co-operate, we immediately organized our committee, of which Mr. B. was appointed president.   On the 5th of April, an account was taken of all the copies of the Holy Scriptures; at the same time noticing the demands for them.   Before the formation of the Society, there were not in all the valley twelve Bibles (almost all from Louvain), and a very small number of New Testaments, most of them Father Amelot's edition, and all in a very bad state.   Since the remittances from the London Society, and especially, since the formation of that in Paris, half of the families have been provided with Bibles, and almost all with New Testaments.   Most of these books have been paid for at the ordinary price, and have reached us through the kindness of Messrs. Lissignol and Laget.   Now, almost all those who still want Bibles, have set down their names for them.   We afford them the accommodation of paying for them by instalments, which, in the case of the poorest, extends to two or three years.   In these countries we must not speak of weekly subscriptions for payments of this sort; the mountaineers scarcely ever touching money, but at the time they sell their cattle; all the rest of the year, most of them have not a *sol* at their disposal. Having reduced all this business into the form of a report, I addressed it to the president of our consistory at Orpierre, in order that he might forward it to the Paris Bible Society; but foreseeing that this course would take some time, I addressed myself directly to the committee for one hundred pocket New Testaments, saying, that we impatiently waited for them, because, as I expressed it, 'the young shepherds of the Alps were languishing to be able to furnish their scrip with the bread that endureth to eternal life.' And now the Christian traveller visiting the glacier valley of Fressinière, will see, not without emotion, the humble shepherdess seated at the foot of a block of granite, and surrounded by her lambs, reading with her eyes bathed in tears, the history of the *Good Shepherd who gave his life for the sheep.*

"On Wednesday, the 6th, I passed the defile of Orsière. Several of my catechumens were my guides. Our conversation was very edifying. I was struck with the Christian reflections, which the difficulties of our way, and the savage aspect of the glaciers that surrounded us, suggested to them. 'How many times,' said one of them, 'have I braved danger in following the wild goat among these precipices! I have spared neither my time nor trouble; I have endured cold, hunger, and fatigue: I have traversed the most frightful rocks, and exposed my life hundreds of times! Shall I do as much for Jesus? Shall I pursue eternal life with as much ardour? And

N

yet, what comparison is there between the two objects !'

"I arrived the same evening at St. Laurent, where I immediately held a meeting. I thought, on coming to Champsaur, to rest a little from the fatigues of the preceding week, but by the grace of God, I had still enough to do. Our excellent Ferdinand had not relaxed his exertions. I found the zeal of the people increased, and their manners improved. These people, so worldly, so proud of their riches, their strength, or their beauty, are not insensible to the voice of the Gospel. Although the Protestants are only a small minority, their example, nevertheless, influences the Roman Catholics. Dancing has disappeared ; gaming and drunkenness, which had passed into a proverb among them, have sensibly diminished ; and one seldom hears any more of those sanguinary quarrels, once so frequent in this valley. On Thursday and Friday I catechised ; I visited the school and several families, and held a meeting each evening. On Saturday, the day of admitting the catechumens, I held a meeting in the morning. Several of them, the least instructed, live in the neighbouring mountains among Roman Catholics, and have no means for their education, and the distance preventing their often repairing to St. Laurent, they are able to be present only at the catechising. I addressed them in the dialect of the country, in a very simple manner, and endeavoured to bring near to them the truths of the Gospel. They appeared very attentive, so did their parents, not less ignorant than themselves, who accompanied them. I afterwards admitted, at the morning service, fifty-two catechumens, for the most part pretty well instructed, and some of them really impressed with divine truth. The afternoon was passed mostly in the church, and on account of the numbers, we were obliged to hold the meeting there in the evening. On Sunday, the 10th, we had a very numerous meeting at the communion. Notwithstanding an opening I had got made in the ceiling of the church, it was with great difficulty that I could breathe. In the afternoon, the meeting was, contrary to usual custom, almost as numerously attended as in the morning, and the upper part of the church was again almost full. I saw only one Protestant playing at bowls. Several of the inhabitants of the neighbouring hamlets, who had come for the first time to the evening meeting, said, as they were returning, ' If this man often came hither, the public-house keepers would not get rich.'

" In the midst of all this outward zeal, the truly spiritual work goes on slowly ; and I think, that excepting Ferdinand, few have become established in grace."

The last observation was forced from the pastor, because he found in the people of Champsaur a levity at times, which rent his heart. For example, in a family where there were several young people, one of whom had shown symptoms of growing piety, he was making some earnest appeals to their religious feelings, and was imploring them to seek God in prayer, when a youth, who was a celebrated sportsman, exclaimed, pointing to his dogs and his gun, " look, these are my gods !"   Such unpromising signs often led him into a train of painful thought, and then he unburthened his mind by committing such mournful reflections to paper as these. " Oh ! when will the Gospel find, in these southern provinces of France, such a soil for its reception, as among the faithful hearers in Alsace.   Even those, who are more fit for the work of an evangelist than I am, find the same difficulties.   The few that seem to be awakened, are for the most part languishing and irresolute.   Lively and trifling, the French peasant appears at first to be moved and influenced by the word of life, but he soon grows tired of it, and he suffers his attention to be distracted.   The most brilliant show of blossoms gives but little fruit, and if the fruit ripens, it is but very slowly."

Some transactions, in which Neff took a very decided part, occurred during one of his visits to Champsaur, towards the latter end of the year 1824, which illustrate both his own character, and the low state of religion among too many of the Protestants of the south of France.   Champsaur was served by Neff provisionally, until a pastor could be found, who would undertake the duties of the commune. A clergyman of very indifferent character, whose proffered services had been rejected by many of the Protestant sections, presented himself as a candidate for the parish of Champsaur. The president of the consistory of Orpierre knew that he was an unfit object for the charge, but, under the influence of that indecision, which too frequently marks the bearing of official persons, who are less the heads than the organs of a representative body, he was disposed to act against his own better judgment, and to yield to the importunity of two members of the board, who were personally interested in behalf of the unworthy applicant. The discussion lasted for several days, and, as is often the case, the pertinacity of the minority triumphed over the indifference of the majority. They were on the eve of gaining their point by dint of out-talking the better thinking. Happily, Neff was in the neighbourhood at the time, and the president sent a messenger to entreat him to repair to Orpierre without loss of time, and to throw his weight into the right scale. A wild mountain was to be traversed at the shortest notice in the month of December, and some very severe weather had affected Neff's health; but he cheerfully set out upon his dreary journey before day-light, to avoid the keen north wind, which usually blew at certain hours. But rude Boreas was earlier than our traveller. He had much difficulty in achieving the ascent, and when he arrived at the summit, he was so weak, and the wind was so violent, and the ridge so slippery with ice and frozen snow, that it was an affair of no small danger to proceed. He persevered, however, and his presence and arguments turned the scale. The undeserving candidate was a man of considerable address and powers of mind, and at a former period of life, before his immoralities unmasked him, had obtained testimonials from some persons of eminence, which he now exhibited. Armed with these, and supported by the suffrages of those, who thought more of talent and lively manners than of sound ministerial usefulness, he would have succeeded, if the remonstrances of Neff had not shamed the consistory into a decision, which saved the flock from one, who would neither have " healed that which was sick, nor bound up that which was broken, nor sought that which was lost."

Note.—In the summer of 1826, Neff paid a visit to the Waldenses of the Valleys of Piedmont. He did not bring away an opinion entirely favourable to their spiritual condition. To those who are inclined to pass severe sentence upon the Vaudois, because they are not all that they ought to be, and who judge of the whole community from a few degenerate descendants of that noble race of confessors and martyrs, I would recommend a perusal of the following remarks, from the conclusion of Captain Cotton's Letter, published in the ninth report of the Continental Society:—

" I should be sorry indeed, if, in informing the committee of what fell under my observation, and of the opinion I have thence formed of the state of religion in the valleys, it should in any degree contribute to stop the current of charity from England : there is much need of foreign assistance. It is of the first necessity that the schoolmasters should be qualified to instil ideas with the lessons they teach the children ; a better pay should be attached to their situations in the hamlets, and they should be themselves instructed. It will be very difficult to find spiritually-minded men proposing to themselves the glory of the Redeemer, in bringing little children to believe on him. They may, however, be trained to follow a good system, and watched over ; and to God must be left the increase. Far from me be the desire to weaken the charitable feeling existing with regard to the Vaudois ; they have, on many grounds, a claim to our sympathy : for their fathers' sake, from whom I believe evangelical light penetrated into England ; for the long period in which they were witnesses for the truth in times of repose as well as of persecution ; for the manifest favour with which God has regarded them in the most critical circumstances of their history ; for their former missionary spirit, their poverty, and their civil disabilities. It has been insinuated, that the pastors are enemies to the truth ; I witnessed no such thing. It does not appear that they took any steps to drive Messrs. ———— and ———— from the valleys. They must have been denounced for admitting strangers into their pulpits ; those two ministers were prevented from preaching any longer by an order from government, and consequently left the valleys. Their visit was not without some degree of fruit : a brother of Mr. ————, to whom I am indebted for an introduction to several pastors, and four or five other converts to the faith. They meet occasionally to edify each other, at the house of an excellent man, Mr. ————, a retired pastor. If the spirit of true religion is become cold, the effects of the religious state of their forefathers have not ceased to be visible. The Vaudois are far superior in moral character to the Roman Catholic inhabitants ; they are from ancient habit, honest, civil, and quiet ; and from their situation and necessity, simple and laborious : it is highly to their credit, that they took no part in the late revolution, although emissaries were sent into the mountains to seduce them. Should foreign assistance be withdrawn, the light still twinkling amid the snows of the Alps may expire ; they may not long resist the encroachments of the Church of Rome, now exerting herself in every quarter to bring again the Christian world into the same subjection as in ancient times ; whereas, by strengthening the Vaudois Church, it may become, in more favourable circumstances, an instrument for enlightening Italy, in which country, though now there appears but a few gleaning grapes on the uppermost boughs, the fruit thereof may, hereafter, shake like Lebanon."

CHAPTER IX.

NEFF'S METHOD AND GOOD UNDERSTANDING WITH THE RO-
MAN CATHOLICS—HIS INTERVIEW WITH A ROMISH PRIEST
—A FAMILY SKETCH—THE CONVERT OF ARVIEUX—A DEATH-
BED SCENE—THE MISSION—CONTROVERSIES—ANECDOTE—
THE CURÉ—PALONS—THE SHEPHERDESS MARIETTE.

UPON several important occasions, the pastor of
the High Alps obtained as much influence by
the sweetness of his temper, as by his firmness,
and by that kindness of manner which never deserted him, however trying might be the juncture,
in which it was necessary to display it. We have
seen, that after the discussion with the Vaudois
minister, who was inclined to take himself away
in a pet, Neff's conciliatory deportment brought
him to his good humour, and they parted with
mutual feelings of respect and good-will. It was
his second nature, if not his original disposition,
to suffer long and to be kind. His charity never
failed—it displayed itself in a thousand trifles, so
much so, that it oftentimes softened the animosity
of those, who had most reason to be jealous of
his presence. As the Mahomedans and Hindoos
crowded round Heber in India, to hear his persuasive and mild reasonings, when they would

have shrunk from angry polemics, so did Roman
Catholics take delight in listening to Neff's truly
Catholic discourses. The popish clergy lost
many of their flock during his sojournment in
Dauphiné, but it was some time before they re-
sented his proselyting exertions. When they
were inclined to give reins to their displeasure,
his meekness took the sting out of their indig-
nation. He never reviled them, or spoke dis-
respectfully of them——on the contrary, he was
forward to place even their errors in the best
light, and whenever he found them labouring
usefully at their posts, he gave them their meed
of praise. It once happened that he preached
at St. Laurent, in Champsaur, on the day of the
patron saint, a festival which, in general, produces a great deal of dissolute conduct. On that
occasion, however, the people were more orderly,
and there were fewer scenes of drunkenness and
disorder than usual. A note in his Journal observes upon this, and attributes it as much to the
exertions of the curé, as to his own, which were
uniformly employed in promoting the sanctity
of the Sabbath. An interesting proof of the
good footing upon which he stood for a long
time with the priests of the other Church, occurred at Fressinière in October of the year now
under notice, 1824. It cannot be better related
than in his own words.

" At Fressinière a strange adventure awaited
me. I was invited to sup with the priest, a

most fanatical and rude sort of person. It is some time since the curé of Chancelas had requested me to pay him a vist in his own parish, which lies on my route. I went there, and we passed several hours in serious conversation. He afterwards accompanied me across the Durance. This young man, who is full of good sense, and well informed, appeared to have a perfect comprehension of the essential principles of the Gospel, and did not depend upon the outward works of devotion, or upon the intercession of the saints for his acceptance with God, but he was a staunch upholder of the sacrifice of the mass, and of the hierarchy of the Roman Church. He had pressed me very much to renew my visit, but I had not seen him again, until the time of which I am going to speak. On this day he came to the house of M. Barridon with the priest of Fressinière. The latter is so intolerant, that every body in the commune thought that he would insult me, if we should ever meet, for he used to revile the Protestants, and all that belonged to them, in the most unsparing terms, and a hundred times he has abused our people in the very grossest language, even at their own doors. I do not know what he thought upon seeing me there, but as he found that his colleague expressed some friendship for me, he could not do otherwise than conduct himself civilly; and the curé of Chancelas having asked me, in his hearing to visit him, he thought he must exercise the same politeness. He there-fore gave M. Barridon and me an invitation, and engaged his brother of Chancelas to stay with him till the next day. We went to his house, and to our great surprise the conversation was quite amicable, although we did not abstain from religious topics. The good effect of this inter-view was visible in the intercourse to which it led between members of the two communions. Who would not have been astonished to see the priest and the pastor discoursing quietly to-gether !"

Many other instances might be selected from his Journals, to show the good understanding which long prevailed among the Roman Catho-lics and Protestants in different parts of his parish, where Bibles and Testaments were read and distributed without interruption.

At a small hamlet near Arvieux, just below the picturesque torrent and the Alpine bridge, which I described in a preceding page, there was a family consisting of an elder brother, a Protestant, who had one son of the same faith ; a second brother, his wife and children, Roman Catholics ; and a third brother, named James, an old bachelor and a Protestant. This family lived together in the greatest harmony, and the son of the elder brother married a daughter of the second. Their uncle James was a remark-ably intelligent man, and, going about the coun-try as a pedlar, he picked up all the old religious books he could lay his hands upon, and nobody was better read than he in the histories of the reformation, and of the popes and councils. He could recite with astonishing accuracy the dates of councils, and of papal bulls and rescripts, and was never so happy as when discussing matters of religion. Neff had previously made acquaintance with this man in the course of his rambles at Mens and Grenoble, and was so pleased with his conversation and his books, that he never passed his house, in his way to or from the presbytery at La Chalp, without calling upon him. This gave him frequent opportunities of holding serious discourse with the different members of the family, and when he spoke to the Protestant branches of it on the solemn duties incumbent on them, the Roman Catholics never failed to listen with marked attention. He prudently displayed no anxiety to convert them; but, by degrees, the mother and daughter began to enter into the spirit of his pious and affectionate style of conversation, and expressed a desire to know more of some of the books, which were the frequent subject of his observations. Two of these were the Bible, and a translation of Doddridge's Rise and Progress of Religion in the Soul. The mother took one of Neff's favourite volumes with her to her mountain chalet, where she spent the summer with her cattle, and during her solitary abode amidst the grandest works of creation, where nothing met her eye but objects proclaiming the immensity and majesty of the Eternal, she grew utterly dissatisfied with the limited views of Divine love and wisdom, to which she had hitherto been confined, and sighed for the liberty wherewith Christ could make her free.   When she returned to her cottage by the torrent side, she made a point of inviting her Roman Catholic friends to come in, whenever Neff was likely to be paying them a visit, and this went on for some time without any interruption or indication of sectarian jealousy.   In the end, the little family became one in faith, as they had ever been one in affection, and some of their neighbours of the other Church left the ministry of the curé for that of the pastor.   The conflicts which some of these proselytes had with their consciences, before they could find peace in Jesus Christ, proved the sincerity of their conversion.   The account which Neff gives of one of them is peculiarly interesting.   It explains his method with the Roman Catholics, and enables us to take a fearful look into that abyss of despair, through which the devout and sensitive mind has to pass, before it can emerge from the darkness of Popery to the clear light of Protestantism.

" You will not have forgotten the name of Maria ———, a young woman whose serious manner I noticed more than a year ago.   She is now, like the sister of Lazarus, sitting at the feet of Jesus, but she has suffered so much before she could reach them, that I am afraid the new birth will be at the cost of her life. She was brought up a Roman Catholic, but having married a Protestant, she adopted her husband's faith. Not having yet received the sacrament of the Lord's Supper, according to the forms of our Church, I have given her the same instructions as my other catechumens, and it is astonishing with what facility she has acquired a knowledge of the subject. But when we came to a personal application of the lessons, I observed that she was most deeply affected by a sense of her condition. During the winter I had many opportunities of seeing her, and every time I found her more and more cast down. Her countenance expressed great dejection, and she appeared to be suffering from illness. Her mother entreated me to visit her as often as I could. 'My poor Maria,' said she, 'has no comfort but when you are here,—at other times she is constantly weeping.' I tried to have a private interview with her, but did not succeed for a long time. One day her husband said to me, in tears, 'My poor wife will die, I do not know what is the matter with her; she takes no nourishment, and is melting away like the snow.' I told him that I hoped this sickness was not unto death, but for the glory of God, and that he himself, and others, would be greatly edified. The same evening Maria appeared more sad than before,—she retired from us on the plea of suffering some internal pain, and her mother then told me that she complained of being unable to pray ; that it was this which so distressed her, and that she was anxious to have some private conversation with me. This was the very thing I wished.

"' Well, Maria,' I began, 'what makes you so melancholy ? what is the matter ?'

"' I am lost !' she exclaimed.

"' No doubt, you are lost, and we are all lost by nature : but did not Christ come to seek and to save that which is lost ?'

"' But it is three years since God first graciously imparted to me a sense of my lost condition, I was all the winter as ill as I am now. I wished for conversion, but I have thrown away the means of grace. I have slumbered and slept, like the foolish virgins of the parable. My hour is gone by, and now my heart is hardened, and God rejects me. God is just, I deserve it !'

" This was said with all the calmness of despair, and I was afraid that the terrible persuasion had taken fast hold of her mind. I asked her, whether at the first indication of a change in her religious sentiments, there had been any body to teach her the way of salvation : for how should you find it yourself, said I. Be not afraid,—to-day is your hour—hitherto you have never fully known the Good Shepherd !

" After this she seemed to be relieved from the apprehension, that she had lost the favourable season, but still she was not assured.   It was in vain that I spoke again and again of God's mercy in Jesus Christ.   She told me that she could neither repent, nor believe, nor pray, as she ought, and that when she endeavoured to draw nigh unto God, a spirit of blasphemy seemed to come across her.   I then suggested every consideration that I thought would avail her, and affected to regard her state as very natural and very common; I prayed with her; still she was not comforted.   I conjured her, in the most earnest and tender manner, to persevere in supplications to God, through Jesus Christ: and she promised that she would.

"The next day I spent part of the morning with her, and returned several times in the course of the days following, but always without success.   She was incapable of making any bodily exertion; she was suffering physically as well as mentally, and literally watered her couch with her tears, always complaining of the same thing, of her want of proper contrition, and of her hardness of heart.   One day when I was going to leave her, she cried out, 'If you depart, I shall die.'   I was forced to remain near her for some time, before her agitation was over. She passed three or four months in this afflicting condition, and though she has at length experienced a sense of the mercy of her God; yet she is still depressed in spirits; her conscience is susceptible and alarmed by the least symptom of sin. One day, when some young girls were frolicking around her, one of them exclaimed, ' Maria, why do not you laugh as we do?' She replied, but with great sweetness, ' I prefer my sadness to your mirth.' She has with difficulty picked up a little strength, but she is still very weak. The soul is consuming the body. I have never seen any one so deeply affected, so enlightened, and yet so simple at the same time. A younger sister of her's, who, up to this period, was a devoted Roman Catholic, but full of levity, has now begun to think seriously of her own responsibility, and to display an increasing repugnance against the Romish worship. I asked her one day, ' Do you think that the priest, or the pope himself, can give you a dispensation of conversion, as he grants you a dispensation to eat meat ? Can he dispense with what is required by Jesus Christ, the new birth ? Do not deceive yourself, it is written, except a man be born again he cannot see the kingdom of God !' "

I am happy to be able to add some information [1] to this affecting account, which Neff's Journals do not supply. It pleased the God of hope to fill Maria —— with all joy and peace in believing, and, at length she abounded in hope, through the power of the Holy Ghost. In August, 1829, after Neff's return to Switzerland, to recruit his shattered health, he heard of the sudden

Collected from " Notice sur Felix Neff."

death of Maria's mother, who, with her sisters, had become sincere converts to the Protestant faith. The pastor wrote a letter of condolence to the afflicted family, in which he declared that he had rarely experienced any grief equal to that, which he suffered on learning this mournful news. "The good Madeline, who was so kind in her attentions to me, who had so much sympathy for the sorrow of others; who received the servants of the Lord with so much joy and love, and who had such pleasure in listening to the word of life, am I then never to meet her again in this world! But why should I thus wound your heart and my own? Is it for us, the inheritors of an incorruptible and heavenly crown, to afflict ourselves, and to be sorry as men without hope?" This letter brought an answer, written by Maria, assisted by her brother, in which she gave the following relation of the sufferings and death of her mother, from which we gather the consolatory assurance, that the pastor's proselyte fell asleep in Jesus, and that her children enjoy the peace which passeth understanding.

"My mother's illness only lasted seven days, but it was exceedingly violent. It was an inflammation of the bowels, attended with a tormenting cholic, which never allowed her to have an hour's rest during the whole of that time. We saw from the first that there was no hope, and talked to her of her approaching end. She used to reply to us with a smile full of hope and joy.

' Have you nothing to attach you to earth?' we asked. ' No,' she replied, with a serene air; 'all that this world contains, passeth away!' ' And have you no fears, at the thought of entering into a new existence, and appearing before the Judge Eternal?' She joined her hands together, and raised her eyes to heaven, and then replied: ' No, there is nothing to fear, Jesus Christ is my atonement and intercessor. I rely upon his promises, and therefore I desire to depart, and to be with Christ!' She often blessed God for having sent you to announce the glad tidings of redemption through Jesus Christ, and invoked the heavenly benediction upon your body and soul. When her strength was almost gone, she said to us: ' I cannot pray aloud—pray for me, my children; pray that the Lord may increase my faith.' She pointed out this verse of an hymn, which she asked to have repeated to her.

Vois l'âme criminelle
A tes pieds, Dieu Sauveur!
Daigne jeter sur elle
Un regard de faveur.

" Soon after, she exclaimed, ' I know in whom I have believed. He is faithful to keep that which is committed unto him. I am weak, but he is strong.' Upon another occasion, she said to us: —' My children, do not weep: offer up your prayers to the Saviour for comfort, and he will not forsake you. I am happy, I shall only precede you a little; you will rejoin me, and we shall meet again in the presence of God.' At a crisis, when her pains were very great, I said to her, 'You are suffering severely, my dear mother.' She answered, ' The sufferings of my Redeemer were much greater.' 'Then you have a firm assurance in his promises now, even in the valley of the shadow of death?' ' Yes, Jesus Christ is my support. He has swallowed up death in victory.' She then made a last effort to join her hands, and lifting up her eyes to heaven, she uttered in broken sentences:—' Thy cross, Thy blood,—Thy death, Jesus, are—my support!' These, my beloved and respected pastor, were my mother's last words. She gave me her two hands, and while I was praying aloud, her soul quitted its earthly tenement and mounted to heaven. I heard nothing around me but weeping and sighing; every thing was sad and mournful, but He who is rich in mercy, poured out his consolations, and helped us to be resigned to his will. For myself he has made me feel assured, that my dear mother is happy in his bosom, and that I shall soon be with her there. Sadness has given place to joy. I must tell you, that since my mother's death, my father has been more attentive to the Word of God, and thinks more about his soul. He listens with pleasure when we tell him of the Saviour. He goes with us to the temple. Oh! what a happy day it will be for me, if, in losing my mother for a short time, I shall obtain my father for eternity. Pray for us that it may be so.

"Your devoted sister in Jesus Christ,
"MARIA ———.""

The reader will perceive in this simple narrative of a death-bed scene, not the wild sentiments of an enthusiast, but the calm piety of a Christian, and he will say, if such were Neff's pupils and converts, what must their instructor have been!

But at length "*The Mission*" disturbed the harmony that had hitherto reigned between the Protestants and the Roman Catholics. Some of the members of the Mission marshalled ostentatious processions, preached incendiary sermons, and pursued such effectual means of exciting an angry and bigoted feeling against the Protestants, that many of the Romanists declined holding any intercourse with them as heretofore, and even crossed themselves whenever they passed a house in which Protestants were dwelling. *The Mission*, is the name under which a religious movement commenced in France in 1819, and continued till the revolution of July, 1830, with the sanction and assistance of the government, and under the direction of ecclesiastics and others, who formed themselves into a religious order. The persons who were employed in the work of reviving the spirit of the Roman Catholic religion, were selected for their zeal and eloquence, and, as they went from town to town, and in some parts from village to village, instructing and confessing the people, it is astonishing what effects were produced by the combined influence of example, exhortation, and authority. They erected colossal crosses, beautifully carved and gilt, on conspicuous spots—they made the circuits of streets and hamlets at the head of splendid processions, swelled by priests and other ecclesiastics gorgeously arrayed[1], and bearing costly banners flaunting and glittering in the sun, and by such of the population as caught the infection of their ardour; and the multitude thus composed made the air resound with their penitential psalms, or sighs and groans of contrition. At the churches decorated with tapestry, at favourite shrines expensively ornamented, and before crucifixes of enormous magnitude, the procession would halt, and some gifted preacher would stand forth and address the congregated thousands, in language best calculated to promote the interests of the Romish faith. If piety revived under the influence of these impressive solemnities, so unhappily did fanaticism, and as

---

[1] " And the woman was arrayed in purple and scarlet colour, and decked with gold and precious stones, and pearls, having a golden cup in her hand. And I saw the woman drunken with the blood of the saints, and with the blood of the martyrs of Jesus."—*Rev.* xvii. 4. 6.

heresy was frequently branded by these peripatetic preachers as something worse than infidelity, the lower orders among the papists were excited to acts of violence against the Protestants, which made some of the latter tremble for their lives, and anticipate a recurrence of former sufferings. The peaceful hamlets, which composed Neff's parish, were greatly disturbed by the Mission; some few weak and wavering brothers were scared into abjuring the creed of their ancestors, who had died martyrs to their faith; and instances were known, not only of Roman Catholics being compelled by their priests to burn their copies of Scripture, but of Protestants committing venerable Bibles to the flame, under the influence of terror, which had escaped the worst of times, and had been transmitted to them, as the only possession which their forefathers had been able to preserve, amidst the wreck of all their little property.

What presumption in man, to dare to put a stop to the free course of God's own word! Be the reason, the sophistry, the pretext what it may, which would render the Bible a sealed book, or a prohibited book, or a book which is to be read under certain limitations, the upshot of the control, and the meaning of the authority which so presumes is this :—" We desire you to accept our creed; believe what we believe. The Bible contains the exposition of the faith proposed to you,—we derive all our own knowledge from it:

but you must not read what we read: it is inexpedient to open to you the fountain, from which we derive our knowledge. We do not permit you to consult those pages indiscriminately, or to read them without our guidance and interpretation." And yet with all this real hostility to the Bible, and practical prohibition of it, some Roman Catholics deny that the Bible is prohibited by their Church. Do they deny the validity of canons of councils? What will they say to the following?

"We forbid any of the laity to have in their possession the books of the Old and New Testament [1]."

In England the Romish priesthood withhold these tell-tale prohibitions of their Church, but in France, at the period of which I am speaking, the Mission openly proclaimed them.

"Some of our poor Protestants are extremely dejected by these proceedings," complained the pastor in his Journal. "They are looking for me in some of my villages with great anxiety, for it has been reported that I too have turned Papist." They had not to wait long, for no sooner did Neff hear that his presence was necessary in any part of his parish, than he immediately repaired thither, and though all his circuits were performed on foot, and in the summer the drought consumed him, and in the winter the

---

[1] Fourteenth canon of the eleventh council of Thoulouse.

frost, yet no apprehension of fatigue or difficulty ever arrested his steps. In consequence of the excitement caused by the Mission, he felt it to be his duty to be still more vigilant and active. "The Lord," said he, in one of his letters from the High Alps, " has permitted me to have the unspeakable joy of seeing some of the Romish Church awakened, and leaving their broken cisterns, to go to the real fountain of living waters. Not that we have easy access to the houses of the Roman Catholics ;—a Protestant, and especially a minister, finds many impediments in the way of declaring the Gospel, for besides the prejudices they entertain, it is impossible to enter into any religious conversation, but they forthwith give it a controversial turn, the result of which is rarely satisfactory to either party. In these mountains the officiating clergy are young priests, exclusive in their notions, and strongly embued with the spirit of the Jesuits, in whose seminaries they have been educated. The Mission, the jubilee, and other exciting causes, have successively revived fanaticism in a region, which was previously too much the scene of intolerance and superstition."

But neither the pastor, nor the more enlightened members of his flock, suspended their exertions: where the timid shrunk from the open avowal of their sentiments, the bold, and such as were truly anxious for the salvation of others, came resolutely forward, and seized every opportunity of giving their testimony to the truth, in the house,—by the way-side,—and even in the presence of the Roman Catholic priests. Their appeals came with all the force of sound sense, and were irresistibly supported by their ready quotation of Scripture. In Champsaur, the Protestants were greatly in the minority, as far as numbers were concerned, but there were two or three sturdy champions of the cause, who were a host of themselves; and fortunately the curé there, though he was a most bigoted Papist, had not fortified himself with any polemical weapons, either from reason or Scripture, which were a match for the offensive and defensive armour of his adversaries. One day, when this curé ventured to ask a Protestant, "Upon what do you build your belief, since you have no authority for your faith?"

"Upon the Bible," was the reply: "if the apostles had left behind them any infallible successors, it would have been unnecessary to bequeath to us so many instructions in writing!"

"The apostles! and why are you to place greater reliance on the apostles, than on their successors?"

"Because the apostles were inspired by the Holy Ghost."

"Well; and we too are inspired!"

"Are you inspired?"

"Yes! I repeat, we too are inspired!"

"Then why do you require to be further instructed in the college of the Jesuits?"

The priest was routed.

Upon another occasion, when a young woman of the valley of Queyras was questioned by a Romish priest upon the object of her faith and hope, and when she constantly made the same reply, and reverently named Jesus Christ, as the ground of her faith and hope, the curé exclaimed impatiently, "Jesus Christ! It is always Jesus Christ! do you think, then, that Jesus Christ is every thing to you?"

The young woman answered with a meekness and solemnity which silenced her interrogator. "Yes; every thing is Jesus Christ—who of God is made unto us wisdom, and righteousness, and sanctification, and redemption, that, according as it is written, he that glorieth, let him glory in the Lord."

A few days afterwards, the curé, before several witnesses, returned to the contest, and among other things, took upon himself to declare, that all sins were not mortal. He named the sins which he called exclusively mortal, and then proceeded to argue himself right by analogy and by authority, and afterwards launched out in defence of purgatory, indulgences, &c. The young woman asked him to tell her, if the sin of Adam, which the curé had not contrived to include in the list of his mortal sins, was mortal or venial?"

This was too much for the controversialist.
Taken by surprise, but yet perceiving the horns
of the dilemma between which he was so ridicu-
lously stuck, and aware of the consequences of
answering such a question, he wisely replied that
he would give an answer another time.

Chancelas is a lovely village at the entrance of
the valley of Fressinière, where the mountains
form a splendid panorama, whose vine-clad sides
stretch on one side down to the Durance, and
where the little hamlets, divided by ravines and
torrents, are seen rising out of forests of larch
trees. This village was often the scene of
triumph to Neff and his converts, and the priests
of that parish had the mortification of seeing
many of their flock fall away from them, and
become proselytes to the powerful reasoning of
the Swiss preacher. There was a family here,
anciently Protestant, which had been forming
connexions among the Roman Catholics, until
they eventually deserted the worship of their
ancestors, and went to mass. Upon the opening
of the new church of Violins, the head of this
family and two of his younger sons attended the
service, and from that time, the young men regularly waited upon Neff's ministry, both public
and private, and one of them attached himself
closely to the pastor, and manifested the most
devoted fidelity both to his person and his doctrines. In his journeys from one valley to
another, Neff frequently passed through Chan-

celas, and visited this family, but the elder son and his wife, invariably left the house, whenever he entered it, and continued to express a rude dislike, which was obvious to all. It so happened, that this man, whom nothing could persuade to listen to Neff, was persuaded to go and hear a friend of Neff, who preached at Palons. He returned home full of what he had been hearing, and as soon as he entered the house, he exclaimed to his wife, "we are lost if we neglect this way of salvation." The woman was moved by his earnestness, and from that time the pastor was no longer treated with rudeness or neglect, but his conversation was eagerly sought for, and his persuasions were so forcible, that the whole family returned to the bosom of the Protestant communion. Many people of the same village followed this example, and though the distance was very considerable from the church at Violins, all the new converts regularly attended public service whenever it was performed. This movement was becoming so general at Chancelas before Neff's health failed him, that it was thought necessary to send another curé there to produce a re-action: but the violence and intolerance of this person confirmed the sensation, which was beginning to be felt, and added to the number of those who questioned the infallibility of the Romish Church. Neff supplied several of the converts with Martin's edition of the New Testament, which is printed with references in the margin to parallel passages, and by the help of these, they used to turn to a variety of corresponding and confirmatory passages, when the priests told them that the texts, which they quoted, were only solitary passages which admitted of explanation.

I was assured, when I was on the spot, two years after Neff's departure, that the flame kindled by him was still spreading, and that Chancelas was likely to become one of the most zealous Protestant villages in the whole region. But Chancelas was not the only place where his persuasive eloquence made converts. In Val Queyras he was equally successful, and upon an occasion when it was thought that he had quitted the country, the curés triumphantly announced the event from their pulpits. The priest of one of the parishes invited his people to bless God, for having removed such a ravening wolf from their fold. "But that poor priest," said Neff, when he heard of it, "was ignorant that none can overturn the work which proceeds from God, and that it can support itself without the assistance of the first instruments, who laboured at it. In fact, three persons of his flock left it, after I went away, to join that of Jesus Christ, and, but a little while before, the younger sister of one of my converts did the same, and several proselytes, who had hitherto been timid, now openly declared themselves."

The narrative of Neff's labours, and of his

successful efforts with the Roman Catholics in the High Alps, might be enriched with many more details of this kind, but I think it will be enough to bring this part of the relation to a conclusion, with the mention of an incident which he himself made known to the world during his life, by transmitting an account of it to one of the periodical publications of his own country.

The two villages of Palons and Chancelas, the scene of several of the pastor's most interesting conversions, lie contiguous to each other at the entrance of the valley of Fressinière. Palons is at the very neck of the defile, and the rocks which overhang "the peasants' nests" command a beautiful prospect both of the valley, which draws up narrower and narrower, as the traveller advances towards Dormilleuse, and of the country which opens down towards the waters of the Durance.

One day Neff met, at Palons, a little shepherdess of twelve or thirteen years of age, whose air and language struck him with surprise. In answer to his inquiries about her, he was told that her name was Mariette Guyon, and that she lived in the adjacent hamlet of Punayer with her grandfather and grandmother, who were Roman Catholics; that she had expressed great anxiety to be instructed in the true principles of the Gospel, and that they could not attribute this desire merely to human influence, and to the persuasions of Protestant acquaintances, for she was not permitted to associate with Protestants. He asked the child if she could read? She burst into tears, and said, "Oh! if they would only let me come here to the Sunday-school, I should soon learn, but they tell me that I already know too much." The pastor's interest was further excited, by learning that what little she knew of the difference between the religion of the two Churches was picked up by accident, and by stealthy conversation with the converts of the neighbourhood.

After his first short interview with the poor girl, he remained some time without hearing any thing more of her. In the interval, she was deprived of all regular means of improvement, but her zeal made her find out a very ingenious expedient. She often kept her flock near a very rocky path which descended to the valley of Fressinière, and when she saw a peasant pass, she would accost him in her patois, and ask "Where do you come from?" If he named a Catholic village, she said no more, and let him pass on. If he came from a Protestant hamlet, she approached him, and put questions to him [1], and if he displayed any zeal and knowledge of the Gospel, she would keep him as long as he would good-naturedly remain, and treasure up

[1] Literally did this child obey the Divine precept, " Stand ye in the paths and see, and ask for the old paths, where is the good way, and walk therein, and ye shall find rest for your souls." Jeremiah vi. 16.

P

all that she heard from his lips. At other times she would make friends with Protestant children, who were watching their sheep or goats near her, and would beg them to bring their Testaments, and read and translate to her. This went on until she saw that she was watched by some of the Roman Catholics, and was obliged to be more cautious. During the long and rigorous winter, which followed after Neff first saw her, the mountains were buried in snow, and the people could not go out of their villages, therefore Mariette had no intercourse with those whose conversation she so much desired to cultivate. Notwithstanding her faith was strengthened and her mind enlightened, and on the return of spring she positively refused to go to mass. In vain they attempted to force her by ill-usage. Her father was then appealed to, and first tried rigorous means, and then persuasion, to engage her to declare from whence she obtained what he called " these new ideas." She persisted in declaring that God alone had first put these things in her heart, and expressed herself with so much meekness and solemnity, in explanation of the motives by which she was actuated, that her father felt constrained to say to those who urged him to exert his authority, " Who am I, to oppose myself to God?" But he left her still under the care of her grandfather and grandmother, who continued to ill-treat her, although without success.

The pastor shall now tell the continuation of the story himself. "Some time after I had learnt all these particulars, I was going to Palons, accompanied by a young man, and Madeleine Pellegrine, a most humble and zealous disciple of Jesus Christ. Whilst stopping near the bridge and cascade of Rimasse, which precipitates itself into a deep abyss, we saw a flock of lambs, which appeared to be hastily driven toward us by a young shepherdess. It was Mariette, who had recognised us from a distance, and who ran up to us breathless with joy. She expressed in language which it is impossible to describe, how happy she was at meeting me. I requested Madeleine to watch the flock while I conversed with Mariette. She thanked me with affectionate earnestness for the visit I had made to her father in her behalf. She spoke of what she had suffered for the Gospel, in a manner so Christian and so touching, that I could hardly believe my ears, knowing that the poor child did not know even the letters of the alphabet. ' It is this,' she said, ' that gives me pain ; the evil spirit tempts me, by insinuating that I resist in vain, and that I am too young and feeble to persevere ; but when I suffer most, then the good God supports me, and I fear nothing. They want me to make the sign of the cross ; they wish to drag me to mass, and because I refuse, they beat me ; and when they have beaten me for the name of Jesus

Christ, and see that I do not cry, but rejoice in
his name, then they become furious, and beat
me still more; but were they to kill me, I would
not cry, since the good God strengthens me.'
She uttered many things equally affecting.
When she left me, she went to join another
young shepherdess, a Protestant, with whom
she oftentimes kept her flock, and who attended
the Sunday-school for both of them, for she
repeated to Mariette verses from the Psalms,
and passages from the New Testament, which
she had learnt there.   A short time afterwards I
held a réunion near Punayer, which Mariette
attended; it was the first time she had ever been
present at Protestant worship.   She blessed
God, who had inspired her with the courage to
do so, and appeared most attentive to the sermon and the prayers, which were in French,
though most probably she was unable to comprehend more than a small part of the service,
not understanding any language but the mountain patois.   Not daring to return to Punayer,
after this, she went to her father, and confessed
to him all that had occurred: he received her
kindly, and took her back to her grandfather
and grandmother, and strenuously forbade them
to ill-treat her for her religious opinions.   This
was something gained, but not sufficient for her;
she earnestly entreated him to allow her to attend the public worship; her constant prayer
during the week was, that God would dispose

her father to grant her permission. Her prayers were heard, and the Sunday following, we had the joy of seeing her come to our temple at Violins, a long way from her home. She was received with every demonstration of joy, and a poor man of Minsas, who had married an aunt of her's, promised to take her to his own house, if they would trust her with him, during the winter, and that he would there teach her to read, and instruct her more perfectly in the truths of the Gospel."

Mariette's perseverance triumphed over the prejudices of her family. She was permitted to receive instruction, and to attend the public services of the Protestant Church, and her singular history having reached the ears of some friends at Mens, they begged her father to be allowed to take charge of her, and her education was conducted under auspices which give us every reason to believe, that she is now a bright ornament of the community, whose faith she thus embraced from the strongest conviction of its purity.

CHAPTER X.

NEFF'S SELF-DENIAL—REMINISCENCES IN VAL FRESSINIÈRE
AND VAL QUEYRAS—THE ALPINE PASTOR'S DUTIES AND
MODE OF LIFE—PASSION WEEK IN DORMILLEUSE AND VAL
FRESSINIÈRE—CAPTAIN COTTON'S ACCOUNT OF AN EXCUR-
SION WITH NEFF.

THE active life which Neff led, must have been
continually bringing scenes of great interest under his notice.   I have before observed, that he
was an ardent lover of nature, from his very boyhood, and an enthusiastic admirer of those, who
had distinguished themselves, by achievements
above the ordinary level of human daring and
perseverance.   And yet, though he was in the
province which is the very land of interesting
recollections, and every excursion, from one
hamlet to another, conducted him over ground
famous in history or romance, it is very rarely
that his Journals or correspondence contain any
allusion to subjects unconnected with the great
object before him.   Occasionally we see a spark-
ling of the early spirit which animated him, but
before it can kindle into a flame, it is suppressed
by his self-denying resolution to know nothing
but Jesus Christ, and him crucified.   Even in

little things, he seems to have been ever keeping himself under, and fixing a steady eye upon the great object of his life. One day he had been traversing one of those glorious Alpine summits, where the purity of the air, and the magnificence of the view, and the buoyancy of feeling so peculiar to mountain scenery, are enjoyed to a degree of exhilaration, which none can imagine, but those who have experienced them, and naturally enough he felt inclined to describe his sensations, when he was writing down the incidents of the day. But he had scarcely penned his first expression of pleasure, before he checked himself, and substituted for the intended apostrophe of delight, a remark on what he considered to be the more proper contemplation of a servant of God, who must have no eye but to his Master's service.

It is necessary to explore the valleys of the Durance and the Guil, and the Ubaye, and of their tributary torrents, and to be well acquainted with the events which still live in the traditions of the natives, to appreciate that forbearance which the pastor exercised, when he abstained from mixing up any commonplace topics in that religious diary, from which I have principally drawn the materials of which this Memoir is composed. He could not pass a defile, which had not been the scene of fierce conflict: every mountain side had rung with the din of arms, in defence of religious liberty,—and every cottage which he entered was the dwelling of a family, who had some memento to show, or some story to tell, of the sufferings or exploits of an ancestor in support of that cause, which he himself came to uphold, though with weapons of a very different warfare.   In the valley of Fressinière, the famous Duke de Lesdiguières, constable of France, left enterprises on record, which are still the theme of every mountaineer's praise. In Val Queyras, the strong passes which guard the frontiers of Italy, were garrisoned by Neff's own countrymen, the Swiss, who, in the stirring times of Francis the First, occupied the Col de la Croix, and all the practicable defiles on the mountain border, and compelled the French monarch, when he menaced Piedmont, to attempt a passage across the Alps, by a route which had never before been attempted by any body of armed men.   This route lay through that part of Neff's parish which was between Guillestre and the Col d'Argentière.   None but the chamois hunter, or the contraband adventurer, had ever traversed the mountain path, by which the chivalry of France then pushed their way into the plains of Piedmont.   How different was the object which led Neff to the deep and dreary ravines, which once rung with the din of pioneers levelling the rocks, cutting down trees to throw bridges across the torrents, and widening the shepherds' paths for the passage of artillery. The romantic courage of the French leaders and soldiers, which was not to be subdued by the difficulties of their enterprise, has been the theme of many a page of eulogy.   That they should have braved " the rushing cataracts, the falling avalanches, the hoarse roar of the mountain winds, which, pent within the rocky walls, might have been imagined to utter forebodings and maledictions, and the appalling accidents by which men and cattle were lost,"——has been the admiration of the world ever since !   How much more ought we to admire the fortitude of our pastor of the Alps, who often braved all these horrors alone, with none by his side to encourage him, or to share his dangers.   Not only at a favourable season of the year, but in winter ; amidst snow and sleet beating in his face, many times did he scale those summits, and cross the torrents, as a messenger of peace.

Neff's second winter in the French Alps was spent very much like the first, for the season was mild and open, and he shifted his ground from hamlet to hamlet, and from house to house, accordingly as he found his presence necessary to strengthen the weak, or to confirm the strong. His journeyings, in the frequent tour of his parish, rendered his life a migratory one in the full sense of the word, and all that our own George Herbert imagined and recommended in his " Country Parson," was realized in the pastor of the High Alps, save his contemplations on " the parson in his house."   He had so much to do out of doors, and away from his own habitation, that home duties, as well as home pleasures, are to be excluded from the list. But we behold in him, " The parson in circuit," —" The parson in journey,"—" The parson comforting,"—" The parson in sentinel,"—" The parson catechizing,"—" The parson's completeness." It was not on Sunday only, that he went the round of his churches, but he was ever visiting now one quarter, and then another : and happy did they esteem themselves at whose table he sat down, and under whose roof he lodged for the night. When his arrival was expected in certain hamlets, whose rotation to be visited was supposed to be coming round, it was beautiful to see the cottages send forth their inhabitants, to watch the coming of the beloved minister. " Come, take your dinner with us."—" Let me prepare your supper."—" Permit me to give up my bed to you,"—were re-echoed from many a voice, and though there was nothing in the repast which denoted a feast-day, yet never was festival observed with greater rejoicing than by those, whose rye-bread and pottage were shared by the pastor Neff. Some-times, when the old people of one cabin were standing at their doors, and straining their eyes to catch the first view of their " guide to heaven," the youngsters of another were perched on the summit of a rock, and stealing a prospect which would afford them an earlier sight of him, and give them the opportunity of offering the first invitation. It was on these occasions, that he obtained a perfect knowledge of the people, questioning them about such of their domestic concerns as he might be supposed to take an interest in, as well as about their spiritual condition, and finding where he could be useful both as a secular adviser and a religious counsellor. " Could all their children read? Did they understand what they read? Did they offer up morning and evening prayers? Had they any wants that he could relieve? Any doubts that he could remove? Any afflictions wherein he could be a comforter?"

It was thus that he was the father of his flock, and master of their affections and their opinions; and when the seniors asked for his blessing, and the children took hold of his hands or his knees, he felt all the fatigue of his long journeys pass away, and became recruited with new strength. But for the high and holy feelings which sustained him, it is impossible that he could have borne up against his numerous toils and exposures, even for the few months in which he thus put his constitution to the trial. Neither rugged paths, nor the inclement weather of these Alps, which would change suddenly from sunshine to rain, and from rain to sleet, and from sleet to snow : nor snow deep under foot, and obscuring the view when dangers lay thick on his road; nothing of this sort deterred him from setting out, with his staff in his hand, and his wallet on his back, when he imagined that his duty summoned him. I have been assured by those who have received him into their houses at such times, that he has come in chilly, wet, and fatigued; or exhausted by heat, and sudden transitions from excessive heat to piercing cold, and that after sitting down a few minutes, his elastic spirits would seem to renovate his sinking frame, and he would enter into discourse with all the mental vigour of one who was neither weary nor languid.

When he was not resident at the presbytery, he was the guest of some peasant, who found him willing to live as he lived, to make a scanty meal of soup-maigre, often without salt or bread, and to retire to rest in the same apartment, where a numerous family were crowded together, amidst all the inconveniences of a dirty and smoky hovel. The people of Arvieux and La ·Chalp were rather dissatisfied with the small share which they had of his company and ministrations. They thought that the habitation, which was provided for him in their commune, gave them a greater claim to his services than any other portion of his parishioners, and one day, when he was preparing to take a journey to a distant hamlet, they remonstrated very earnestly with him, and complained that he did not make the presbytery his home. The pastor endeavoured to explain to them, that they could not reasonably expect him to devote more of his time to them, than to the rest of the population; that he must divide his services according to the number of those who required them, and that, so long as he did not take up his abode in any other part of the parish capriciously, or for a longer period than was necessary, they had no just cause of complaint. The inhabitants of the upper part of the same section, San Veran, Pierre-Grosse, and Fousillarde, to whom he communicated the murmurs of those of Arvieux, assured him, that they too had great cause to regret the little time that he could devote to them, but that they were well aware of the extent of his charge, and of the necessity, which was laid upon him, of giving all his flock an equal share of his attention, as far as it was practicable to do so.

But independently of the sense of duty, which led him to shift his residence from one place to another, there was nothing in Arvieux to tempt him to prolong his sojournment there. The repose and enjoyment of domestic life had no attractions for him, and the natives of Arvieux were, with few exceptions, so little improved by his instructions, that he thought his time was better employed in other places. "More and more," said he, to an intimate friend, "do I experience the truth of the declaration, that he who planteth, and he who watereth is nothing. How often I sigh to think of these poor Arvieusians?

but it is one of the severe trials to which a pastor must submit, to find that he is labouring in vain."

Upon another occasion he wrote thus: "I left this stony place for Fressinière, (Monday, March 28th, 1825,) where the Eternal had prepared more comfort for me." It took him three days, on that occasion, before he could get through the lower hamlets of the valley, for though it was only twenty days since he had paid them a previous visit, yet he was obliged to make many stops on the route, to receive the demonstrations of affection, which they were anxious to offer him. It was Passion Week, an interesting season, when both the pastor and his flock were preparing themselves for the observance of the most solemn festival of the Christian Church, the Easter communion; and among these simple people, the preparation and the ceremonial itself were conducted with all the solemnity, with which the primitive Christians were wont to observe it.

Every person, who intended to present himself at the Lord's table, was expected to give intimation to the minister, and those young persons, who were to communicate for the first time, were subjected to a most rigid examination. I have used the word ceremonial, but it was far from being a mere outward observance.

As the pastor was slowly wending his way from Minsas towards the abrupt steep which conducts to Dormilleuse, and pondering in his mind on the spiritual improvement, which he hoped to find in his catechumens since his last instructions, he suddenly beheld a sight which called all his strong feelings into action. His return to Dormilleuse was welcomed, like that of Stouber to the Ban de la Roche, when all the inhabitants, old and young, ascended the top of the mountain to watch his approach. A large company of the villagers did more than wait Neff's coming, they were descending the rock to meet him, and to greet his arrival. In vain he beckoned to them to stop, and not give themselves the trouble of remounting the whole of that formidable acclivity. The faithful creatures ventured to disobey their beloved guide this once, and hurried down the slippery and treacherous path, literally to throw themselves into his arms. When he gently blamed them for putting themselves to this unnecessary fatigue, one of them gave utterance to a sentiment to which they all responded. " It is not often that we have the enjoyment of walking with you, and we value it too much to lose it." It was a beautiful opportunity of obeying the Divine precept, and the pastor did not lose it. " And those words that I command thee shall be in thy heart, and thou shalt talk of them when thou sittest in thine house, and when thou walkest by the way."

I collect from the tenor of his Journal, that
7

Neff and those of his young flock, who were to
commemorate their Lord's death on the following Sunday, (Easter day,) by eating bread and
drinking wine, according to Christ's solemn in-
junction, in remembrance of him, spent the
whole of the anniversary of " the night of trea-
son," in exercises of devotion.   At midnight
they walked out to take the air, and as they
passed a house where some young women were
assembled, they heard sounds which told them
that the inmates were engaged in sacred duties.
They heard the voice of weeping and lamenta-
tion, but they were not those wild and extravagant sounds, which sometimes proceed from persons who are wrought up to bursts of passion,
which more resemble the ecstacies of Bacchan-
tes than the emotions of Christian penitence.
" I listened," said the pastor, " for a moment to
those plaintive expressions, and affecting rythmical apostrophes, which are peculiar to the patois of this country, and which cannot be translated into French.   The French language is not
rich enough to bear the transfusion.   I would
not interrupt them, but went by silently, and
perceived that the young companions of my walk
were as much affected as I was.   So passed this
night, which the Lamb without stain or spot
consecrated by his agony and passion ! If that
Holy One was obliged to taste of the cup of his
Father's wrath, if his soul was exceedingly sor-
rowful even unto death, to think of the condemn-

ation under which all the world lay, must not the really guilty tremble when they think of the weight of a trespassed covenant?"

At day-break, on Good Friday, Neff's unbroken perseverance urged him to descend from Dormilleuse to Minsas, to examine the intended communicants there, and at ten o'clock he performed public service at the new church of Violins. It was crowded. Every Protestant of the valley seemed to be present, and the heart of the pastor must have been deeply moved, to see the seats opposite to the pulpit occupied by about a hundred young persons, who were preparing themselves to appear at the Lord's table on the approaching solemnity. In fact, of all the youth of the valley of Fressinière, who were of the proper age, and who were able to attend, not one was absent. Perhaps such a scene was never witnessed in any Christian community before, and nothing could attest more forcibly the indefatigable labours of the spiritual shepherd of the flock, who when "the sheep wandered through all the mountains, and upon every high hill, searched for them, and fed them, and brought them to a good fold."

Upon these solemnities, after the sermon, the intended communicants are called upon to repeat their baptismal vows : a custom most worthy of imitation and of more general practice ; especially when it is done with the impressive seriousness which distinguishes the service in the

Q

Alpine Churches of France and Italy. But upon this occasion, when the young people should have made the declaration of their faith and obedience, not a voice was heard. A few stifled sounds, and half-smothered sobs were all that struck the pastor's ear. He was obliged to recite the words for them, and to suppose that their awful, mute assent, was the deliberate renewal of their engagements. The formulary used by Neff in his Alpine Churches on this occasion, and on others, when young persons were received at the Lord's table for the first time, resembled that of the old Genevan Church. After the sermon, the pastor, addressing the congregation, says, " We shall presently receive at the Lord's table those young persons whom you now behold, who have given sufficient proof, after a solemn examination, that they have been properly instructed in the nature of the ordinance. They come to take upon themselves the most sacred engagements : to make an open profession of the Gospel,——and to undertake the discharge of its duties, in order that they may henceforth enjoy all the privileges which Christ vouchsafes to those that are his.

" We will begin by reminding these young people what they have engaged to do.

" You then, who desire to be received at the Lord's table, and who have been instructed in the truths of the Gospel, are you so thoroughly convinced of these truths, that nothing could induce you to renounce the Christian religion, and that you are ready to suffer any thing rather than abandon your Christian profession?

" Yes.

" Have you examined yourselves, and are you resolved to renounce sin, and to regulate your lives according to the commandments of God?

" Yes.

" As in the sacrament of the Last Supper, we profess to be all of one body, do you desire to live in peace and charity, to love your brethren, and to give them proofs of your love in all things?

" Yes.

" To confirm your faith and your piety, do you promise to apply yourselves diligently to read and meditate upon the word of God—and to prayer—to frequent the holy assemblies, and to employ all the means which Providence has imparted to you of advancing your salvation?

" Yes.

" Do you sincerely ratify your baptismal vows, which oblige you to resist your evil inclinations, and to consecrate yourselves to God and Jesus Christ your Saviour, and to live in his communion, in temperance, righteousness, and piety?

" Yes."

Then follows a solemn address to them. On the occasion which I have been describing, when the service was over, the greater part of the congregation remained for a time upon their knees, so absorbed were they in the devotional feelings of the hour.

Some Protestant Churches and congregations, that they may keep at the greatest possible distance from the Church of Rome, and from the Church of England, which has, in her discretion, retained all that she judged to be unobjectionable in the Romish ritual, reject all observance of Christmas-day, Good Friday, Ascension-day, and other festivals of the ancient Christians. Not so the Alpine Churches—those remains of the primitive Christians; they observe these days with marked attention; and thus we find that Neff, and his mountain flock of the valley of Fressinière, consecrated the whole of the day of the crucifixion to acts of devotion. At two o'clock they re-assembled in the church of Violins. " And then," Neff observes in his Journal, " I performed the service according to the form used by the Moravian brethren, that is to say, by reading a harmonized narrative of the events of the Passion-week, compiled from the four Evangelists. This was interrupted occasionally by the singing of psalms, selected with a view to their conformity with the Gospel relation. The impression was even greater than that which was made in the morning ; very few of the congregation could command themselves sufficiently to sing—two of the leading singers could not raise a note. Mr. B——— said to me when the church was over——" This is a most simple and affecting service. The finest sermon could not produce the same effect!"

Having spent the Thursday of Passion-week at Dormilleuse, and Good-Friday at Minsas and Violins, the pastor thought it right to give Saturday to the inhabitants of Fressinière and Palons. On Easter Sunday he again officiated in the new church at Violins, and administered the sacrament to an assembly so numerous, that it was remarked by the oldest people, that they had never before seen half the same number of communicants. On Easter Monday the untired minister performed three public services at Dormilleuse, at which the whole of the Protestant population of the valley, who could climb the rock, were present.

"So passed this happy week," wrote the pastor, " this holy week, for such it really was in this valley. The inhabitants spent it in penitence and prayer, or in pious reading or conversation. All the young people seemed to be animated by the same spirit: a flame of holy fire appeared to spread from one to another, like an electric spark. During the whole of the eight days, I had not thirty hours' rest. Before and after, and in the interval of the public services, the young people might be seen sitting in groups among the huge rocks of granite, with which the place is covered, edifying each other by serious reading or conversation. I was absolutely astonished by this sudden awakening. I could scarcely collect my scattered thoughts. The rocks, the cascades, even the surrounding ice, seemed to present a new and less dreary aspect. This savage country became agreeable and dear to me : it was at once the home of my brethren ; the beloved Jerusalem of my affection [1]. But I must not forget, that at first awakening, many appear to be converted, who are only drawn along by the general movement. It is like the burning flint in the midst of the brazier, which looks like the flaming charcoal. But, however it may turn out, it is the work of the Eternal. He can only recognise those who are his, and knows how to make it manifest that they are his. To him be the praise and the glory for ever and ever. *Amen*."

I select this place for the insertion of a communication from Captain Cotton, whose interesting account of an excursion in company with Neff, when he was making a circuit of his parish, will be received as a valuable addition to the reminiscences contained in this chapter.

[2] "I spent several days with Neff in visiting the scattered hamlets of which he had taken the spiritual oversight, and I was thus afforded a good opportunity of observing the zeal of that excellent man, his affection for the objects of his care, his singular fitness for ministering in a country

[1] Psalm cxxii.
[2] In the first edition, this interesting account, communicated

of such peculiar natural and moral features, and the regard which his simple flock had for him.

"At Pallon, at the entrance of the Valley of Fressinière, I first met with Neff, who, full of spirits at my arrival, proposed climbing to the caverns that had served the inhabitants, in former times, both as places of refuge and of worship. Among others visited by us under the guidance of a native, there was one still called the *Glesia* or *Eglise,* whence many a time the prayers of the people, obliged to retire out of the reach of their oppressors, went up to the throne of mercy; —it is now but a small place, owing, it is said, to a slide of the rock. The opening is on the crest of a frightful precipice. The guide fearlessly entered it, though the rugged rock afforded scarce a hand's breadth to reach it by; we squeezed through another opening. I do not know that I ever felt the power of association more strongly than when Neff and another, who accompanied us, chaunted Te Deum in that wild temple, the guide appearing the representative of the persecuted race. We entered also another cavern, said to have been used for a similar purpose, during the persecutions in the reign of Louis XIV. The last we entered seemed from below inaccessible. We gained it by the use of hands as well as feet. On returning to Pallon I offered our guide a franc, but instead of taking it, he called Neff's attention to the circumstance,

by Captain Cotton, was placed as a Postcript to the Memoir, having been received too late for an earlier insertion.

who bade me put the money into my pocket, and not teach the people bad habits.   It was also with difficulty that I forced some money on the young man, who had been my guide from St. Laurent du Cros, when he returned; for three days' labour, he felt himself repaid in the gratification derived from the journey, and in helping forward my object.   From Pallon we mounted to La Ribe, the next village, where we were received by M. Barridon. 'percepteur des impôts' in the district.

" Neff held a réunion in his house in the course of the evening: it is by means of meetings of this kind principally that he effects the good he does in the mountains.   His congregations are so dispersed, that he is of necessity in continual motion from one village to another.   On arriving, perhaps after a toilsome walk of several leagues over the mountains, he calls the inhabitants together, and commences his service improviso. Those who assemble first, when in a private house, or stable, where the assembly usually takes place in the winter, pass the time in singing hymns, the women spinning or knitting, till he appears.   It is a simple service among simple people, several of whose hearts, however, are impressed with the Gospel.   A table is placed for the minister; some forms or chairs are brought for the rest, all sitting with a thick carpet of manure under their feet; one or two lamps, suspended by strings, throw their light on the plain-featured, and plainly-attired group, and show the cattle ranged at their mangers behind. Sometimes the hymns, that the congregation are singing at his entrance, furnish a subject for Neff's discourse, sometimes he expounds a chapter of the Bible, or preaches from a text: singing and extempore prayer preceding and concluding the service; at other times he questions his auditory from a chapter, a mode of teaching well-suited for private assemblies.   For a minister to be useful among a population so situated as that of the high Alps, it is necessary to have a heart overflowing with the Gospel, a lively solicitude for his people's souls, and a mouth which never tires of those doctrines that convert, console, and edify, however weary the body may be, and which, after the service performed, still loves to dwell on the all-important theme.

" 1st November.—Having slept and breakfasted at Barridon's, we went to Violins, a village situated at the Combe : this word signifies, as in Devonshire, an abrupt narrow valley in the mountains.   Let the etymologist discover how the inhabitants of Devon and Dauphiny came to possess the word in common.   Divine service was performed by Neff in the new temple at Violins, after which we proceeded upwards to Minsals, another small village, then enjoying during the day only half an hour's sunshine, and about to lose the glorious luminary till the month of March: during the intervening cold months he never rises above the mountains so high as to dart his rays down to the poor cluster of cottages at Minsals.   There is no comfort in the houses; they are vaulted, perhaps to resist an extraordinary accumulation of snow; the walls, though thick, are badly built, and within black with soot, and a single small window sheds a partial light into the gloomy apartment.   We paid, notwithstanding, a very interesting visit, in one of these dark dwellings, to a family named Besson, nine or ten in number; all of them, I believe, are blessed with the light of the Sun of Righteousness, to cheer them in the absence of his type in the firmament.   The inhabitants in all the valleys in this severe climate are accustomed to pass the winter in the stable along with their cows, sleeping in cribs erected for that purpose.

"———— After this we returned to La Chalpe, where Neff presided at another meeting, previously to bidding adieu to our friends; we then descended the valley to Philippe, our friend at Moulins: here again a meeting of the neighbours was held in Philippe's stable; they were mostly, if not all, Catholics. The example of the miller's family has doubtless excited some of these persons to think seriously about their salvation, and the interesting nature of Neff's meetings; prayers which they can comprehend, and the mercies of God in Christ, plainly and affectionately set before them, occasion those who have heard once to desire to hear again, and to bring others.   The different services of this day, except a few prayers in the temple, were all extempore.   Whether tired or not, Neff is at all times ready to begin, thinking he never does enough. We passed the evening by Philippe's fire-side, the women retiring behind to afford us the best places, and after a cheerful meal we retired for the night.

" Early next morning we left our kind host's cottage, who evinced considerable emotion at parting. Returning to the point where we had left the valley of Queyras, we ascended by Château Queyras, which is a small fortress on a rock, commanding the passage up and down the valley, to Fousillarde, and were received with great joy by a warm-hearted and zealous convert, named André Vasserot, who was prepared to undertake a school in the winter. It is one of Neff's plans of amelioration to form and place pious school-masters in the villages, who may in some measure supply the want of a minister, and especially implant, betimes, religious principles in the minds of the young. There was a lame youth so trained whom I saw at La Chalpe. The villagers were brought together for service in the temple, and we then proceeded through the snow, crossing and recrossing a wood of mélèze, a species of fir, to San Veran. A meeting was held here also, in a stable belonging to Pierre Sybille, in whose house we slept for the night, being at no great distance from the top of the ridge separating France from the valleys of Piedmont. By daylight next morning, we were on our way back, through the snow, to

Guillestre, descending by the channel of the Guil to that town. After dining there, I mounted a wretched mule, and set off again for Fressinière, Neff still walking. It was dusk before we reached Champcella, a village not far from Pallon. We put up here with a family of the name of Arnaus, who were, I believe, lately Roman Catholics, and much opposed to Neff's proceedings, but now greatly altered. Although Neff had been on foot from daylight, except during the time of breakfast and dinner, he called a meeting together in a neighbouring house, at which, notwithstanding the lateness of the hour, a considerable number of persons attended, and among them several Catholics. To this hastily-assembled crowd, he addressed the Divine word, and then spent some time with a sick person. Through the activity of Neff, I was on the back of a mule on the way to our friend Barridon's, at La Ribe, before daylight. We walked from thence to Minsals, and visited again the Christian family of Besson in their stable, where it was so dark that we could not see all the inmates, till they came near the small window to show themselves. We mounted from this place, in company with some others, to Dormilleuse, the highest of all the villages in Fressinière. One would imagine that no motive, but that of personal security, could have led to the construction of a village in that place. One side of the valley, as we ascended, appeared impracticable to the foot of man; the mélezè waves there on lofty ledges which seem inaccessible, yet the chasseur climbs among them, and the inhabitants I believe, derive from thence a supply of fuel: on the other side, between the mountain and the stream, enormous fragments are piled together or thrown about the small extent of flat ground which is susceptible of cultivation ; farther on we climbed by a tedious zig-zag path on the face of the mountain, over ruins, that having been split off by the frost or rain, had rolled from above.   The nature of the slope was almost hid from the eye by a deep layer of snow ; large icicles were hanging from the cliff.   As winter advances these increase in size and form, as I was assured, to stupendous columns, far more wonderful than the porticos effected by human labour, which are intended to occupy the public eye from age to age, whereas those of the Almighty are renewed and dissolved year after year.

" After a very toilsome walk we at length reached the remote village of Dormilleuse, one of the least and most retired of the many thousands of France, but particularly distinguished by Him, who seeth not as man seeth, in being preserved inviolate from the papal abomination. The houses are ranged above each other on a steep hill; the inhabitants are inoffensive and kind, and some of them are pious characters. The snow lying deep, several of the villagers

were warming themselves on the sunny side of
their cottages as we approached.   The people
were soon assembled in the church for service,
and here I observed the women kneel in those
parts of the service in which the men stood.
The church was built by government previous
to the revolution, with a parsonage-house, and
a curé was appointed for the village, in hopes by
mild measures to gain over the people to the
Roman religion; but persuasion was as ineffec-
tual in this attempt as persecution in former
instances—the priest met with no success; he
disappeared at the revolution, and has never
been replaced : the inhabitants have free possession both of the church and of the house.
Neff uses the latter as a school, having little
need of a house, as he is continually on a journey; he has here both a school for boys and for
adults during the winter; there is also a Sunday-
school and a school for infants.

"A crowd of people came into the house
where we had taken up a place by the fire ; and
Neff asking me if I had the courage to pass over
the Col d'Orcières to Saint Laurent du Cros, to
avoid making so great a circuit as we should do
in going by the valley, the practicability of the
measure was debated, and the opinion of an experienced chasseur taken : his decision was that
the passage might be performed if the weather
should be clear and without wind.   The danger
from cloudy weather is the probability of snow

7

falling: that from wind is greater, as it often causes so thick a cloud of snow as to hinder the traveller from seeing his way. A perfect knowledge of the mountains is also requisite, as the drifted snow frequently conceals the danger of the path by lying lightly perhaps against a precipice; and should the unwary traveller set his foot upon it, the mass is instantly set in motion, he is carried away with it, and never rises again. We saw, while ascending to Dormilleuse, the effect of the wind, or, as it is called in the Alps, the tourmente, on the snowy summits of the mountains, they seemed to smoke like so many volcanoes. We intended by the laborious journey of the following day to save time, but we were as long in performing it as we should have been in going round about. I supped this evening on a marmot, and found it by no means bad fare; it is a rich food, more like pork than any thing else.

" The morning following proving clear and free from wind, we prepared for the fatigues of the day by a good breakfast; my thick and heavy-nailed shoes were covered with linen socks, and a string passed across my gaiters and round my ancles, to prevent the snow from entering. The mountaineers always take the precaution of securing their feet from the admission of snow in a similar way. I was furnished, like the rest, with a staff, and we set out, eleven in number, the peasants having the laborious task of tracing the way for us. The first of the party had a very laborious task, appearing sometimes to be breast high, and it was necessary for the others successively to take the lead : in this manner we passed over the dreary white and trackless waste, crossing several considerable eminences, though we were in a valley, compared with the ridges on each side. It might seem impossible for any living beings to make this their natural abode, yet the wild is not left untenanted : the wolf and the bear are natives of the Alps, but require more shelter than is to be found in the tract we were passing over; the lynx is sometimes, but rarely, to be found; the marmot keeps himself as warm as he can in the earth; the chamois ranges over the loftiest summits at perfect liberty—we saw a flock of them on the mountain to our right, far out of the reach of man. I was exceedingly fatigued and vexed to be continually sinking when the others trod firm. There is an art in following the leader's track; great care must be taken to place the foot in the trace of him that goes before, and to follow with the same foot. At length the Col appeared before us. We had hoped to reach it before it would be necessary to take refreshment, but our progress was so slow and our whole party so exhausted, as to render a meal necessary; it being impossible to sit, we trod down the snow, and ate our bread and cheese and drank our wine standing, after which we started again.

Neff sometimes took the place of leader, and in the most laborious part of the journey roused the spirits of the people by chanting hymns.   At last the height was won, but not till two or three in the afternoon.   A new waste of snow presented itself on the other side, but the labour of descending was comparatively trifling ; having rested a short time, Neff, myself, and three mountaineers, on their way to Mens also, proceeded downwards from the Col. The kind people watched from the top till we were out of sight, being anxious about me, whom they saw to be an inexpert mountaineer and quite tired. Instead of being in a valley as before, we passed over a country of an undulating surface, and descended very rapidly.   Proceeding more by the general bearings of the country than by any landmarks, we descended several precipices, where I should never have hazarded myself alone, even had there been no snow.   Some small lakes lie between the hills, probably furnishing the sources of the Drac, which originates hereabouts. Some notion of the height, at which we were, may be formed from the circumstance of one of these lakes having been passed incautiously in the month of July by a man, who did not know he had been on the ice till he had crossed it. We came afterwards among stone fences of fields under the snow, and a little lower down to a village, and shortly after reached the inn at Orcières."   E. A. C.

R

CHAPTER XI.

NEFF'S EXTRAORDINARY INFLUENCE OVER HIS FLOCK—HOW
OBTAINED—HIS IMPROVEMENTS INTRODUCED INTO THE
CONDITION OF THE ALPINES—THEIR WRETCHED STATE
PREVIOUSLY TO HIS ARRIVAL—PROPOSES TO HIMSELF THE
EXAMPLE OF OBERLIN—THE AQUEDUCT—THE CHRISTIAN
ADVOCATE—NEFF A TEACHER OF AGRICULTURE—NEFF AT
THE FAIR OF ST. CREFIN—OBSERVATIONS.

TIME and eternity will show, whether the pastor of the high Alps had such a blessing upon his labours, as enabled him to produce a lasting impression upon the minds of those simple mountaineers, who devoted themselves with such impulsive ardour to the cause of the Gospel. His full usefulness will be known in that glorious day when the number of God's elect shall be completed. It is certain, however, that his influence over them was something quite extraordinary. This influence would have been less a matter of wonder, had he resorted to any of those extravagances, which too often succeed by turning the heads of the ignorant and fanatical. But it was not so: the whole course of his ministry was sustained by the same even and sober piety: his preaching was forcible, and faithful to the doctrine of redemption through a crucified Saviour; but never solicited attention by stirring up the wild passions, or vain-glorious and fond conceits of his hearers. He made no use of those arts by which "silly women," and silly men are led captive. His Journals make us fully acquainted with his doctrine, his manner of life, his purpose, his faith, his long-suffering, his charity, and his patience; and to these virtues, the influence, which he obtained, must be attributed in a very great degree.

Neff was not merely the Sabbath day minister and instructor: nor was he the religious guide only. He was every thing to his mountaineers: he interested himself warmly in all their concerns, and when they saw that his sole object and unwearied endeavour was to make them happier and better in all the relations of life, than he found them, he bowed their hearts as the heart of one man, and they reverenced the Mentor, who was always busy in adding to their stock of comfort [1].

Like the philosopher with the shipwrecked

---

[1] " By evincing a sincere interest in their concerns, I would endeavour to gain their confidence, and induce them to regard me as their friend: and then having once obtained this confidence, and a proportionate degree of influence, I would exert it to the utmost of my ability to their advantage, both in the instruction of the young, and the conversion of the old, seeking to win their affections by my earnest desire to promote their spiritual interests. If you adopt this method, my dear friend, God will take care of the rest." Stouber's Advice to Oberlin. *Memoirs of Oberlin*, p. 71.

crew, in the uninhabited island, his example, his
contrivances, his persuasions, his suggestions,
were ever leading the way to some new improvement in their condition.   He taught them to
improve their dwellings, to cultivate their lands
to greater advantage, to employ time profitably
and agreeably that had previously hung heavy
upon their hands, and to find occupation and
amusement in numberless resources, of which
they had no conception till his arrival among
them.   He was their schoolmaster in short, not
only to bring them unto Christ, but to instruct
them in whatever was useful and advantageous.
They saw that he had their best interests at
heart—and the current of their affections naturally flowed towards him, in the full tide of confidence and veneration.

The natives of Val Fressinière had, perhaps,
greater reason than the rest of his flock, to attach
themselves most affectionately to their pastor,
for finding them in a more forlorn condition than
the others, he did more for them in the way of
general improvement.   Their persevering fidelity
to the faith and discipline of their ancestors,
when their nearest neighbours, the inhabitants
of Val Louise had been exterminated, and when
the people of Val Queyras had conformed outwardly to the religion of Rome, had cut them off
so effectually from all human society [1], during a

---

[1] I transcribe the following edict of Louis XII. in proof of

long period of time, and from all the conveniences of civilized life, that on Neff's arrival at Dormilleuse, he found them the same half-barbarous tribe, which De Thou represented them to be 250 years before. One proof of their utter wretchedness affected him sensibly. Long habits of suspicion, and the dread of ill-treatment, had become so natural to them, that at the sight of a stranger, they ran into their huts, particularly the young people, like marmots into their holes. Their houses, clothes, food, and method of cultivation, were four or five centuries behind the rest of France, and to this hour, after all his exertions to ameliorate their state, if a stranger could be carried asleep to the village, on waking

the unmerited sufferings of the Protestants of this region, when the iron hand of their oppressors lay most heavy upon them.

" Lewis, by the grace of God, king of France.

" Forasmuch as it is come to our knowledge that the inhabitants of Fressinière have endured great troubles, vexations, and punishments, we, desiring to relieve them, and to cause their property to be restored to them, do, by these presents, command all those that retain such property, to restore it without delay. And in case of refusal or delay, we, having regard to their poverty and misery, and inability to obtain justice, will take cognizance thereof in our own person, warning all those who shall continue to do them wrong, to appear before us. Given at Lyon, the 12th of October, 1501." The original is in vol. H. of the Waldensian MSS. in the Cambridge library. The edict is cited by Perrin and Morland.

This edict was after the celebrated papal bull of 1487, when the Protestants of Val Fressinière were pursued like wild beasts, and had their property confiscated.

he never would believe that he was in the land of civilized Frenchmen.   The pastor had to begin with first principles, and in this his scientific knowledge, and the systematic rules of command and obedience, in which he had himself been so well schooled in the garrison at Geneva, came seasonably to his help.   He knew how to set about arranging and giving directions.

His first attempt was to impart an idea of domestic convenience.   Chimneys and windows to their hovels were luxuries to which few of them had aspired, till he showed them how easy it was to make a passage for the smoke, and admittance for the light and air.   He next convinced them that warmth might be obtained more healthily, than by pigging together for six or seven months in stables, from which the muck of the cattle was removed but once during the year.   For their coarse and unwholesome food, he had, indeed, no substitute; because the sterility of the soil would produce no other; but he pointed out a mode of tillage, by which they increased the quantity; and in cases of illness, where they had no conception of applying the simplest remedies, he pointed out the comfort which a sick person may derive from light and warm soups and ptisans, and other soothing assistance.   So ignorant were they of what was hurtful or beneficial in acute disorders, that wine and brandy were no unusual prescriptions in the height of a raging fever.

Strange enough, and still more characteristic

of savage life, the women, till Neff taught the men better manners, were treated with so much disregard, that they never sat at table with their husbands or brothers, but stood behind them, and received morsels from their hands with obeisance and profound reverence.

" But with all this, they participated in the general corruption of human nature, as far as their poverty would let them. Gaming, dancing, swearing, and quarrelling, were not uncommon, though the Papists, who occupied the lower part of the valley, were certainly much more corrupt. Nevertheless, the wretchedness of this people commends them to our compassion, and ought to excite the deepest interest, when we consider, that it is the result of their ancestors' fidelity to our cause. Persecution has penned them up, like frightened and helpless sheep, in a narrow gorge, where there is scarcely an habitation which is not exposed to avalanches of snow, or falling rocks. From the first moment of my arrival, I took them as it were to my heart, and I ardently desired to be unto them, even as another *Oberlin.* Unfortunately I could not then give them more than a week in each month, whereas, such is the length of the valley, and the number of the hamlets, that I ought to be constantly there. But the Almighty has been pleased to bless the little care that I could bestow upon them, and to permit a change to be produced in more respects than one."

So affectionately, so apologetically, when he was constrained by the force of truth to touch on their failings, and so modestly, when he was recording his own exertions, did this excellent man write down his thoughts, when the Val Fressinière was the subject of his Journal.

The character of Oberlin was Neff's delight and his model, and if it did not first awaken his desire to become eminent in the same way, it confirmed his good resolutions. The good which is done by the recital of labours like those of Oberlin, and by giving circulation to the memoir of such a life, was singularly illustrated in the case now before us. The pastor of the Alps had by some means become acquainted [1] with the history of the pastor of the Vosges, and of his improvements in the Ban de la Roche; several publications had noticed Oberlin's beneficial labours in his mountain parish, and Neff's bosom glowed with a noble emulation to imitate his doings. Therefore, without derogating in the least degree from Neff's merits, it may be said, that much of his usefulness may be attributed to the practical lesson, which Oberlin had previously taught. It is for this reason, that few

---

[1] Probably by reading the letter printed in a German magazine in 1793, and some accounts of him in the Bible Society's Reports, or " Promenades Alsaciennes," par M. Merlin, and " Rapport fait à la Société Royale d'Agriculture, par M. Le Comte de Neuf-Chateau, sur l'Agriculture et la Civilization du Ban de la Roche."

greater boons can be conferred on society, than by giving all possible notoriety to the labours of such benefactors of mankind, as our own Bernard Gilpin, and George Herbert, or Frederick Oberlin, who in their humble stations of parish priests, promoted the temporal and spiritual good of their people at the same time. Many a young clergyman has received the same impression as Neff, from reading such biography, and has lighted his candle at such glorious lamps, and has been inspired with the noblest of all ambition, that of distributing happiness and comfort within the immediate circle of his duties.

The amiable biographer, who collected the memorials of Oberlin, may enjoy the exquisite satisfaction of believing, that her record of his blameless life, and indefatigable labours, will be like a voice exclaiming in the ears of many, who begin to feel the pleasure of being useful, " Go and do thou likewise," and will thus be the means of perpetuating to future generations, the influence of Oberlin's beneficent exertions, more effectually than any monument to his memory.

In his private memoranda, Neff frequently made allusion to the same fact, that in remote, and particularly in Alpine villages, the life of a minister of the Gospel resembles that of a missionary in uncivilized countries, and to use his own expression, " It is necessary to be a Frederick Oberlin, to do all that is required of him." From the first, therefore, he made it his study to conciliate the affections and confidence of the peasants, by employing all his attainments for their improvement, and by showing them that there were many things, in which his general knowledge might be rendered serviceable to them. He not only did not hesitate, but he sought occasions, to put his hand to the tool of the mechanic and artisan, and to the husband-man's implement, and thus to drill the peasantry into better management, and to instruct them in the best mode of adding to their stock of conveniences and comfort. We have already seen him working with the masons and carpenters, to give the last air of architectural beauty to the new Church of Violins, and now I will exhibit him in the character of an agriculturist, introducing an improved method of irrigation, and a system of sowing and planting, which doubled the quantity of production.

One of the principal resources of the valley of Fressinière, is the breeding and pasturage of cattle. But the winter is so long, and the tracts of land capable of producing fodder are so scanty, that every blade of grass that can be raised, and made into hay, is a very treasure. A dry summer often left them unprovided with hay, and compelled the poor creatures to part with their stock at an inadequate price. Neff's eye perceived that a direction might be given to the streams in one part, which would improve the ground in another, and furnish the proprietors with constant means of keeping the grass fresh and moist. But he found the utmost difficulty in explaining the simplest principles of hydraulics, and in persuading his ignorant listeners that the water might be made to rise and fall, and might be dammed up and distributed, accordingly as it might be required for use. The imaginary expense stared them in the face like certain ruin; and the labour appalled them, as being perfectly insuperable. When their pastor first advised them to construct the canals necessary for the purpose, they absolutely refused to attempt it, and he was obliged to tell them, that they were equally deaf to temporal and spiritual counsel. Pointing to the rushing waters, which were capable of being diverted from their course to the parched and sterile soil, which he wished to see improved, he exclaimed, " You make as little use of those ample streams, as you do of the water of life. God has vouchsafed to offer you both in abundance, but your pastures, like your hearts, are languishing with drought !"

In the spring of 1825, there had been so little snow, that there was every appearance of the soil yielding even less than its usual scanty increase : its wonted supply of moisture had failed. Neff took advantage of the state of the season, and once more pressed them to adopt his mode of irrigation. But still the reluctance and the excuses were the same. If the canals and aqueducts were made, they would soon get out of order: if one proprietor adopted them, another would not: the next neighbour would not permit them to cross his land, and one opponent of the measure might stop the whole proceeding: but if all should agree, and the work were to be brought to a happy conclusion, an avalanche, or a crumbling mass of granite, would soon crush or interrupt the constructions, and reduce them to their old condition.   In vain did the pastor endeavour to convince them of the weakness of these arguments, particularly of the last: they might as well refuse to plant and sow, or to build houses, for nothing was safe from avalanches. Finding that he could not prevail, when he addressed them in a body, he took them separately, and asked, "Will you consent if your neighbour will?   Will you put your shoulder to the work, if the occupiers of the next property will join you?"   They were ashamed to refuse, when they were thus personally appealed to, and an unwilling acquiescence was thus gradually obtained.   But then arose another and more formidable objection.   "Suppose the aqueducts are completed, and the water flows, will the distribution be equal?   Will not my neighbour get more of the water than I shall? How do I know that he will not exhaust the supply, before my land has had a drop."   Neff was too ready at expedients to be easily foiled.   He proposed that there should be a committee, and an arbiter, to determine what share of the public benefit each occupier should enjoy, and how long, and on what days, and at what hours, the stream should be permitted to pour its waters into the different sections and branches of its course.

At length all preliminaries were settled, and the work was agreed to be done. The line was marked out, and the proprietors consented that the main channel should cross and recross their lands accordingly as it should be required. But again there was some demur. The people would only labour at that part of the construction which was to irrigate their own ground. "Be it so," said Neff, "only let us make a beginning." He saw that he could easily bring them to good humour and compliance, if he could only once set them on. Every thing having been arranged, the working party, consisting of forty, met at daybreak, and with the pastor at their head [1], proceeded to examine the remains of an ancient aqueduct, which it was thought might be rendered in some degree available to their purpose, if they could so far make out the direction as to follow its line. Some few traces were discernible,

[1] How Oberlin lived again in this incident! "Oberlin had already traced the plan (of the bridge across the Bouche) and no sooner had he pronounced the words, 'Let all who feel the importance of my proposition come and work with me,' than with a pickaxe on his shoulder, he proceeded to the spot, while the astonished peasants, animated by his example, forgot their excuses, and hastened with unanimous consent to fetch their tools and follow him."—*Memoirs of Oberlin*, p. 65.

but the sight of them seemed to dishearten rather than encourage the conscripts.

"We shall be three days," said one, "before we can complete this part of our work!"

"It will take us not less than six," said another: "ten," grumbled a third.

"Not quite so many," said the pastor, mildly, and with his benevolent smile.

Neff divided his troop into little detachments, of five or six, with a commander at the head of each, and, taking upon himself the direction in chief, he allotted a distinct proportion of the work to each. Presently all were busy, some digging and excavating, others clearing away; the pastor himself was at one time plying his pickaxe, aud another time moving from place to place, and superintending the progress of others. At ten o'clock the party expressed a desire to discontinue their labour and go home to their breakfast. But this would not do for their chief. He foresaw that there would be stragglers, and perhaps deserters, if they should once lose sight of each other; therefore, still setting them the example, he sent for his own breakfast, continued at his work, and persuaded the rest to do the same.

It was a toilsome undertaking. In some places they had to elevate the floor of the main channel to the height of eight feet, and in others to lower it as much. In the course of the first day's labour, it was necessary to carry the construction across the rocky beds of three or four torrents, and often when the work appeared to be effectually done, Neff detected a default in the level, or in the inclination of the water course, which obliged him to insist upon their going over it again. At four o'clock the men were rewarded by seeing the first fruits of their labours: one line of aqueduct was completed; the dam was raised, and the water rushed into the nearest meadow amidst the joyful shouts of workmen and spectators. The next day some cross cuts were made, and proprietors, who were supposed to be secretly hostile and incredulous, saw the works carried over their ground without offering any opposition to the measure, for who could indulge his obstinate or dogged humour, when the benevolent stranger, the warm-hearted minister, was toiling in the sweat of his brow to achieve a public good, which never could be of the least advantage to himself? It was the good shepherd, not taking the fleece, but exhausting his own strength, and wearing himself out for the sheep. On the third, and on the following days, small transverse lines were formed, and a long channel was made across the face of the mountain, to supply three village fountains with water. This last was a very formidable enterprise. It was necessary to undermine the rock, to blast it, and to construct a passage for the stream in granite of the very hardest kind. " I had never done any thing like it before," is the pastor's note upon this achievement, "but it was necessary to assume an air of scientific confidence, and to give my orders like an experienced engineer."

The work was brought to a most prosperous issue, and the pastor was thenceforward a sovereign, who reigned so triumphantly and absolutely, that his word was law. This power was exercised in a manner worthy of a Christian guide, and particularly in one instance. The Roman Catholic bishop of Embrun had some territorial rights in the valley of Fressinière; but such was the general unwillingness to permit any of his agents to exercise them, and to collect the dues, that his property in Dormilleuse and its contiguous villages added little or nothing to his revenues. What could the prelate do in a region, where the persecutors of centuries had found a rampart thrown up against their oppression : where the blood-hounds of Louis the Fourteenth could pursue their chase no further : and where Napoleon himself was baffled, when he attempted to fill up his conscription list with the youth of these mountains ? But what neither force nor stratagem could effect, persuasion accomplished, and at Neff's request, the agents from Embrun made a return to the archiepiscopal treasury to which it was totally unaccustomed [1].

[1] A similar anecdote is told of Oberlin (see Memoirs, p. 195.) How unlike the proceedings in Ireland, where a popish

The valley of Fressinière, like the Ban de la Roche, had need of the potatoe, to supply the deficiencies of its native productions, and in extension of the resemblance, it was cultivated so wretchedly, that both the quantity and quality were lamentably bad. The pastor would fain have put the people in the way of obtaining a better root, and more of it. But his proposed means were so foolish, according to their notions of husbandry, that before the aqueduct lesson, they thought they might just as well let their ground lie fallow, as throw it away upon his system. Their own mode was to set their plants so close to each other, that there was no room for growth or expansion, and not the slightest chance of being able to weed the land, or to keep it clean with the crop upon it. In vain therefore were they recommended to set the plants at a proper distance : they could not believe that they should get as much as their seed back again. Neff's expedient to teach them wisdom partook of his usual decision. He devoted several days to traversing the valley in the planting season, and went into gardens and fields where they were setting potatoes, and taking the hoe, or the spade out of the labourer's hands, he planted two or three rows himself. This was permitted with great reluctance : a few

bishop is encouraging the Roman Catholics to withhold their rights from Protestant claimants.

let them remain as he left them, others took
them up, and set them again after their own
fashion, as soon as his back was turned.   But
the next year the malcontents were too happy to
learn their pastor's method; they saw the astonishing increase which his rows yielded, and the
potatoe is now one of the most valuable productions of a soil, which gives but a scanty return
at the most.   In Val Queyras, where the pastor
had a garden of his own, his system was adopted
earlier, for when his neighbours saw him take
up nine or ten tubercles from one plant, they
were not easy until they had tried the same art
of obtaining the same increase.

We have seen upon more occasions than one,
that our unwearied pastor was in the habit of
going out of his way to be useful.   He was not
satisfied with doing good as opportunities might
arise; but he sought, and even made those opportunities.   Thus, in the case just related, he
went through his hamlets, and searched through
field after field, that he might put the ignorant
and obstinate peasants in the way of improving
their mode of cultivation.   He promoted their
spiritual good by similar means.   " Seeing the
distressed state of so many poor souls," said he
in one of his letters, " I sent for a hundred copies
of the tract, ' *Honey flowing from the Rock.*'   On
the 23d they arrived, and on the 25th I repaired
to St. Crepin, on the Durance, where they were
then holding a fair, which brings together a

great number of the inhabitants of the province. I carried my packet to the inn, where I could obtain a room for half an hour only. This time, however, was sufficient for me to distribute my tracts, which were carried off in a few minutes. This book, small as it is, contains some excellent things for souls thirsting for eternal life ; and as I have always distributed them prudently, they have seldom failed to produce good effects. All our friends of the High Alps carry it about with them, and we often see them in groups reading and commenting on it, in the midst of the fields, or in the cross-ways of the villages. Several of them know it by heart, and quote from it entire passages very appropriately. I think I ought, on this occasion, to mention what I have long observed, that a preacher of the Gospel would do well often to frequent fairs and great markets, where persons assemble from different parts. I there distribute many books and religious tracts, and I have opportunities of communicating with the brethren of the different valleys, who are delighted with becoming acquainted with each other."

It was thus, in his manifold schemes of usefulness, that Neff resembled the amiable and admirable pastor of the Ban de la Roche, whose character he took such pleasure in contemplating ; and had not the scene of his labours been so remote, and inaccessible, we might have had many such interesting anecdotes to communi-

cate, as those which grace the Memoirs of Oberlin. But in his widely extended parish, and in
his homeless mode of life, there was no one centre
of attraction, like the parsonage of Waldbach, to
draw admiring strangers, whose letters or journals might have recorded many an incident,
honourable both to the pastor and his flock, and
might sooner have drawn the character of the
self-denying, and ever working, minister out of
its obscurity into beautiful relief. He was removed from life almost before he was appreciated; and assuredly there are many more such,
even at this moment, and in our own country,
who are pursuing their noiseless course, as humble and indefatigable country clergymen, and
who are living for others, while their sole motives are the sense of responsibility attached to
their stations and means of usefulness, and the
love of God, working in them the purest love of
their fellow creatures. Many such as these are
acting their parts nobly, and are upholding the
credit of their Church, and are, in fact, the
labourers in the vineyard, to whom thanks are
due for the ingathering of the harvest, while the
literary champions of the same Church are run-
ning away with all the honour of being its sup-
porters.

At the moment I am writing this, my mind is
full of the meritorious and self-denying services,
which a young clergyman, who took the highest
honours at Cambridge, is now rendering to the

cause of religion, as a village curate in the west of England. If "Oxford" had not been the title of one of R. Montgomery's beautiful poems, in which the subject is introduced with all the force of poetry and truth, I should have thought that Mr. M. had been in his eye, when he composed the subjoined lines:—

> " Ah little know they, when the harsh declaim,
> Or folly leads to scorn a curate's name,
> In hamlets lone what lofty minds abound,
> To spread the smiles of charity around !
> It was not that a frowning chance denied
> An early wreath of honourable pride :
> In college rolls triumphantly they shine,
> And proudly Alma Mater calls them, mine !
> But heav'nlier dreams than ever fame inspired
> Their spirits haunted, as the world retired :
> The fameless quiet of parochial care
> And sylvan home, their fancy stooped to share :
> And when arrived, no deeper bliss they sought
> Than that which undenying heaven had brought.
> On such, perchance, renown may never beam,
> Though oft it glittered in some college dream :
> But theirs the fame no worldly scenes supply,
> Who teach us how to live and how to die."
>
> **Page 69.**

CHAPTER XII.

NEFF'S CAUTION IN THE CHOICE OF HIS CATECHISTS—NEFF
IN HIS SCHOOLS—WORKS AT THE BUILDING OF A SCHOOL-
ROOM IN DORMILLEUSE—ESTABLISHES AND CONDUCTS A
NORMAL SCHOOL FOR THE TRAINING OF CATECHISTS AND
SCHOOLMASTERS—THE DIFFICULTIES OF THIS UNDER-
TAKING—THE FAREWELL REPAST—NEFF'S REMARKS ON
THE CHARACTERS OF THE YOUNG MEN OF HIS ADULT
SCHOOL, AND ON THE EFFECTS PRODUCED BY IT—OBSER-
VATIONS ON THE STATE OF PUBLIC INSTRUCTION IN
FRANCE.

VERY few men of Neff's vehement and sanguine
temperament have displayed a happier union of
zeal and discretion. He seldom permitted his
enthusiasm to get the better of his judgment.
When his influence was at its zenith, and the
extraordinary improvement, in the Protestant
population of Val Fressinière, would have led
most persons to exult in their success, and to
flatter themselves that such striking effects produced by their ministry must be permanent, he
distrusted appearances, and anxiously revolved
in his own mind the best means of bringing his
neophytes to ripeness and perfectness in Christ.
Instead of urging on such as desired to become
his fellow-helpers and catechists, and acceler-
ating their pace, he kept them in check, and

endeavoured to convince them, that it was still a day of small things with them, and that they must undergo much preparation, before they could take upon themselves to guide others. Several young persons expressed an ardent wish to communicate the impressions which they themselves had received, and to hold little social meetings for that purpose. The pastor's decided opinion of the value of such meetings has already been noticed; I shall now show that he tried to keep them under proper control and superintendence, and that he did not give encouragement to the effusions of zeal without knowledge. One of his Journals contains the following observations upon this subject.

" Those who are dazzled by the first blaze of a new religious light, and who, imagining that zeal, however fervent, can supply the want of study and information, confide the most difficult part of God's work to persons, who have nothing but their faith and spiritual experience to guide them, will not be long before they discover their mistake. Nothing can be more erroneous. For my own part, I think the principle must be generally admitted, that knowledge and preparation are indispensably requisite for a labourer in the Lord's vineyard, that he may pursue his work efficaciously. He must combine sound discretion with fervent Christian piety. The truth of this has long been felt by me, but especially since my abode among these secluded people.

Their profound ignorance is, at present, an insuperable obstacle to the usefulness of those who are most zealous, and who have the best inclinations."

Neff has here said enough to confirm an opinion which I expressed in a former chapter [1], as to the risk of encouraging prayer meetings, and similar associations, composed of promiscuous persons, under no influential guidance; where all may speak, " those that are unlearned, or are unbelievers, and where every one hath a psalm, hath a doctrine, hath a tongue, hath a revelation, hath an interpretation [2]," and where there is no check upon those who are inclined to take a lead, whether qualified by character and attainments, or not [3]. On the other hand, nothing can be more conducive to piety and religious improvement, than well ordered, and well selected meetings of Christian friends, who devote certain portions of time to mutual conference and scriptural exposition, with prayer. These are strong links of union and fellowship, and powerful helps and encouragements, which animate the individuals who form them, and carry them forward in their Christian progress.

In another place, Neff complained that there was scarcely one in the whole valley, who could read the pure French language with any tolerable degree of fluency, much less speak it.

---

[1] See Chapter VII.   [2] 1 Cor. xiv. 23. 26.
[3] Baxter called it " a sinful humouring of rash professors."

"They learn to read, and they profess to read, but they have very few books; and it is the most disagreeable thing in the world to hear them attempt to recite a passage in Scripture, with their discordant tones, and vile pronunciation. They pitch their voices so high, and their articulation, from bad habit, is so imperfect, that it is scarcely possible to understand them, when they utter any thing but their own patois. Even the schoolmasters, whom I have found in the mountain villages, would not be thought worthy of being classed above learners of rudiments in any other place."

But what could be expected of functionaries, whose stipend was only twenty-four francs, or less than twenty shillings for the year : and of scholars, whose studies were always interrupted at the return of the open weather, and who were sent from their books to the flocks and herds, as soon as the snow was off the ground? The pastor saw that every thing must be done by himself: that he must give lessons, not only in the first principles of religion, but in the elements of ordinary scholarship, and that he must condescend to become an Abecedarian, before he could lay a good foundation of sound religious learning. With his usual unbroken perseverance he went to work, determined to give primary instruction to all, to old as well as young; to as many as were willing to be taught to read. But it was first necessary that he should make himself thorough master of the provincial dialect of the country, and in this he succeeded.

The unwearied diligence, with which Neff devoted himself to the acquirement of the patois of Dauphiné, is one of the efforts most creditable both to his judgment and his powers of application. It is recorded of Irenæus, the first Protestant bishop, (as that prelate may fairly be called, who first rebuked the bishop of Rome for his uncatholic spirit, in attempting to lord it over God's heritage,) that he learned the language of the province, before he preached Christ in these Alpine regions. Every body feels his reverence for the apostolical Heber increased upon reading Kohlhoff's account of his confirming the Tamul congregation in their own language. " After the conclusion of the sermon, he pronounced the blessing in Tamul, from the altar, correctly and distinctly, to the great surprise and joy of the whole native congregation. Fifty of the native congregation were confirmed by him in the Tamul language. The correctness with which he pronounced every word in Tamul, was not only striking, but will be always remembered by our native Christians, as a proof of the apostolic spirit which was in him, a proof of his fervent zeal and benevolent disposition to promote the eternal welfare, not only of the Europeans, but also of the poor natives." The humble pastor of the Alps is entitled to the same praise in all the churches.

Behold the preacher surrounded by his classes in a miserable stable, correcting the tone of one, the pronunciation of another, and the articulation of a third: patiently dinning sounds and sense into their ears, and making them spell the words, and divide by syllables, and repeat by sentences again and again, until he had put them into something like a fair training. Behold him also, to keep his pupils in good humour, and to mingle something pleasing with the dull routine of reading and spelling, putting aside his books, and giving lessons in music. This was a most successful as well as agreeable expedient; it was soon found that the best singers were also the best readers, and application to the more attractive lesson was usually accompanied by proficiency in the duller acquirement.

There was another scheme of the pastor which answered admirably well, and displayed the resources of his active mind. The inhabitants of Val Queyras were the best instructed, and the most ready scholars: those of Val Fressinière were the most devout Christians; he therefore judged that it would tend to their mutual improvement, if he could transplant a few of the well informed of the former into the villages of the latter, and employ their services as his assistants in the schools. " I hoped," said he, " that in exchange for their human learning, they would bring back from the valley of Fressinière some of the more precious knowledge

which makes one wise unto salvation." He was
not deceived; Andrew Vasserati of Molines, and
Stephen Matthew of San Veran, and others who
went to Dormilleuse and Minsas, were so pricked
to the heart by the simple and fervent piety of
the young people, whom they were employed to
instruct, that they returned to their homes exactly in that frame of mind which Neff anticipated, and they endeavoured to inspire in others
the feelings, which they themselves had acquired.

It was thus among the grandest and sternest
features of mountain scenery, that Neff not only
found food for his own religious contemplations,
and felt that his whole soul was filled with the
majesty of the ever present God, but here also
he discovered, that religious impressions were
more readily received, and retained more deeply
than elsewhere by others. In this rugged field
of rock and ice, the Alpine summit, and its glittering pinnacles, the eternal snows and glaciers,
the appalling clefts and abysses, the mighty
cataract, the rushing waters, the frequent perils
of avalanches and of tumbling rocks, the total
absence of every soft feature of nature, were always reading an impressive lesson, and illustrat-
ing the littleness of man, and the greatness of
the Almighty.

The happy result of his experiments made
the pastor feel anxious, to have a more convenient
place for his scholastic exertions than a dark and

dirty stable; and here again the characteristic and never-failing energies of his mind were fully displayed. The same hand, which had been employed in regulating the interior arrangements of a Church, in constructing aqueducts and canals of irrigation, and in the husbandman's work of sowing and planting, was now turned to the labour of building a school-room. He persuaded each family in Dormilleuse to furnish a man, who should consent to work under his directions, and having first marked out the spot with line and plummet, and levelled the ground, he marched at the head of his company to the torrent, and selected stones fit for the building. The pastor placed one of the heaviest upon his own shoulders, —the others did the same, and away they went with their burthens, toiling up the steep acclivity, till they reached the site of the proposed building. This labour was continued until the materials were all ready at hand; the walls then began to rise, and in one week from the first commencement, the exterior masonry work was completed, and the roof was put upon the room. The windows, chimney, door, tables, and seats, were not long before they also were finished. A convenient stove added its accommodation to the apartment, and Dormilleuse, for the first time probably in its history, saw a public school-room erected, and the process of instruction conducted with all possible regularity and comfort.

I had the satisfaction of visiting and inspect-

ing this monument of Neff's judicious exertions
for his dear Dormilleusians:—but it was a melancholy pleasure.   The shape, the dimensions, the
materials of the room, the chair on which he sat,
the floor which had been laid in part by his own
hands, the window-frame and desks, at which he
had worked with cheerful alacrity, were all objects of intense interest, and I gazed on these
relics of " the Apostle of the Alps," with feelings
little short of veneration.   It was here that he
sacrificed his life. The severe winters of 1826-7,
and the unremitted attention which he paid to
his duties, more especially to those of his school-
room, were his death-blow.

The course of the narrative, which I proposed
to myself as being best calculated to illustrate
Neff's singular character, and the very important
nature of his labours, now brings me to what
may be considered his crowning work,—the system by which he trained adults, and taught them
how to teach.   It was so in every sense of the
word; it was his most difficult, and his most unpleasant, but at the same time his most necessary
work, anxious as he was to leave permanent
effects of his ministry behind him, when he should
be removed from that scene of action; and it
was his last, for it broke up his shattered constitution, and hastened his death. But before I permit myself to dwell, with delighted admiration,
on the wisdom of this complement of his pastoral career, I must let him give his own account

of the motives which induced him to undertake the severest of all drudgery.

" I foresaw with sorrow," said he, " that the Gospel, which I had been permitted to preach in these mountains, would not only not spread, but might even be lost, unless something should be done to promote its continuance. I bethought me how it might be preserved in some degree ; and after mature deliberation I determined to become a training master, and to form a winter school, composed of the most intelligent and well disposed young men of the different villages of my parish, more particularly of those who, notwithstanding their lamentable ignorance, had already determined to become teachers. Many of these aspirants to the scholastic office were in the habit of leaving their mountain homes in the winter, to open schools in the warmer and more sheltered hamlets, and of returning in the spring to cultivate their own little heritages. I communicated my design to the most sanguine of these, and they entered into the spirit of it most joyfully. But I foresaw that the execution of the plan would entail expenses such as my poor mountaineers, who expatriate themselves during the winter season to obtain a precarious subsistence, could by no means incur. I therefore wrote to some friends at Geneva, who generously promised to promote my views, and to send some remittances in aid of them [1]. Dor-

[1] I believe Mr. Guassen, who is now so actively promoting

7

milleuse was the spot which I chose for my
scene of action, on account of its seclusion, and
because its whole population is Protestant, and a
local habitation was already provided here for
the purpose.   I reckoned at first that I should
have about a dozen élèves; but finding that
they were rapidly offering themselves, and would
probably amount to double that number, at the
least, I thought it right to engage an assistant,
not only that I might be at liberty to go and
look after my own Churches and villages, but
that I might not be exposed to any molestation,
for in France nobody can lawfully exercise the
office of a schoolmaster without a license, and
this cannot be granted either to a foreigner or a
pastor.   For these reasons I applied to Ferdinand Martin, who was then pursuing his studies
at Mens, to qualify himself for the institution of
M. Oliver, in Paris.   It was a great sacrifice
on his part to interrupt his studies, and to lose
the opportunity of an early admission to the institution; nor was it a small matter to ask him
to come and take up his residence, at the worst
season of the year, in the midst of the ice and
frightful rocks of Dormilleuse.   But he was sensible of the importance of the work, and, without any hesitation, he joined our party at the

the new academical institution at Geneva, was one of these
friends; and that the lady who has assisted me in the compilation of this Memoir, by lending me Neff's Journals, was greatly
instrumental in raising funds in England in aid of our pastor's
plans.

beginning of November. The short space of time, which we had before us, rendered every moment precious. We divided the day into three parts. The first was from sunrise to eleven o'clock, when we breakfasted. The second from noon to sunset, when we supped. The third from supper till ten or eleven o'clock at night, making in all fourteen or fifteen hours of study in the twenty-four. We devoted much of this time to lessons in reading, which the wretched manner in which they had been taught, their detestable accent, and strange tone of voice, rendered a most necessary, but tiresome duty. The grammar, too, of which not one of them had the least idea, occupied much of our time. People who have been brought up in towns, can have no conception of the difficulty which mountaineers and rustics, whose ideas are confined to those objects only, to which they have been familiarized, find in learning this branch of science. There is scarcely any way of conveying the meaning of it to them. All the usual terms and definitions, and the means which are commonly employed in schools, are utterly unintelligible here. But the curious and novel devices which must be employed, have this advantage,—they exercise their understanding, and help to form their judgment. Dictation was one of the methods to which I had recourse : without it they would have made no progress in grammar and orthography ; but they wrote so miserably, and

T

slowly, that this consumed a great portion of valuable time.   Observing that they were ignorant of the signification of a great number of French words, of constant use and recurrence, I made a selection from the vocabulary, and I set them to write down, in little copy-books[1], words which were in most frequent use; but the explanations contained in the dictionary were not enough, and I was obliged to rack my brain for new and brief definitions which they could understand, and to make them transcribe these.   Arithmetic was another branch of knowledge which required many a weary hour.   Geography was considered a matter of recreation after dinner: and they pored over the maps with a feeling of delight and amusement, which was quite new to them. I also busied myself in giving them some notions of the sphere, and of the form and motion of the earth; of the seasons and the climates, and of the heavenly bodies.   Every thing of this sort was as perfectly novel to them, as it would have been to the islanders of Otaheite; and even the elementary books, which are usually put into the hands of children, were at first as unintelligible as the most abstruse treatises on mathematics.   I was consequently forced to use the simplest, and plainest modes of demonstration;

[1] They have no slates in this country—nor in the valleys of Piedmont.—Two benevolent benefactors to the Protestant cause in Italy, who wished to confer a benefit upon the schools of Piedmont, have enabled me to supply the Vaudois schools with this useful and economical article.

but these amused and instructed them at the same time.   A ball made of the box tree, with a hole through it, and moving on an axle, and on which I had traced the principal circles; some large potatoes hollowed out; a candle, and sometimes the skulls of my scholars, served for the instruments, by which I illustrated the movement of the heavenly bodies, and of the earth itself.   Proceeding from one step to another, I pointed out the situation of different countries on the chart of the world, and in separate maps, and took pains to give some slight idea, as we went on, of the characteristics, religions, customs, and history of each nation.   These details fixed topics of moment in their recollection.   Up to this time I had been astonished by the little interest they took, Christian-minded as they were, in the subject of Christian missions, but, when they began to have some idea of geography, I discovered, that their former ignorance of this science, and of the very existence of many foreign nations in distant quarters of the globe, was the cause of such indifference.   But as soon as they began to learn who the people are, who require to have the Gospel preached to them, and in what part of the globe they dwell, they felt the same concern for the circulation of the Gospel that other Christians entertain.   These new acquirements, in fact, enlarged their spirit, made new creatures of them, and seemed to triple their very existence.

" In the end, I advanced so far as to give some lectures in geometry, and this too produced a happy moral development.

" Lessons in music formed part of our evening employment, and those being, like geography, a sort of amusement, they were regularly succeeded by grave and edifying reading, and by such reflections as I took care to suggest for their improvement.

" Most of the young adults of the village were present at such lessons, as were within the reach of their comprehension, and as the children had a separate instructor, the young women and girls of Dormilleuse, who were growing up to womanhood, were now the only persons for whom a system of instruction was unprovided. But these stood in as great need of it as the others, and more particularly as most of them were now manifesting Christian dispositions. I therefore proposed that they should assemble of an evening in the room, which the children occupied during the day, and I engaged some of my students to give them lessons in reading and writing. We soon had twenty young women from fifteen to twenty-five years of age in attendance, of whom two or three only had any notion of writing, and not half them could read a book of any difficulty. While Ferdinand Martin was practising the rest of my students in music, I myself and two of the most advanced, by turns, were employed in teaching these young women, so that the whole routine of instruction went on regularly, and I was thus able to exercise the future schoolmasters in their destined profession, and both to observe their method of teaching, and to improve it. I thus superintended teachers and scholars at the same time."

It is quite impossible for those who have not seen the country, to appreciate the devotedness to the Christian cause, which could induce Neff to entertain even the thought of making the dreary and savage Dormilleuse his own headquarters, from November to April, and of persuading others to be the companions of his dismal sojournment there. I learn from a memorandum in his Journal, that the severity of that winter commenced early. "We have been in snow and ice since the first of November, on this steep and rugged spot, whose aspect is more terrible and severe than any thing can be supposed to be in France." He himself was the native of a delightful soil and climate, and even some of the mountaineers, whom he drew to that stern spot, were inhabitants of a far less repulsive district, but had yet made it their custom to seek a milder region than their own, during the inclemency of an Alpine winter. To secure attendance and application, when once his students were embarked in their undertaking, he selected this rock, where neither amusement, nor other occupations, nor the possibility of frequent egress or regress, could tempt them to interrupt their studies :—and he had influence enough to induce them to commit themselves to a five months' rigid confinement within a prison-house, as it were, walled up with ice and snow. Nothing can be compared to the resolution and self-denial of the volunteers, who enrolled their names under Neff for this service, but the similar qualities, which were called into action by our own gallant officers and seamen, who embarked in the polar expeditions, with the certainty before them of being snowed or iced up during many months of privation. In their case the hope of promotion and of reputation, and the ardour of scientific research, were the moving inducement. In that of the pastor and his young friends, a sense of duty, and thoughts fixed on heavenly things constituted the impulse. To Neff himself it was a season of incessant toil, and that of the most irksome kind. He did violence to his natural inclination every way. His mind and body were kept in subjection. He was devoted to his profession, as a minister and preacher of the Gospel, and yet he suspended the pursuits, which were more congenial to his tastes and habits, and went back to first principles, and consented to teach the simplest rudiments, and meekly sunk down to the practice of the humblest elementary drudgery, when he saw the necessity of laying a foundation for a system of instruction different to that, which had hitherto prevailed in this neglected region. His patience, his humility, his good-humour and perseverance, his

numberless expedients to expand the intellect of
his pupils, to store their minds, and to keep up
a good understanding among them, are all subjects of admiration, which it is beyond the power
of language to express. Whose heart does not
warm towards this true disciple of the good
Shepherd, who thus followed his Divine Master's
path, and gathered the lambs with his arm, and
carried them in his bosom, and gently led them:
this amiable teacher, who practised all the lessons he taught on the first day of the week, and
rose with the morning sun of the six other days,
to pursue his routine of active benevolence,—
this wise master builder, who saw that the
spiritual condition of his Church would be improved, by laying a foundation for the high and
holy things of the Gospel, with the precious
stones of common-place information: who prepared the minds of his flock for the reception
and comprehension of sacred truths, by giving
them an insight into those secrets of knowledge,
which some are weak enough to imagine are too
profound for the simple, and too attractive for
the religious.

The young men, who submitted to their pastor's system of discipline at Dormilleuse, must
have their share also of our admiration. We
cannot but feel respect for students, who willingly
shut themselves up amidst the most comfortless
scenes in nature, and submitted to the severity
of not less than fourteen hours of hard study a

day, where the only recreation was to go from dryer lessons to lectures in geography and music. It was a long probation of hardship. Their fare was in strict accordance with the rest of their situation. It consisted of a store of salted meat, and rye bread, which had been baked in autumn, and when they came to use it, was so hard, that it required to be chopped up with hatchets, and to be moistened with hot water. Meal and flour will not keep in this mountain atmosphere, but would become mouldy,—they are, therefore, obliged to bake it soon after the corn is threshed out. Our youthful anchorites were lodged gratuitously by the people of Dormilleuse, who also liberally supplied them with wood for fuel, scarce as it was, but if the pastor had not laid in a stock of provisions, the scanty resources of the village could not have met the demands of so many mouths, in addition to its native population. The party consisted of five from Val Queyras, one from Vars, five from Champsaur, two from Chancelas, four from the lower part of the valley of Fressinière, and eight from the immediate neighbourhood of Dormilleuse.

Neff had the satisfaction to find that his plan answered well, and this was reward enough. " I never," said he, " can be sufficiently thankful to Almighty God for the blessing, which he has vouchsafed to shed upon this undertaking, and for the strength he has given me to enable me to bear the fatigue of it. Oh! may he continue to extend his gracious protection, and to support me under my infirmities, or rather, to deliver me from them, that I may be able to devote myself to his service and glory, to my life's end!"

A note of the expenditure upon this occasion will excite some wonder in the minds of many readers, who are not aware how much good may be done at a small cost, when the stream of bounty is made to pass through proper channels.

" Our disbursements for the adult school, including candles, ink, and paper, the salary of an assistant master, and food for the sixteen or seventeen students who came from a distance, did not exceed 560 francs (about 22*l*. 10*s*.) for four months. Of this sum I can replace a little more than two-thirds, because some of the students have repaid their share of the expense, and even the poorest furnished their quota of bread. We did not provide commons for those who belonged to Dormilleuse, because they boarded at home."

The separation of this little party is not the least interesting part in the history of their proceedings. Towards Easter, the opening spring gave the signal for their return to their several communes, and the studies of the school-room gave place to manual labour in the fields and woods. The breaking up of a society, which had been united by the strongest ties of mutual respect and affection, could not be contemplated without feelings of reluctance on all sides—but it was an event which was regarded with peculiar regret by the inhabitants of the secluded Dormilleuse. It was a perfect epoch in its history to have received in its bosom a company of young men, who, though they were of grave habits and serious demeanour, yet gave a dash of unwonted cheerfulness to the dull routine of Alpine life. To see them in the village sanctuary, to hear their voices at the close of day, and to listen to the swelling harmony, when their evening hymn of praise was raised to the throne of the Most High, to receive them in their humble dwellings, and to meet them by the torrent side, when the weather would permit them to take exercise,—these were so many incidents to change the sameness of their usually unvaried existence, and the day, on which they were to bid farewell to their guests, was one of painful anticipation to the Dormilleusians. On the evening before they took their leave, the young men of the village prepared a supper for their new friends, and invited them to the parting banquet. It was a simple and a frugal repast, consisting of the productions of the chase. The bold hunter contributed his salted chamois, the less enterprising sportsman of the mountain laid a dried marmot upon the table, and one or two of the most successful rangers of the forest produced a bear's ham, as a farewell offering in honour of the last evening, on which the conversation of this interesting group was to be enjoyed. It was at the same time a pleasing, and a melancholy festival, but I do not find, in the pastor's Journal, that either the achievements of their ancestors, who had garrisoned this rocky citadel, and had repulsed numberless attempts to storm it, or the exploits of the chasseurs, who had furnished the festive board, formed the conversation of the evening. It seems to have savoured rather of the object, which originally brought them together, and when one of the party remarked,—" What a delightful sight, to behold so many young friends met together—but it is not likely that we shall ever meet all together again !" The pastor took the words up like a text, and enlarged upon the consolatory thought, that though they might see each other's faces no more in this life, they would most assuredly meet again in a joyful state of existence in the world to come, if they would persevere in their Christian course. He then gave them a parting benediction, and, after a long and mournful silence, which each seemed unwilling to interrupt, either by uttering the dreaded good-bye, or moving from his seat, the valedictory words and embraces passed from one to another, and they separated. The next morning at an early hour, they were seen winding down the mountain path to their several homes ; they of Dormilleuse gazed after them till their figures were lost in the distance, and the village on the rock appeared more dreary and desolate than ever.

Neff left behind him some remarks touching the progress which these students made, and their several capacities, and dispositions, from which I select the following passages.

" With regard to the improvement which I observed, this varied according to the character of the individuals. The greater part of them were so illiterate and so raw, and the time was so short, that it did not suffice for the inculcation of the first elements of human knowledge. But yet we had seven or eight, who will, I trust, answer the proposed object, that is to say, they will become qualified to discharge the functions of village catechists, and to diffuse around them the precious knowledge of Jesus Christ. As many more, without taking upon themselves the same office, will consecrate the knowledge they have acquired to the glory of God : and the rest, though less advanced, will yet be likely to profit in every respect by the information they have picked up, and by the edifying things which they have learnt. Two young women of Dormilleuse, (Anna Maria Arnouf, and Susannah Baridon,) have made very great progress, and will be extremely useful to the Sunday-school, which has been established in their village. They are the centre and soul of a religious life to all in Dormilleuse, and even in the other hamlets of the valley, by means of the religious correspondence which they keep up with many persons, whom they have never seen. Many others have perseveringly continued to seek for the kingdom of God and his righteousness. Hitherto none of my young élèves have been placed out as regular schoolmasters, because the schools are not open in the summer-time, but many of them preside over Sunday-schools, which now begin to take in this country. At Arvieux in Val Queyras, Barthélimi Albert of Brunichard, aged nineteen, who is lame in both feet, but in other respects strong and healthy, and intelligent, and gifted with a good ear for music, (a very rare accomplishment in these mountains) reads and sings in the church at Arvieux, and performs two services [1] at Bruni-chard every Sunday. He will also be at the head of the Sunday-school which I hope to establish there. This youth contends firmly against the apathy and rudeness of his com-panions, and against the levity of some young men who bring from Marseilles, (where they generally go to work during the winter) some of the corruption of a populous city. He does much to confirm the good intentions of those who are well disposed. At San Veran, Chaffrey Matthew and Joseph Jouve take charge of the public services and the Sunday-school. The latter is clever and well informed, and has a great deal of originality of character and firm-

[1] In all the Protestant churches of France and Italy, a great part of the public service, such as reading the chapters and the commandments, and giving out and leading the psalms, is regu-larly performed by laymen.

ness of purpose : during the winter he advanced rapidly in spiritual attainments, and from being proud and self-willed, is become a faithful follower of the Lamb of God. Daniel Isnel, also of San Veran, who intends to be a schoolmaster, is about fifteen years old, and is going to Languedoc, to place himself under a relation who is following this vocation, continues to manifest an excellent disposition, without being a very great proficient as yet. Stephen Matthew, whom they wished to retain at Mens as precentor, when he accompanied me there on his last visit, is the most promising youth of his village, and I have reason to hope, that he will be the means of spreading the light of the Gospel, wherever he goes. At Fousillarde, Andrew Vasserotti performs three Sunday services, and holds two meetings during the week. He sings well, reads impressively, expresses himself fluently, even in French, and but for some few defects of style, would frequently be thought to be a regular preacher. The valley of Fressinière, to my great astonishment, has not furnished a single individual, who is even moderately gifted. Even those, who in the ordinary affairs of life, and in matters purely spiritual manifest great judgment, are incapable of acquiring a knowledge of any of the sciences. Notwithstanding all the pains I have taken with them, and their own application, their progress is by no means satisfactory. The most intelligent of them is James Baridon of Dormilleuse, who, until lately, was only distinguished for his great bodily strength, and the violence of his character, and the irregularity of his conduct. From the time that he began to frequent our school, he became a changed man, and has been doing all he can to edify others ; but his past life prevents his gaining the confidence of his neighbours, and I think it would be a good thing if he would take himself away for a short time. Peter Baridon, also of Dormilleuse, is perhaps the most steady and Christianminded youth of the whole village; it is he who has undertaken the charge of the boys' Sunday-school there.

" At Minsas, the two brothers Besson, and at Violins, John Baridon, have opened Sunday-schools, and evening meetings. Francis Bertholon of La Ribe, the first-born of the valley, attended the school during the winter, but he despises all human acquirements, I know not why, and regrets the time he has spent in them. This is the more to be lamented, because with his zeal and Christian attainments, he would be able to do much good, if he would make himself master of the languages, and would learn to read better. Champsaur sent us five students, and my assistant master, Ferdinand Martin, who has since taken his departure for Paris. If he is well encouraged and directed, he will make rapid progress in all his studies. He is beloved and regretted wherever he has been, and especially in his native valley. One of the most promising youths of Champsaur is Peter Albert, who burns to consecrate himself to the ministry, but his relations, though they are rich, will probably refuse their consent. But the most surprising person is Alexander Valon of St. Laurent, who, previously to last autumn, made a boast of being the wildest and most profligate man in all that country. He had even suffered imprisonment for eight months, for nearly killing a man. He [1] is now at the head of the Lord's work in Champsaur, and supplies the place of Ferdinand Martin. His former companions scarcely recognise him as the same person. He passed the winter with us, and though he is now thirty-three years of age, the progress he made was very extraordinary. He reads remarkably well, and will make a good schoolmaster. He has already had several places offered to him. The valley of Vars [2], between

[1] Nefi's great prudence and discernment induce me to hope, that he was not deceived in the change wrought in this person.

[2] Brockeden's animated description will help the reader to comprehend the nature of the country about Vars, which I had not an opportunity of visiting myself.

"The descent of the Col de Vars is gradual over a fine pasturage, thence passing through St. Marie, and the village of Vars, the traveller descends the mountain brow, between the valleys of the Vars and D'Eserans, and a magnificent scene opens upon him of Guillestre, and the fort of Mount Dauphin, the valley of the Durance, and the mountains covered with glaciers, which flank the Col de Lautaret.

" From Barcellonette, a path by the Col de la Vachère, leads

Guillestre and Barcelonette, contains but very few Protestants, and sent us only one student, John Rostan, aged eighteen, of a very decided character, and of good abilities; he will either go to Paris and place himself under M. Olivier, or he will become a schoolmaster. There is another very deserving young man at Vars, Peter Tolosan, who is a cultivator of land in the summer, and a colporteur, or pedlar, in the winter, travelling the country about Nismes. He has the resolution to avoid that species of falsehood, which most men practise in his line of life, and to demand a fixed price for his articles. At first, after making this determination, he sold nothing, but by persevering in it, he has had better custom than others in the same business, so that many of them have been obliged to follow his practice."

This is the second time that mention has been made of the colporteurs of Dauphiné, and here I will take the opportunity of remarking that some of the religious Societies have made great

across the mountains to Embrun, but the *chemin royal*, as Bourcet calls it, lies by the course of the Ubaye, though in many places not a vestige of a *chemin* remains, for the violence of the Ubaye, and the streams which fall into it, is so great in the winter, as to leave the entire valley for miles a bed of stones and black mud. After crossing a hill, and descending a zigzag road at the pass of La Tour, in losing sight of Laurent, all is again sterile. On looking back, the deep course of the Ubaye is seen issuing from the defile of La Tour, and the grand forms of the mountain of *Cugulion des Trois Evêques*, present a scene which is savage, mountainous, and dreary."

U

use of these itinerant venders, who follow their
wandering occupation on the borders of France,
Italy, and Switzerland, and supply the mountaineers, and inhabitants of villages remote from
towns, with almost all the small articles of convenience which they require.   These men are
employed in the circulation of Bibles, Testaments, and tracts, which they generally sell at
reduced prices, but in some cases they are
allowed to distribute them gratis; and, when
disposing of their other commodities, they have
often produced very beneficial effects, by drop-
ping a word in good season, concerning the
more precious stores with which their packs are
furnished.

I know an officer of high rank in the British
service, and of whose Christian labours I never
can think without the deepest sentiments of respect, whose time and talents, since the peace,
have been devoted to translating the Gospels
into the patois [1] of one of the Alpine provinces,
and whose principal dependence, for the circulation of his selections of Scripture, in corners
where it is difficult to obtain access for them,

---

[1] The Bible Society has lately printed the Gospels of St.
Luke and St. John, with the French version in one column,
and a translation in the Waldensian patois in another column.
" Li Sént Evangilé de notre Seigneur Gésu Christ counfourms
Sént Luc et Sént Giann rendù en Lengua Valdesa, par Pierre
Bert, ancien modérateur des Eglises Vaudoises, et Pasteur de
a Tour." Such is the title of the Patois version.

rests on the fidelity and zeal of the colporteurs. "It would be tedious," says the Report of the Continental Society, "to give the detail of all the operations of the colporteurs, but it may not be uninteresting to state, that one individual in a range of country comprising fourteen towns, disposed of 3,900 of Leander Van Ess's New Testament, 500 of Gossner's, and 1,700 of De Sacy's [1]."

I cannot bring this chapter, on Neff's scholastic labours, to a conclusion, without offering some remarks upon the state of education in France, and the difficulty of putting any system of national education on a firm and good footing there. "To establish a new school," says Vincent in his Vues sur le Protestantism, "in France [2], is a work of enormous labour, in which patience the most persevering must not always expect to succeed. It is necessary to create schoolmasters. We have absolutely none. It is necessary to know how to teach, and therefore Normal, or Model, Schools we must have for the instruction of Schoolmasters, in which they may be made acquainted with the best methods of imparting knowledge : in a word, in which themselves may learn the most difficult of all arts, the art of

[1] A letter which I have lately received from Geneva contains this bold prediction—" Il nous parait presqu' évident que le renversement du Papisme en France est réservé au Colportage."—*July* 5, 1833.

[2] Vol. ii. p. 32.

teaching." It was this that Neff undertook to do, at a time when the attempt was more arduous than at the period when Vincent published his work, (in 1829,) for the parti-prêtre, which had been opposing every comprehensive system of education, was then on the decline. This writer has stated, on the authority of M. Soulier's Statistique, that the scarcity of Protestant schools was so great, that on an average, there was only one school for 2857 Protestants, or supposing that each school contained thirty scholars, a population of one hundred, reckoning by round numbers, would only have one scholar. M. Vincent allows for some exaggeration in this statement, but with every allowance it shows how want of funds, want of zeal, and want of well qualified instructors, have combined to keep the inhabitants of that country, which professes to be the most civilized in the world, in a state of the most woeful neglect. A still more recent publication [1], complains not only that France ranks considerably below England, Switzerland, great part of Germany, and of the north of Europe, Holland, and North America, in the scale of nations, where provision is made for public education, but that there is scarcely any country, except Spain and Portugal, and others where the Romanism of the middle ages still prevails, which does not rise above her. It then states

----

[1] The Semeur, of November, 1831.

that more than two-thirds of the entire French population are unable to read; that in many departments there are whole villages, where not more than three or four of the inhabitants can read, and that according to the official reports of the Minister of Public Instruction, there are a great many communes, where there are no elementary schools. In the pursuit of this interesting inquiry, the Semeur quotes the statistical table of M. C. Dupin to show that Great Britain, with a population less by half than that of France, has more scholars in her gratuitous Sunday-schools only, than France in all her schools put together, and concludes with the observation, that the difference between the state of education in those parts of the kingdom which are Protestant, and those which are Roman Catholic, is something enormous. Such is the condition of France revolutionary, France sceptical, France Roman Catholic, France refined and philosophic, when compared with countries under the influence of more steady and more scriptural religious principles. " Wherever the true principles of the Gospel are obscured," says the same journal [1], " either by scepticism or by Romish superstition, there intellectual progress is retarded, and we may lay it down as a general rule, with all the precision of a mathematical problem, that national instruction and the num-

[1] The Semeur.

ber of scholars vary in every country, in a direct
ratio with the influence of the Gospel, and in an
inverse ratio with the influence of Popery and
monkery, or with sceptical philosophy." The
Semeur assigns the highest rank in the scale of
educated nations to Protestant Scotland; but the
Protestant population of the Valleys of Piedmont
may take an equally, if not a more honourable
place still, for there provision is made for the
elementary instruction of every child, without
any exception: and from all that I can collect,
it is a very rare case of neglect on the part of
the parents, if a single child can be found among
the Waldensian peasantry, of age sufficient to
learn, who cannot read.

In fact it has been reserved for Protestantism
only, to produce what the wise and the good of
all ages and countries have desired to see,
namely, an entire population furnished with the
means of receiving education. The Gospel, in
its pure form, has done what philosophy and
philanthropy have made the subject of their
eulogies, and of their recommendation, but have
never been able to achieve: it has raised up a
race of men, who have consecrated themselves
to the task of making others acquainted with the
most valuable part of their own knowledge, and
have laboured to do so, not in the graceful walks
of the refined, the clever, and the docile, but in
the haunts of the squalid, the dull, and the in-
tractable. It was for the sages of old, to attract

admiration, and to add to their fame, by lecturing to young patricians, on the popular literature of their day, and it is for the learned and the liberal of our own times, to praise and to patronize, and to promote by their writings, and by their open purses, the systems of instruction, which they think will be extensively useful. None, however, but such men as Oberlin, and Neff, none but those who, like them, have been under the strong influence of Christian motives, have ever done violence to their natural tastes and inclinations, and have left the more agreeable, and equally legitimate duties of their profession, to assume the functions of the humble pedagogue and of the village dame, and to teach the lowest rudiments to the lowest poor ; not before the admiring eyes of the world, but in seclusion, and amidst all the disheartening circumstances of dirt and stench, of chilling cold or suffocating heat. Those who profess to be the benefactors of their country, and the utilitarians of the day, whose names are constantly before the public, and who run away with all the praise of philanthropy and wisdom, will, we trust, continue to form plans for the amelioration of mankind, and for the advancement of human knowledge; but, unless they are actuated by the highest and holiest motives, they will not be any thing more than theorists : they will not be the working parties in a cause, which never can be effectually promoted, but by those, who, feeling the power of the Gospel, are constrained to acts of self-denying charity, and to busy, practical benevolence, by Christian love, and a deep sense of religious obligation [1].   It was this that led Neff to the dismal solitudes of Dormilleuse, and shut him up with his twenty-five pupils, and urged him to abandon for a time those pursuits, which were most congenial to his mind and habits, in order that he might lay a foundation of knowledge and happiness, and contribute something to the stock of general prosperity in a district, which was separated from the more habitable parts of the world by rocks and mountains, cold and sterility.

[1] The Journal of Education, No. 3, contains information on the subject of education in France, confirmatory of what I have advanced on this subject.   It states that very little has yet been done for the education of the lower orders, that " almost every thing remains to be done," but that nothing will be done till a sufficient number of schools shall be formed for the education of masters.   It intimates that " the theocratic or absolutist party" has been the means of keeping the country in this wretched state.

CHAPTER XIII.

NEFF'S STRENGTH FAILS—WINTER HORRORS OF DORMIL-
LEUSE—NEFF OBLIGED TO RETURN TO SWITZERLAND—
PARTING SCENES—NEFF GOES TO THE BATHS OF PLOM-
BIÈRES—HIS LAST ADDRESS TO HIS ALPINE FLOCK—HIS
SUFFERINGS AND PATIENCE—HIS LAST HOURS—HIS DEATH
AT GENEVA.

IT was after the winter of 1825, and the cold
spring of 1826, when the severe duty of presiding over the Normal School at Dormilleuse,
and of visiting his distant Churches at regular intervals, overwhelmed him with fatigue, that Neff
began to feel that his career must soon end. The
long-continued excitement and anxiety, the oft-
repeated journeys on foot in all weathers, the
sharpness of the external air, and the suffocating
heat of a small-room, in which so many persons,
not remarkable for their cleanliness, were crowded
together, day after day, these, together with
the exertion of daily, and almost hourly, lectures,
would have undermined the most robust frame.
Deprivation added to hard work, and the irregularity, as well as the coarse unwholesome quality
of his meals, brought on a weakness of stomach,
which was followed by a total derangement of
the digestive organs. Had he relaxed his exer-

tions in time, he might have been saved, but in the destitute state of the Alpine Churches, he could not reconcile it to his mind to desert his post of duty, so long as he had any strength remaining. He struggled through the summer of 1826 pretty well, but when the winter came, and he resumed his labours both in the school, upon the rock, and in visiting his scattered hamlets, while the snow blocked up some of the more direct passes, and rendered all difficult of access, it was more and more manifest that the conflict could not last long. The internal pains, which he suffered from indigestion, were aggravated by an accidental disaster. To avoid the danger of an avalanche, he traversed a *débris* of rock; his foot slipped, and he sprained his knee so badly, that the effects were felt long and severely. His letters, written from Dormilleuse in the early part of 1827, breathe the same devout and resigned spirit as before, but I fancy that I trace in some of them a melancholy foreboding, that his projects had just been completed in time, and that the erection of his school-room, and the instructions which he had been enabled to give to those, who were destined to the catechetical and scholastic office, were seasonably completed before his race was run. The following gives an animated description of the wintry horrors of Dormilleuse.

" Thanks to the generosity of my friends, our little school is now floored and glazed—the benches and seats are finished, and while all the other schools in this country are held in damp and dark stables, where the scholars are stifled with smoke, and interrupted by the babble of people, and the noise of the cattle, and are obliged to be constantly quarrelling with the kids and fowls in defence of their copy-books, or shifting their position to avoid the droppings from the roof, we have here a comfortable and well-warmed apartment. I am again conducting a school for the education of those, whose business it will be to educate others—it now consists of about twenty young men from the different villages. We are buried in snow more than four feet deep. At this moment a terrible hurricane is raging, which dashes the snow about in clouds,—we can scarcely put our feet out of the house, and I know not when my letter will reach you. During the late abundant falls of snow, and the violence of the wind, our communication with the other valleys has been both difficult and dangerous. The avalanches threaten us on all sides. They have been falling thick, especially about Dormilleuse.

" One Sunday evening our students, and many of the inhabitants of Dormilleuse, were returning home after the sermon at Violins, when they narrowly escaped an avalanche. It rolled down into a very narrow defile, and fell between two groups of people. Had it fallen a moment sooner or later, it would have rolled one of the parties into the abyss below, and would thus have destroyed the flower of the youth of this region. But the Eternal, who rules over the waves of the sea, commands also the ice and the snow, and protects his children in the midst of peril. The villages are every where menaced with the impending danger. Upon several occasions lately, I have seen even our calm and daring Alpines express anxiety. In fact, there are very few habitations in these parts which are not liable to be swept away, for there is not a spot in the narrow corner of the valley, which can be considered absolutely safe. But terrible as their situation is, they owe to it their religion, and perhaps their physical existence. If their country had been more secure and more accessible, they would have been exterminated like the inhabitants of Val Louise."

When his élèves separated for the second time, the pastor returned to Arvieux, and nursed his sprained knee, but his stomach had so entirely lost its tone, that it could receive nothing but liquids. " I perceived," said he, when he spoke of himself afterwards, " that my strength was diminishing rapidly : for the first time I became conscious that it was time to seek for that succour, which, with all their kindness, these poor mountaineers could not procure me."

It was heart-rending to him to think of quitting the valleys, where he had been of so much use, and where he had been received and treated so affectionately: but he submitted to the absolute necessity of a removal to his own native climate, and made preparation for a return to Geneva by slow journeys. From henceforth, during his short continuance on earth, we shall find him exercising the passive virtues of a suffering Christian, as eminently as he had displayed the active qualities of a zealous man of God.

Neff took leave, for ever, of his presbytery at La Chalp, on the 17th of April, 1827. He was surrounded by so many afflicted friends, that he was constrained to repeat the Apostle's tender rebuke. "What, mean ye to weep, and to break mine heart?" At the distance of about three miles from Arvieux, just before he entered the gloomiest part of the pass of the Guil, he was met by four young men, from Dormilleuse, who had then walked eight leagues since sunrise, to have the melancholy satisfaction of paying their farewell attentions to their beloved pastor. They considered it no fatigue to continue walking by his side till they arrived at Guillestre. The next morning, with the earliest dawn, one of the faithful creatures, who had observed how painful it was for Neff, in his exhausted state, to pursue his journey on foot, set out for Fressinière to procure a horse for the invalid. He met a party consisting of the heads of families, who were on their way to bid adieu to the pastor, and great was their joy, when they learnt, that the painful good-bye would yet be deferred for a short time, and that it was his intention to pass through the valley of Fressinière on his route to Mens, from whence he was to proceed to Switzerland by the easier direction of the high-road.   But that none of his flock might feel themselves forgotten, or neglected, Neff turned his face towards Vars, the furthest out-post on the south of his vast parish, and there preached a farewell sermon to the weeping Protestants of that village.   His last charge to John Rostan of Vars, of whom honourable mention is made in Neff's Journal, and whose zeal and attainments gave him hopes, that he would become a useful minister of the Church, was, that he should make frequent tours through the several hamlets during the summer, and keep things in order.   He also left that young man some money to bear his expenses, and there is every reason to believe that the expectations entertained of him will be realized.

On my way to Dormilleuse, from the Piedmontese Valleys, in 1829, Rostan heard of my arrival at Guillestre, and accompanied me from thence to Val Fressinière.   I was struck with the affectionate and respectful manner in which the young catechist was greeted, as we passed through the several hamlets, and judged that his services would be extremely beneficial in the valleys, if he could get ordained.   He had been to the university of Montauban for a term or two, but had found it too expensive to continue his studies

7

there, it is therefore to be feared that his hopes of ministerial advancement will be disappointed, and that he must remain in the humbler station of a catechist.

When Neff proceeded through Chancelas, and Palons, and Fressinière, and Violins, and Minsas, and Dormilleuse, on his way to Mens, the struggle between his emotions, excited by a farewell visit to the cottages of his friends, and his sense of the necessity of keeping up their spirits and his own, was a terrible conflict for his weakened frame. "However, I was not sorry," said he in one of his letters, "to have seen once more my friends of the mountains. I observed with joy, that, amidst the sadness caused by my departure, those who were truly established in religious principles, bore it with the greatest fortitude, and joined their voices to mine, in assuring the more dejected that Jesus Christ, the chief Shepherd, never leaves us, and that with him, we can want nothing : that the ministers of the Gospel are like so many John Baptists, whose mission should be considered as done, when they have pointed out the Lamb of God, and that they, and dependence on them, ought to diminish, in proportion as Jesus increases in the heart. Several of those who felt the greatest affection for me, exclaimed, ' had you always remained with those among whom you first laboured, we might have continued in darkness until now ; it is fair that some others should now have the benefit of your ministry. May the Lord accompany you, and bless your labours, every where, for his name's sake.' "

The invalid stopped for a short time at Mens, where he was again deeply affected by the attentions of his friends in that town, and in its vicinity; and his anxiety, to address them once more from the pulpit, induced him to exert himself in a manner which added considerably to his debility. When he arrived at Geneva, he was in a state of extreme languor and suffering, but his native air produced a temporary improvement, which gave some faint hopes that he might yet be restored. The ever busy spirit, however, would not suffer the body to rest; he imprudently attempted to do things beyond his strength, and in a very short time his malady had increased so much, that he found himself utterly unable to take any solid food: the digestive organs seemed to be completely paralyzed. In this miserable condition he dragged through the remainder of the year 1827, and the spring of 1828, when, as a last expedient, it was recommended to him to try the effects of mineral waters.

Neff was not deceived respecting his own condition; he had very little hope of his recovery; but he did not think it right to neglect the advice of his physician, who ordered him to go to the baths of Plombières. He left Geneva on the 19th of June, to travel thither by short

stages, and journeyed slowly through the cantons of Vaud, Neufchâtel, Berne, and Bâle,
where he had preached the Gospel, eight years
before. It was soothing to his mind, to meet
again the acquaintances he had made there, and
to be cordially greeted by many others, who were
strangers to him, but who gathered round him
with affection, for the sake of the good work in
which he had been engaged.

The journey, or rather the joy he felt, at the
reception he met every where, having reani-
mated him, he had strength to preach in every
place where he stopped. At Plombières, he
found what is to be met with at all watering
places, a confused mixture of every moral and
physical evil, and he felt himself called upon
to publish the word of life amidst this throng of
persons, whose minds were occupied chiefly by
their sufferings, or their pleasures, ‘ where no
one,’ said he, ‘ seemed to think of eternity.’
Madame de C——, wife of the prefect of the Vosges, a Protestant lady, proposed to him to establish a public service on Sundays, and she made
it known to all the Protestants of the place.
The congregation was large, and he had never
before preached to so brilliant an audience, yet
he spoke with as much freedom and simplicity,
as he had done to the mountaineers of the Alps.
On the succeeding Sundays there was a great
number of Roman Catholics in attendance, and
two large apartments could scarcely contain the

hearers.   Many persons of both persuasions appeared to take delight in these services.

The use of the waters and the baths promised at first to produce a good effect.   His strength and his appetite improved, and it was thought adviseable to add solids to the milk, which, for a whole year, had been his only nourishment, but this experiment proved highly injurious. After some days he suffered more severely than ever, and it was evident that the most skilful care could not arrest the progress of the disorder for many weeks more.   On the approach of the bad season at Plombières, it would have been right to have moved him away at once, but his total loss of strength rendered every exertion more and more hazardous: yet in this melancholy situation, his letters contained such sentiments as these :—" I cannot sufficiently thank God for his goodness to me !   What composure, what peace, he permits me to enjoy ! Until lately it appeared to me impossible to support the idea of being cut off from the number of Christ's labourers, and of being condemned to absolute inaction ; but the Lord no sooner saw fit to call upon me to make this sacrifice, than he made me sensible that, what is impossible with man, is possible with him.   Sustained by his grace, I can say Amen to his decrees."   Whilst he was confined to his bed, he received several visits from one of the curés of Plombières, and from some young Romish ec-

NEFF RETURNS TO GENEVA.   307

clesiastics. ' Had they come for controversy,'
said Neff, ' I should not have been able to receive them, weak as I was; but they carefully
avoided every thing that could fatigue me, and
even listened willingly to the few words I addressed to them. They were surprised to hear
a Protestant speak of the conversion of the heart
and of spiritual life, in the same terms as some
of their most eminent divines. I have often observed that with such persons, it is much better,
if possible, to build up and to plant, than to tear
away and to destroy; most of their prejudices
proceed from their ignorance of all that concerns
true Protestantism, and they are half disarmed,
when we speak to them, without any argument,
of that which constitutes the life, the strength,
and the peace of the soul.'

Certain prescriptions having, in some degree,
restored his strength, he quitted Plombières, but
not without expressing his regret at being deprived of the affectionate care of his medical at-
tendant, Dr. Turck, who is well known to the
visitors at Plombières, for his humane disposition, as well as for his professional talents. This
time too, the journey again seemed to revive the
invalid a little, and on his arrival at Geneva, some
faint hopes were cherished; "but very soon," said
one of his friends, "as though the strength of
his body had been absorbed by that of his mind,
he became worse than before."

The period of his sufferings, at which we are

now arrived, was long and dreary; his stomach
could scarcely bear a little milk whey, for even
with this he often suffered terribly from indigestion, and the pain it caused was so violent, that
he could not venture to take this slight nourishment, until after he had endured the pangs of
hunger for many hours. When he was no longer
able to go out of doors, they contrived all kinds
of manual occupation to assist his digestion.
Conversation was forbidden him: only a small
number of his friends were permitted to enjoy
the privilege of seeing him, and during these
visits, they could only press his hand, and render him some trifling service. He loved to see
them for a few moments, and when he was fatigued, he made a sign for them to leave him.
" It was most heart-rending," said a spectator of
his sufferings, " to behold him, thus pale and
emaciated, his large eyes beaming with an expression of fortitude and pain; covered, from
head to foot, with four or five woollen garments,
which he was obliged to change frequently;
submitting, in silence, and with the greatest
calmness, to the application of the moxas [1], a
painful operation, which was constantly repeated;
suffering the pangs of hunger; counting the
hours, and at last venturing to take something,
then waiting with anxiety till the food, such as
it was, should digest, and thus passing all his

---

[1] An Indian or Chinese moss, used in the cure of some disorders, by burning it on the part affected.

days and nights during a long succession of re-lapses, and of physical prostration, which we sometimes looked upon as a relief."

As he became more and more debilitated and exhausted by hunger, new kinds of decoctions were continually tried, but what he at first took with apparent pleasure he soon refused. His thoughts were perpetually turning towards the Alps, and there he seemed to have centered all his anxieties. If he still cherished an earthly wish, and ventured to hope against hope, it was that the Almighty would again vouchsafe to employ him, in the work which he had there commenced. When he could no longer write to his Alpines himself, he requested his mother to become his amanuensis, and to her he dictated his energetic exhortations, and the touching expression of his never-ceasing solicitude on their account.

In the following extracts from two of these letters, the reader will perceive how strong his feelings were even in death, and will be able to understand something of the force of Christian affections and anxieties, and may study them, as a tablet on which were written the pure and real sentiments of a minister of religion, when all worldly considerations had passed away.

From a Letter, dated October 6th, 1828.

" In the state of complete isolation in which I am kept by my long sickness, a portion of my time is employed in imaginary excursions into Dauphiné. My mind wanders, as in a dream, over the high Alps and the Triève[1]. My heart accompanies it in its progress, and finds itself (not without emotion) in all those places, where it has experienced so many delightful sensations; especially where it has beat for the conversion of poor sinners, and where I have been in the society of precious souls, eager for the word of salvation. Again, I pass through the valleys, and over the mountains, and along the shepherds' paths which I have so often trodden alone, or with my friends. I find myself again in the cottages, in the stables, in the orchards, where I have conversed of heavenly things with all those, who are dear to me in Jesus Christ. I see them all separately or together. I hear them and speak to them. In such moments as these, the feelings which then animated me, naturally resume their influence, and as I did then, I lift up my soul to the Father of every perfect gift, in prayer for his dear children. In this retrospect also, the remembrance of my brethren who are no more, presents itself to my mind, and I sigh deeply, but soon I bless God for them, and I rejoice to see them in the sheepfold, sheltered from all evil, and guarded against any wandering. Doubtless I cannot thus recal times and places, without feeling many very humiliating

[1] The country about Mens is so called.

recollections, nor without thinking that, if now I am, as it were, set aside, and cut off from the service of Christ, I have well deserved to be so. These reflections are salutary ones, and I should be wrong to banish them. But that which throws the deepest shade over the picture, is the number of those who have perished in the wilderness, who, after having come out of Egypt, have returned thither in their hearts, not having had courage to press forward to possess the good land! How many unhappy souls do I remember amongst you, who have been shaken by the preaching of the word, who have trembled at the foot of Sinai, who have exclaimed in anguish, ' what shall I do to be saved?' who have for a time renounced the world, borne its hatred, and suffered affliction with the people of God. Who have then become tired of the way, have no longer dreaded the wrath to come, have forgotten alike the threats and the promises, and have fallen asleep, after having watched, long enough, alas! to be without excuse, and to prepare for themselves eternal sorrow, and the most terrible condemnation! Oh! how the remembrance of them grieves me! how deeply I lament the loss of those dear children, of whom my heart has been long in travail, and who have not been able to attain to the new birth, who have appeared bright as flowers, but like barren flowers, have produced no fruit! But what shall I say of those who have yielded some fruit, who have begun a new life, who have tasted the heavenly gift, who have borne witness to the truth, who have even brought many to the light of it, and who have returned, like the sow to her wallowing in the mire, who have forgotten the purification of their past sins; who have forsaken the right way like Balaam, and have done despite unto the Spirit of grace, wherewith they have been sanctified? Take heed, dear friends, of that expression of the Saviour: ' Abide in me, as the branch abides in the vine.' He does not only say there, as he did elsewhere: ' Come unto me,' but, ' Abide in me!' And how? As the branch, which never separates itself from the vine; without which, and apart from which, it has no life."

From a second Letter, dated March 1829.

" Five months have passed away since you received the address, of which this letter is the sequel, and during that time I have had much experience. I am considerably weaker than I was then, and I shall not be able to arrange methodically what remains for me to say to you, indeed I shall have power to say very little; but I am most anxious to address you. I feel constrained to confirm to-day all that I have before spoken, and all that I preached to you and told you when I was with you; for I have now proved those truths which I then taught you. Yes, now, more than ever, I feel the importance, the absolute importance, of being a Christian indeed, of living in habitual communion with the Saviour, of abiding in him.   It is in the time of trial, that we can speak of these things as we ought.   A Christian without affliction is only a soldier on parade; but I experience it now, and I will openly bear witness of it, whilst God still gives me strength so to do.   It is strictly true, that, through much tribulation, we must enter the kingdom of heaven, and we must personally feel what is said of the Prince of our salvation, ‘ that it became him to be made perfect through affliction.’   Though he were the Son of God, yet ‘ learned he obedience by the things which he suffered.’   How much more need have we ourselves of this instruction.   Yes, I can now say, it is good for me that I have been afflicted; this trial was needful for me.   I felt beforehand that it was requisite, and I do not fear to tell you, that I prayed to the Lord for it.   My situation is indeed painful; I, who delighted so much in an active, stirring life, have long been reduced to the most complete inertion, scarcely able to eat, drink, sleep, speak, or to listen to reading, or to receive the visits of my brethren, and feeling it a great effort to dictate these few lines: I am weighed down by the pains of sickness, and often I am deprived, by agonies, or by the wiles of Satan and my own heart, of the sense of God’s presence, and of the consolations which it would afford me. I can, however, without hesitation declare, that I would not exchange this state of trial, for that in which some of my years have been passed, even in the midst of my ministerial labours ; for though my life may have been spent in the service of Christ, and may have appeared exemplary to the eyes of men, I find in it so much unfaithfulness, so many sins, so many things which, in my sight, and above all, in the sight of the Lord, have polluted my work,—I have passed so much time in forgetfulness of God, that had I still thirty years to live, I should prefer a hundred times over passing them on this bed of languor and anguish, to recovering my health and strength, and not to lead a life more truly Christian, more holy, more entirely devoted to God, than I have done hitherto. Ah! my dear friends! how much time we lose, of how many blessings and graces we deprive ourselves, when we live far from God, in levity and thoughtlessness, in seeking after perishable things, in the gratification of the flesh, and of self-love. Now I feel that it is so, and you will feel it also in the day of trial. Redeem then the time : I cannot repeat it too often ; live unto God, by faith, by prayer, and by serious conversation. But can I recommend duties to you without noticing those, which you are bound to fulfil towards that multitude, who live in the darkness, out of which the Lord has brought you by his grace. Should the Church of Christ be contented, like the garrison of a besieged town, to defend herself and preserve her own territory ? Ought she not, on the contrary, to make continual sallies, and to advance, like a victorious army, over the enemy's land? So soon as a tree ceases to grow, it begins to wither away ; so soon as a Church ceases to advance, it becomes torpid, and begins to decline. Ah ! if you feel the infinite worth of your heavenly calling; if you know that love of Christ which passeth all understanding, and the riches of the glory of his inheritance in the saints, and what is the excellent greatness of his power towards us who believe, if you have tasted how good the Lord is, and how precious is the lot which is fallen to us, if at the same time you know the value of immortal souls, and how dreadful is the fate of those, who know not Jesus, can you ever forget the worth of that glorious title, child of God, which you bear? Can you ever be any thing but Christians, if you have felt what infinite happiness it is to be a Christian ? You will be such, in all things and in all places ; you will wish the world to become such ; each one of you will become, in some wise, a witness of God's grace, a missionary, a preacher, a minister of Christ. Your heart will burn with zeal for the salvation of souls, and from it will ascend, without ceasing, as from a burning altar, sighs and prayers in their behalf. Labour then in the kingdom of God ; be courageous in this holy warfare, give no rest to yourselves. Cease not to importune the Lord, till he re-establish Jerusalem, and till he make it to flourish again upon the earth.

"As to myself, I have every reason to believe that my task is finished; I wait, until by means of trials and afflictions, the Lord shall accomplish within me that work of patience, which must be perfected; and may he then take me, how and when he pleases, to his eternal rest. Having then no hope of seeing you again in this world, and not thinking that I shall be able to write more, I must take leave of you, commending you from this time forward to God and the word of his grace.

"Oh, my dear friends, how many things still remain for me to say to you! to how many things would I still call your attention! but the Lord will supply them.

"Sometimes peruse again and again these last exhortations, which I have given you, and beseech the Lord to enable you to put them in practice. Above all read the Bible: go constantly to that tree of life which bears fruit in all seasons: you will always find there some fruit ripe for you, some word which will do good to your souls. If you have opportunities for any other reading, let it be chosen agreeably to the will of God: I should wish, for instance, that each of you should possess the *Pilgrim's Progress*, and the *Life of Bunyan*, that conscientious and experienced Christian. Try to read also in the Paris Missionary Journal, (second year, No. 3.) the *Life of the Missionary Brainerd.* I hope that they will soon publish those excellent *Letters of the Minister Charles Rieu,* who died in Denmark. Another work which I expect will soon appear, and which I cannot too strongly recommend beforehand, is the *Ancient and Modern History of the Bohemian and Moravian Brethren.* There you will see what a Christian ought to be, and what a true Church of Jesus Christ may be. This work will be too expensive for each one of you to purchase it for himself; but some of you can contribute jointly to have it in common. Lastly, I shall recommend to you, as a book of prayer and edification, as well as a collection of hymns, the compilation published at Geneva, under the title of *Psalms, Hymns, Spiritual Songs, &c.* [1]

" I wish, my very dear friends, my dear brothers and sisters, that I could designate each of you by name; but, thank God, there would be too much to do, and I desire that each of you may read these letters, as if they were addressed to himself in particular; for you know my affection for you all, and how ardently I wish to meet you all again in that kingdom, where ' God will

[1] I have lately had the satisfaction of receiving 12*l.* from a Lady at Sedgwick, and 10*l.* from a Lady at Shrewsbury, to be applied in the purchase of Bibles, and of the Books here recommended by Neff, for these Protestants of the Alps.

wipe away all tears from our eyes, where there will be no more death, neither sorrow, nor crying.'

" Be of good courage, then, my dear friends ! We shall soon meet again, and it will be for ever, for ever ! Think upon this, and grieve not at our short separation. Once more adieu, my dear brothers and sisters in Jesus Christ ! May the Lord bless and keep you ! May he give you that peace and joy, which the world cannot take away !

" Your very affectionate brother,

" FELIX NEFF."

The interest which Neff expressed so forcibly, in his letters, in the fate of his beloved Alpines, led them to believe, that his strength was renovated, and encouraged them to hope, that they should yet see him again in the midst of them [1]. Some of his friends, therefore, wrote to Mens, and to the valleys of Fressinière, and Queyras, and prepared them to expect the worst. The answers, which were received, were full of grief and consternation. In one of them, addressed

---

[1] A few days before his death, he was asked by one of his most intimate friends, if he still adhered to the sentiments, which he had expressed in his two farewell letters to his Alpines, of October and March. His answer was given with all the force that his debilitated frame would permit him to use, " I feel as if I should wish to preach those things even in paradise," and he then asked for a pen that he might sign a confession to that effect, but it was very properly judged that he was too weak for such an effort.

to Neff himself, there was this simple, but fervent expression of affliction and self-reproach.

"It is we, it is we, who are the cause of your long illness. Had we been more ready to listen to you, you would not have had occasion to fatigue yourself in the deep snow, nor to exhaust your lungs, and all the powers of your body. Oh, how much pain has it cost you to teach us: like our good Saviour, you forgot yourself for our sakes. Dear pastor, sensible of the affection you have always manifested towards us, we desire, with all our hearts, to be useful to you. We can say, with truth, that if our lives could be of service to you, we would give them, and then we should not be doing more for you than you have done for us. May the Lord bless you, and grant you patience in this long trial. May he shower upon you a thousand benedictions from on high, and recompense you for all the pains you have taken for us! Your reward is in heaven: an immortal crown awaits you. We will conclude by intreating your prayers in our behalf; unworthy as we are, we do not forget you in ours. Every family, without exception, from the heights of Romas to the foot of the Influs, salutes you, and you will see the names of some of them in this letter. We are your unworthy, but entirely devoted brothers."

These artless and tender lines were followed by a great number of signatures, those of the heads of the families of Dormilleuse and its vicinity, and probably of all who could sign their name. In the same letter these good men proposed to depute two persons from among them to see him once more, or to send him the money, which such a journey would cost, if he needed it; but Neff refused both these offers, lest he should be a charge to them. He displayed his disinterestedness in another way about this time. Having received a bill of 400 francs, which were due to him, he said, " This money is no longer mine, it is for the missionary of the Alps," and he sent it to M. Blanc at Mens, to be employed as the donors had intended.

During this prolonged illness, his friends watched by him by turns, but until the few last nights of his life he would not allow them to remain standing about his bed: he even suffered inconvenience rather than call to them. By day, however, it was necessary to be constantly near him, to lift him up, and to moisten his lips with a sponge steeped in milk, mixed with a little lemon-juice; he took nothing else. They applied friction to his stomach to soothe the pains of hunger, and even in this extremity he retained such a playfulness of mind, that when he would ask one of them to rub him, he called out "give me my dinner."

" [1] His voice became so weak that it was necessary to go very close to him in order to hear

[1] This account of Neff's last days is taken from the " Notice sur Felix Neff" published at Geneva in 1831.

10

it; he spoke with great difficulty and with severe pain, yet he willingly endured this suffering when he had any salutary advice to give us."

"We had the satisfaction," said a narrator of the dying scene, "of being much with him towards the close of his painful career, and we never heard a murmur escape from his lips. He was grateful for the affection shown towards him, and returned it abundantly. Often, after our poor services, he threw his arms round our necks, embraced us, thanked us, and exhorted us with all his soul to devote ourselves to God. 'Believe my experience,' said he, 'He only is your sure trust, He only is truly to be loved. If you should one day be employed in the preaching of the Gospel, take heed not to work to be seen of men. Oh, with how many things of this kind do I reproach myself! My life, which appears to some to have been well employed, has not been a quarter so much so as it might have been! How much precious time have I lost!' He accused himself of unfaithfulness in the employment of his time, and of having been vain-glorious: he, whose labours were scarcely known to a few friends! who had refused to marry, that his heart might be entirely devoted to his Master, and whose ardent charity for his fellow-creatures had brought him, at the age of thirty-one, to his bed of death! Knowing his love for sacred music, we frequently assembled in a room near his own, and sung, in an under tone, verses of his favour-

Y

ite hymns, particularly ' Rien ô Jesus que ta grace,' and a paraphrase on the thirty-first chapter of Jeremiah, which he had himself composed. This singing filled his soul with a thousand feelings and recollections, and affected him so much, that we were obliged to discontinue it, though he did not see us, and he heard us but faintly.

" About a fortnight before his death, he looked on a mirror, and discovering unequivocal signs of dissolution in his countenance, he gave utterance to his joy : ' Oh, yes ! soon, soon I shall be going to my God !' From that time he took no more care of himself : his door was open to all, and the last hours of the missionary became a powerful mission. His chamber was never empty, he had a word for every one, until he was exhausted by it. In the full enjoyment of all his mental faculties, every thing was present to his memory : the most trivial circumstances ; even conversations which he had held many years previously, and he made use of them with extraordinary energy in his exhortations. On his mother's account only did he show the least inquietude : old, feeble, and devoted to him, she could not restrain her tears. Before her, he assumed a firmness which amounted even to reproach ; then, when she left him, no longer able to refrain from weeping himself, his eyes followed her with tenderness, and he would exclaim ' my poor mother !'

" He made presents to his friends, and set

apart some religious books for many persons to whom he still hoped to be useful; after having underlined several passages, he thus wrote the address:——Felix Neff, dying, to ————

" We shall have an indelible recollection of the last letter that he wrote; it was a few days before his death. He was supported by two persons, and, hardly able to see, he traced at intervals, and in large and irregular characters which filled a page, the lines which follow, addressed to some of his beloved friends in the Alps. What must have been the feelings of those who received them, with the persuasion that he, who had traced them, was no more!

" ' Adieu, dear friend, André Blanc, Antoine Blanc, all my friends the Pelissiers, whom I love tenderly; Francis Dumont and his wife; Isaac and his wife; beloved Deslois, Emilie Bonnet, &c. &c.; Alexandrine and her mother; all, all the brethren and sisters of Mens, adieu, adieu. I ascend to our Father in entire peace! Victory! victory! victory! through Jesus Christ.

FELIX NEFF.'

" The last night of his life, we and some other persons remained to sit up with him. Never shall we forget those hours of anguish, so well called the valley of the shadow of death. It was necessary to attend to him constantly, and to

Y 2

hold him in his convulsive struggles; to support his fainting head in our arms, to wipe the cold drops from his forehead, to bend or to straighten his stiffened limbs; the centre of his body only retained any warmth. For a short time he seemed to be choking, and we dare not give him any thing: A few words of Scripture were read to him, but he did not appear to hear; once only, when some one was lamenting to see him suffer so much, and said, ' poor Neff,' he raised his head for an instant, fixed his large eyes full of affection upon his friend, and again closed them. During the long night of agony we could only pray and support him. In the morning, the fresh air having a little revived him, he made a sign that he should be carried to a higher bed; they placed him on this bed in a sitting posture, and the struggles of death began. For four hours we saw his eyes raised to heaven; each breath, that escaped from his panting bosom, seemed accompanied with a prayer; and at that awful period, when the heaviness of death was upon him, in the ardent expression of his supplication he appeared more animated than any of us. We stood around him weeping, and almost murmuring at the duration of his sufferings, but the power of his faith was so visible in his countenance, that our faith too was restored by it, it seemed as though we could see his soul hovering on his lips, impatient for eternity.

At last we so well understood what his vehement desire was, that with one impulse we all exclaimed : Come, Lord Jesus, come quickly.

" Two days afterwards, (his death took place 12th of April, 1829,) we accompanied his remains to the tomb. Over his resting-place were read some beautiful verses of that Word which shall never pass away. We then prayed, and in compliance with his wish, his numerous friends, who were assembled at the grave, sang together those lines of M. Vinet, of which the stanzas conclude thus :—

" Ils ne sont pas perdus, ils nous ont devancés."

CHAPTER XIV.

REVIEW OF NEFF'S CHARACTER—ITS VALUE AS AN EXAMPLE—HIS PRACTICAL WISDOM AND USEFULNESS—HIS PRUDENCE AND CAUTION—HIS GENTLENESS OF SPIRIT—HIS CONCILIATING MANNERS—TWO REMARKABLE TRAITS—NEFF COMPARED WITH BERNARD GILPIN, GEORGE HERBERT, OBERLIN AND HENRY MARTYN—TESTIMONIES TO NEFF'S SERVICES.

WHEN I determined to publish the preceding Memoir, I had two objects in view; first to make known the existence of another mountain church [1]

[1] The existence of branches of the Christian Church not *sects*, to which, and through which apostolical Christianity has been transmitted from age to age, without any admixture of Romish error, is a truth in history, which must be agitated, until more justice shall be done to the question by ecclesiastical writers. The author of a " History of the Church," published under the superintendence of the Society for the Diffusion of Useful Knowledge, the best Church history which has yet appeared, will, I am sure, receive this hint with the same spirit of candour and inquiry, which he has displayed throughout the whole of his work. In chapter xviii. pp. 353—355, has he not misapplied the terms, *heresy, heretics*, and *sect*, in application to the Waldenses of Piedmont, for example? My object, of which he has kindly made honourable mention, was not to prove the apostolical *descent* of the Vaudois, for this would be a vain attempt, but to prove their *apostolical Christianity*, from time im-

in the Alps, besides that of the Waldenses of Piedmont, which has continued independent of Rome, and free from its corruptions, ever since it was first planted; and secondly, to hold up the example of a village pastor, who in our own times has displayed " the zeal of an apostle, and the constancy of a martyr."

Whoever has a station in the Christian Church to fill, and appointed duties to discharge, may find something in Neff's character, which is worthy of imitation, and those, whose place it is to receive with meekness the engrafted word, may learn to estimate its importance, from the earnestness with which that devoted servant of God delivered it.

The striking peculiarity in Neff's character, which I will now endeavour to draw out into its full breadth, was his practical wisdom and usefulness as a Christian minister. No man ever preached, or insisted upon the main and essential doctrinal points of the Gospel, more strongly than he did; these were put prominently forward in all his sermons, in his conversations, in

memorial, and their independence of Rome, at periods when the Church of Rome pretends that all, who professed to be Christians, were either in communion with her, or were heretics. Now if I have proved this their perpetual apostolical Christianity, how could the Vaudois be *heretics*, when they were professing the true faith? and why call them a *sect*, when they were always a branch of the vine, abiding in the vine, and never cut themselves off from any community, of which they were once a part?

his correspondence, and in his private diaries :
but at the same time he exacted attention to the
ordinary duties of life, with all the strenuous-
ness of one who would admit of no compromise.
It was his anxiety to build up the Christian on a
foundation, where self-dependence, vain-glory,
and imaginary merit, were to have no place
whatever; and yet every act of his ministry
proved, that he set a just value on knowledge
and attainments.   It was his labour of love to
show, that whenever any addition is made to our
stock of knowledge, we not only gain something
in the way of enjoyment, but are laying up a
store for the improvement of our moral and religious feelings, and of our general habits of
industry.   The spiritual advancement of his
flock was the great end and object of all his
toils; but no man ever took a warmer interest
in the temporal comforts of those about him, and
this he evinced by instructing them in the management of their fields and gardens, in the construction of their cottages, and in employing all
his own acquirements, in philosophy and science,
for the amelioration of their condition.   He was
not only the Apostle, but as somebody said of
Oberlin, " he was also the Triptolemus" of the
High Alps.

To discharge the proper duties of a preacher
of the Gospel, was a vehement desire with Neff,
strong as a passion : his heart and soul were in
them ; yet he often left this walk, so glorious in

his eyes, to follow another track, and to point out those things to the notice of his people, which related to their worldly conveniences. It was his high and lofty ambition to elevate their thoughts and hopes to the noblest objects, to which immortal beings can aspire, and to raise the standard, until they should reach to the fulness of the stature of Christ : and yet he so condescended to things of low estate, as to become a teacher of a, b, c, not only to ignorant infancy, but to the dull and unpliant capacities of adults. Beginning with the most tiresome rudiments, he proceeded upwards, leading on his scholars methodically, kindly, and patiently, until he had made them proficients in reading, writing, and arithmetic, and could lead them into the pleasanter paths of music, geography, history, and astronomy. His mind was too enlarged to fear that he should be teaching his peasant boys too much. It was his aim to show what a variety of enjoyments may be extracted out of knowledge, and that even the shepherd, and the goatherd of the mountain side, will be all the happier and the better for every piece of solid information that he can acquire.

Neff was a man of the most ardent and elastic zeal, else he never could have dedicated himself so entirely to the work of a missionary pastor in a foreign country : yet he brought the good sense of a masculine understanding to bear upon all his religious projects : he exercised a degree of prudence seldom witnessed in conjunction with such ardour, and he was constantly checking the ebullitions of his spirit, and tempering his zeal with salutary prudence. The nicest discretion, and the most judicious caution, distinguished his proceedings. This was especially manifested in the selection and training of his catechists. He knew that a few young men, well prepared, would do more good among their countrymen, than a host of undisciplined enthusiasts and ill-taught novices.

The broad distinctions and uncompromising truths of Protestantism were matters of awful sanctity with Neff; and yet, though he was the pastor of a flock opposed to Popery by all the strong prejudices of hereditary separation, I might almost say of deep-rooted aversion, with dogmatical and polemical Protestantism he would have nothing to do. He made number-less converts from Romanism, not so much by argument and discussion, as by mildly inculcating the true spirit of the Gospel; not by dwelling on topics of strife, or on points of difference, but on points of universal agreement, and by exhibiting our common Christianity in its most persuasive form, until their hearts melted before the one Mediator and Intercessor, and they said, your God shall be our God, and your creed shall be our creed.

He was rigid in his notions of Christian deportment; yet there was a meekness and a kindness of manner about him, which conciliated all, and convinced them that he had their best interests at heart; so much so, that perhaps no man was ever more reverenced and loved. When I traversed the villages and hamlets which had constituted his charge, two years after his removal from them, the recollection of his services was still cherished with so much fondness and veneration, that his name was never pronounced but with a seriousness and tenderness of voice, which assured me, that he still lived in their affections, and that he will form the subject of discourse and admiration, as long as one of the present race shall survive.

Such was the pastor of the Alps in his extensive parish, consisting of scattered and remote hamlets. Now, if Neff,—his ministerial duties spreading over such length and breadth; the boundary lines of his charge stretching far and wide over mountains, and barriers of ice and snow, and across rapid rivers and deep ravines, and having to encounter all the difficulties of distance, climate, unknown language, and those other impediments usually thrown in the way of a foreigner,—if Neff could yet propose to himself, and could effect such improvements as were the objects of his ministry, may not the clergy of our own Church look upon their field of labour with hope and courage. With the same promise of support from above: with parishes for the most part of moderate extent, with all the

advantages of endowment [1]: with facilities derived from scholastic establishments of old standing—from institutions, where teachers are trained
to their profession,—from societies which supply
cheap and useful books: with the aid of an
authorized version of Scripture, where every
copy that is used is the same, word for word,
(an advantage this, which is unknown upon the
continent,) and with innumerable other resources, what may not yet be done to extend our
usefulness, and to make us to grow in favour

[1] The tendency of endowments has often been discussed.
Some are inclined to think that they are not beneficial to the
cause of religion, and it has been argued, that a minister of the
word may be safely left to the generosity of his flock, that a
congregation will never suffer an active and pious clergyman
to be insufficiently provided for.   The name of Oberlin is now
proverbial, and synonymous for that of an eminent and meritorious pastor.   At the revolution, Oberlin, like the rest of the
established clergy of France, was deprived of his scanty income.
This was in 1789.   At first his parishioners came forward with
generous alacrity, and declared that their excellent minister
should be none the worse—that they would raise 1400 francs,
or about 56l. a year for him at the least.   The first year they
subscribed a purse of 1133 francs: the second year their libe-
rality fell down to 400 francs (16l.)   The pastor saw how things
were going on, and requested that there might be no more
annual collections for him: he was unwilling to appear to be
drawing from the poor or the reluctant; he would leave it
entirely to their free will, unsolicited offerings: they knew the
way to his house, he said, and might bring to him what and
when they pleased.   In 1794, few as were Oberlin's wants, his
own resources and his parishioners' bounty had so far failed
him, that he was obliged to undertake the charge of ten or
twelve pupils for his subsistence!

with God and man, if we will but diligently and thankfully employ all the means, with which we are so abundantly supplied !

It has been stated by one of Neff's most intimate friends, that there were two traits in his character, which are seldom found in one possessed of such powers of mind as himself, and whose whole life, from the period of his maturity, had been a career of activity and usefulness. The first, that he was entirely free from any ambitious views, he had no desire to be the first, that thorn in the side of the Christian Church; and though his labours had in reality been more abundant than those of most of his brethren, yet he never undervalued the performances of others, and it never seemed to be a feeling in his own mind, that he had "laboured more abundantly than they all." The second was, such extreme humility, that he even regarded his own energy and activity, as something that partook of the nature of sin; as being an obstacle in the way of his more frequent communion with God; as distracting his thoughts from himself, and those secret contemplations which are needful for the individual. He was fully sensible that an active spirit, and an affectionate concern for the temporal and spiritual concerns of others, are qualities excellent in themselves, and indispensable for the good of the Christian commonwealth, and for the extension of Christ's kingdom; but in his own case, he was afraid that they absorbed other qualities.   He knew that it was not the establishment of schools, the conducting of missions, or the preaching to others, which of themselves constitute the life of the soul : on the contrary, that the strenuous pursuit of great usefulness often becomes a snare and a pitfall, and a covering under which pride lurks : and he felt, with the apostle, the necessity of bringing himself under subjection, lest, when he had preached to others, he himself might become a castaway.   It was under the influence of this feeling, that he was inclined to set small value upon his own labours.

From his very youth he seems to have had continual conflicts with himself : the life of the chamois hunter would have been most in accordance with the natural flight of his spirits, and his ardent attachment to mountain pursuits : but he controlled his wishes, when he was first of an age to seek employment, and he submitted to the confinement, and to the dull sameness of a nursery garden.   Afterwards, when circumstances placed him in the army, and a path was opened to him that was leading rapidly to military reputation, and to the indulgence of some of his early schemes, he turned aside from the tempting prospect, and determined not to know any thing save Jesus Christ, and him crucified. "His temper," said another of his friends, after his death, "naturally violent and unbending, was completely subdued."

It is not venturing too much to say, that Neff's character will bear comparison with four of the most distinguished ornaments in his own profession : with Bernard Gilpin, George Herbert, Frederick Oberlin, and Henry Martyn.

His sphere of action was not, indeed, so concentrated as that of the three first; and we have not the parsonage tales and anecdotes to adorn the page of his history, which grace the biography of the pastors of Houghton, Bemerton, and Waldbach;—nor was it so extensive as that of the missionary Martyn; it partook, however, of the fixed charge of the three first, and of the difficulties of the last.

In the Memoirs of Gilpin, there are several particulars to which passages in Neff's life bear resemblance. Gilpin's parish, Houghton, contained no less than fourteen villages, and had been much neglected before his arrival. Neff's contained as many, or more, and its religion was little more than traditionary. The people of Houghton had been so long excluded from all means of information, that king Edward's proclamation, for a change in the religious services of the country, had not even been heard of at the time of that prince's death. So, in parts of Val Queyras, the edict of toleration of Louis XVI. was not known till four years after its publication. Gilpin's admonitions and example were so impressive, and were so well received, that in a few years a most extraordinary change was observed in the whole neighbourhood of his church: and so among Neff's flock.   Gilpin thought that kindness and moderation, on his part, would produce more conversions than the strife of controversy: and it appears from the accounts of his intercourse with non-conformists, how much he was opposed to all intolerant principles, and how wrong he thought it, on the one hand, to assail an established Church with violent hands, and on the other to molest and vex a quiet separatist. Neff's letter [1] on establishments and separation, and the whole page of his ministerial history, will show that they were kindred spirits.

The following extract from the Life of Gilpin, compared with De Thou's [2] account of Val Fressinière in his time, and with Neff's description of the poverty and ignorance of his Alpines, of his " obtruding Christianity on the notice of the people," by following them to their habitations, when the winter season confined them within doors; and to the fairs and places of resort, when they were likely to be found there; and of preaching to them in any place most convenient for his purpose:—this will extend the parallel. In fact, there is ever the closest resemblance between the means, which all wise, and pious, and active-minded pastors employ, under similar circumstances."

" Gilpin used frequently to visit the most neglected parts.   In each place he stayed two

[1] See p. 25.   [2] See p. 82.

or three days: and his method was to call the people about him, and lay before them, in as plain a way as possible, the danger of leading wicked, or even careless lives: explaining to them the nature of true religion, instructing them in the duties they owed to God, their neighbour, and themselves, and showing how greatly a moral and religious conduct would contribute to their present as well as future happiness.   There is a tract of country upon the borders of Northumberland, called Redesdale and Tynedale, of all barbarous places in the north, at that time, the most barbarous.   In this dreadful country, where no man would ever travel that could help it, Mr. Gilpin [1] never failed to spend some part of every year.   He generally chose the Christmas holidays for this journey, because he found the people at that season most disengaged, and most easily assembled. He had set places for preaching, which were as regularly attended as the assize towns on a circuit.   If he came where there was a church, he made use of it: if not, he made use of barns, or any other large building, where great crowds of people were sure to attend him, some for his instruction, and others for his charity.   This was a very difficult and laborious employment.   The

[1] Owing to the dearth of fit and able men in those times, persons of Mr. Gilpin's character and talents had licences to preach in different parts of the diocese, out of their own parishes.

z

country was so poor, that what provision he could get extreme hunger only made palatable. The badness of the weather, and the badness of the roads, through a mountainous country, and at that season covered with snow, exposed him often to great hardships. All this he cheerfully underwent, esteeming such sufferings well compensated by the advantages, which he hoped might accrue from them to his uninstructed fellow-creatures [1]."

The resemblance between George Herbert and Neff will be seen at once by comparing the ministry of the latter with Herbert's description, and his own exemplification of the " Country Parson:" in his performance of the great and neglected duty of catechising, in the true sense of the word; in his display of all the sympathies and affections of a pastor, and in the corresponding reverence of his parishioners, who would leave their ploughs when his church bell rang for morning prayers, to attend the summons; in his extraordinary love of sacred music, and persuasion that the introduction of it at hours of devotion is a strong help to piety; and lastly, in the briefness of his career, which was shortened by his ministerial labours. Herbert's and Neff's bed of sickness were to each a school of discipline, for which they were thankful and rejoiced. " I do not repine," said Herbert, " but am pleased with my want of health; my heart is

[1] Gilpin's Life of Bernard Gilpin.

now fixed on that place, where true joy is only to be found. I praise God I am prepared to make my bed in the dark: I praise him, that I have practised mortification, and have endeavoured to die daily, that I may not die eternally." We have seen what Neff's dying bed was.

Neff professed to make Oberlin his pattern, and the parallel between the two appears—in their charge of mountain parishes of wide extent, and in the prudent manner, in which each devoted himself to the improvement of a half civilized and indigent population. So much has been said on this subject in the course of the present work, that it need not be further enlarged on.

With equal justice may Neff, in his character of a missionary, be likened unto the devoted and self-denying Henry Martyn. Like him he left his home for a distant country, when he was yet in his youth, and when his heart was still fondly clinging to objects of affection in his own dear land. Without any object of ambition, curiosity, or avarice, he took up his pilgrim's staff, and went forth among a strange people, whose habits and language were new to him; and laying all that he had,—his time, his abilities, his knowledge,—and all that he was, on the altar of his Redeemer, he encountered deprivations and hardships of every kind, for a race who had no other claim upon him, than that they were of the human species, and of the Protestant faith.

z 2

" With the Gospel in his hand, and the Saviour
in his heart," he went his way, braving the rage
of climates, and submitting to the drudgery of
learning an unknown tongue, and to the disagreeable necessity of seeking society which was
oftentimes offensive to him, and of enduring all
things, and becoming all things, in the patient
hope of being the means of saving some.   But
as it was with Martyn, so with Neff, when he
was once embarked in the cause to which he had
consecrated himself, nothing then moved or disgusted him, but every living creature, in whom
he took an interest, was soon entwined around
his affectionate heart.   There are many things
in the sort of life which a missionary pastor
must lead, which are so revolting to the natural
man, that no feelings of mere kindness or benevolence can enable him to endure them.   It is the
power of the Gospel working in his heart, which
can alone sustain the Christian under them.

The following testimonies to the conduct, and
services of the estimable subject of this Memoir,
will close this review of his character.   They are
taken from the Reports of the Continental Society, whose agent he was for many years.   Without professing to approve of all the measures of
this association, or to subscribe to all the sentiments [1] advanced in their printed statements, I

[1] Is it wise, is it just, to make such sweeping charges as the
following ?—the first is contained in one of the Reports of the
Society, and the second in a speech delivered at the Society's

cannot forbear taking this opportunity of observing, that the thanks of every true Christian are due to a Society, which brought forward and fostered such a man as Felix Neff, which furnished him with the pecuniary means of discharging the duties of an authorised pastor of the established Protestant Church of France, when the regular stipend was withheld for want of letters of naturalization which the govern-

general meeting, and published in one of its annual statements :

" And it is of the utmost importance that all persons, who desire that the preaching of the Gospel may be heard on the Continent, should bear continually in mind, that there the word ' PROTESTANT' means nothing but a person who does not go through the ceremonies prescribed by the Church of Rome, and who has, together with the *superstitions*, for the most part, renounced also every *fundamental* of *Christianity*."

" We have also heard to-day, what Continental Protestantism is. And if I were to state what, in my opinion, it is, from my own examination, I would say, it is composed half of the *Deist*, and half of the persecuting spirit of the *Papist*. In fact, the very spirit of persecution on the Continent is not only allowed, but *encouraged*, by those very persons who call themselves *Protestants !* When we hear of Protestantism, we think it is something like our own Protestantism, which is the Protestantism of the Bible : but that is not the Protestantism of the Continent ; the Protestantism of the Continent is a system, from which the whole of true Christianity is excluded but the forms. In fact, Sir, of the two, if I were to judge, I should say, I do believe that Popery is the best. Is not, then, the institution of such a society as this indispensably necessary ?"

Such statements as these are discreditable both to the individual who makes them, and to the Society which gives them a place in its Reports.

ment offices vexatiously delayed to send him, and which generously continued to remit his salary to him, during his last illness, for many months after he had ceased to be one of its labourers. Something, objectionable to our own pre-conceived opinions of what is most expedient, may be found in every religious and benevolent society, but we are not justified in seeking an excuse in this, for refusing our just praise to what is truly good and beneficial.

" One of the agents of the Society, Mr. Neff, labours as suffragan to a Protestant pastor, among these mountainous districts, and visits different places where the truth was formerly held so pure, amidst all the corruptions of the days of antichristian tyranny, but where now little else than mere nominal Christianity is to be found. With indefatigable zeal he ascends the mountains, and descends into the valleys, to preach and catechise the children of the inhabitants; often meeting with great opposition, and many difficulties arising from their ignorance and prejudice against the Gospel. He has been the instrument of a considerable revival in some parts, and in one district, more than two hundred children are under his superintendence as catechumens, of whom he speaks in the following terms :—' I cannot too earnestly recommend to your remembrance at the throne of God, and of the Lamb, this numerous family.' Probably, there is not on the whole Continent another flock of two hundred catechumens, under the care of the same pastor, instructed in pure doctrine with so much simplicity, and solely founded on the New Testament."

" Neff is the spiritual father of these and also of several others in the Churches I afterwards visited. He is particularly calculated for this parish, being capable of undergoing fatigue, indifferent about the conveniences of life, full of zeal, preaching at the end of a long day's march, in the mountains, with unabated energy. The Churches being separated far from each other, in a difficult and miserable country, only a person of such qualities could discharge with efficiency the duty of a minister. The inhabitants are a race of the most simple habits, and until Neff came amongst them, quite ignorant. Dormilleuse, Minsas, and Violins, are altogether Protestant; the lower valleys contain many Catholics. Dormilleuse is the highest of all, and of difficult access; the snow, I am told, lies eight months on the ground, and they have but a small tract of poor land to furnish their subsistence; this retreat has been at all times inaccessible to the superstition of Rome, whether acting by violence or persuasion. The last attempt to convert them was of the latter nature; a Church was built, and a curé sent to reside among the simple inhabitants, but he was not able to

10

gain a single proselyte. The committee will not rightly appreciate the valuable services of Neff, without taking into their view the revival that has taken place in the parish of ———. Mr. ———, the pastor, owes his own self, also, to Neff."

" Before concluding, I have to mention to you the existence of a few more Protestant communities, inhabiting the mountains of Haut Dauphiné, near Briançon in France, and only separated by a high Alp from the valleys of the Vaudois. I was within a few hours' walk of them, and if the passage had not still been blocked up by snow, I should have gone thither. There is at present a Mr. Neff amongst them, who does the duty alternately at the six different churches. From all I have heard of him, he seems to be pervaded by a truly evangelical spirit, and has been the means of producing a great awakening amongst the people. I was confirmed in my opinion by the account given of him by the venerable Mr. M———: ' Monsieur Neff, (he said) étoit ici il n'y a pas long temps, et il a prêché dans mon Eglise. C'étoit un discours excellent et d'accord avec l'évangile ; bien calculé de faire une bonne impression. C'est un véritable enfant de Dieu et qui fait beaucoup de bien ; il ne craint ni de fatigues, ni de froid, ni de privations d'aucune sorte. Il a passé tout l'hiver dans les montagnes, et on ne joue plus comme auparavant, on ne danse plus les dimanches, les gens semblent inspirés par un esprit et un zéle pour la religion, comme on ne se rappelle d'aucune autre époque.'   May his labours be crowned with still more and more success, and may he be the blessed instrument of turning many, many more from ' darkness unto light, and from the power of Satan unto God.' "

Such were the testimonies rendered to the services of Felix Neff, whilst he was yet alive, and in the exercise of his ministry.   Now that he is gone to his rest, may this record of his Christian Virtues have the effect of commending him, not only to the esteem, but also to the imitation of those, to whom the memory of such men is dear.

POSTSCRIPT

TO

THE SECOND EDITION.

A SHORT time after the publication of this Memoir, I had the satisfaction of conversing with the excellent Mr. Gaussen, late pastor at Satigny, and now Professor of Divinity, in the New School of Theology at Geneva. Mr. Gaussen was one of those dear friends of Felix Neff, who was acquainted with him when he first thought of being consecrated to the service of his Redeemer, who corresponded with him while he was labouring in the midst of his Alpine flock, who was with him during his last illness, and who followed his remains to the grave. He assured me, that the character of this highly-gifted and devoted servant of God could not be appreciated too warmly, or described in colours too strong; and he gave me reason to hope, that I should receive some communications from Geneva respecting Neff's early career, which would fill up those gaps in the Memoir, which have been thought to leave it meagre and unsatisfactory upon some points. These, however, have not yet reached me ; but there were a few reminiscences in illustration of Neff's ardent character, and peculiar turn of mind, which I collected from Mr. Gaussen, and which I am now glad to record.

Neff attributed great efficacy to a question which was solemnly put to him, by Mr. Gallard, if I remember right, whilst he was in the barracks at Geneva.—— Are *you* in Christ ? Do you belong to Christ ? He used to represent the searching effects produced at the moment, and the after convictions and scrutiny of conscience and condition, to which the question led. The whole force of the inquiry rushed upon his mind, and it suggested a most serious reference, with prayer for guidance and grace, to those passages in Scripture which speak of " hope in Christ," " Consolation in Christ," " of being made alive in Christ," and of becoming a " new creature," by being " in Christ."

Neff afterwards became instrumental himself in awakening a soldier to a sense of his spiritual danger, by placing the whole truth of his situation before him, in one or two strong sentences. The soldier, in a moment of strong excitement, had killed a man ; but having been a great favourite with his companions, those, who were permitted to visit him in prison, lulled his conscience to sleep by telling him that his crime was venial, as being the result of sudden and unpremeditated violence. Neff pursued a very different course. As soon as he accosted him, he charged him with the enormity of his guilt, and told him that it was his habitual forgetfulness of God, which had led to the commission of his crime. The man's heart was softened, he beheld himself in his full deformity, and from that time began to seek for pardon and reconciliation in the atonement and intercession of Jesus Christ.

Neff had taken great pains with a drummer, while he was in the army, and believed that he had been instrumental in improving him. Some years after, hearing that he had left the army, and was employed as a herdsman on the Jura, he undertook a journey of fifteen or sixteen miles to a mountain chalet, in quest of the object of his former pious interest, and did not give up the search until he found him, and ascertained that his soul was right with God.

It was a matter of conscience with him never to lose an opportunity of conversing on serious subjects with those, who were thrown in his way, and he was particularly attentive in addressing his " word in season" to the domestics of the families where he was visiting. His happy tact of seizing the right moment, his insight into character, his talent of discoursing in a style most suitable to the person and occasion, his wonderful command of scriptural language and illustration, and his facility of falling into the tone of conversation, which was likely to be impressive, gave him singular advantage in conveying colloquial instruction. With the soldier he would converse in military language, and explain his meaning by images and similes drawn from the garrison, or the camp, or the field of battle, or the implements and engines of warfare. With the mountaineer he would embellish his discourse with allusions to the sublimest objects in nature. With persons of polished manners he would talk in a strain, which displayed the variety of his information, and the refinement of his taste, without losing for one moment the simplicity of a faithful minister of the Gospel. On the other hand, with the peasant and the rustic he would use the most familiar comparisons, without compromising the solemnity of his subject. Remonstrating one day with some country people, who were calling their better-disposed neighbours Puritans, and Momiers (Methodists), he told them that they were like silly hens, whose folly induces them to prevent the young ducklings, which they have hatched from taking to the water, and who cannot understand the enjoyment of the element, to which their young brood would commit themselves.

When Neff found it hopeless to make an impression, by charging the individual directly with his obduracy or vicious propensities, he would dexterously mask his attack, by directing his observations not against the person himself, but against another of similar frame of mind. Speaking of his own success by this mode of instruction, he used to say, " Je brosse les gens sur l'habit d'un autre."

" Ne faites pas les doctrines carrées," was another of his sayings : and proofs of his great anxiety to convert, and not to proselytize, to win over to Christ, and not to a sect or party, have been already given (in the letter where he complained of the rage for controversy, which displayed itself so much in the intercourse of some of his Protestant friends with Roman Catholics, and in the observation which he made at Plombières, after his discourse with some young Romish ecclesiastics), but a more striking example remains to be adduced. While Neff was in France he accidentally found himself in the company of a Roman Catholic curé, who did not know him. Their route lay towards the same place, and as they journeyed together the conversation took a religious turn. Our pastor, with his usual good sense and right feeling, spoke fervently on the faith and duties of a minister of the Gospel, but he did not drop a single word which could offend the prejudices, or rouse the suspicion of his companion, who was gradually moved to take a deep interest in the new views of a spiritual life, which were opened before him. They came to a Roman Catholic church, and the curé invited his unknown counsellor to enter the sanctuary, and to implore God's blessing on their conversation. Neff readily complied, they breathed their silent prayers before the altar, and they parted without the curé being aware of any difference in their religious opinions. " I perceived," said Neff, when he related this anecdote, " that the priest's heart was touched, and I did not disturb the pious feelings of the moment, by avowing myself, or by attempting to square his religious sentiments by my own."

Such was the life and conversation of this extraordinary man ; such was his " wisdom to win souls," making himself " servant unto all, that he might gain the more," " and all things to all men, that he might by all means save some."

THE END.

LONDON:
GILBERT AND RIVINGTON, PRINTERS,
ST. JOHN'S SQUARE.

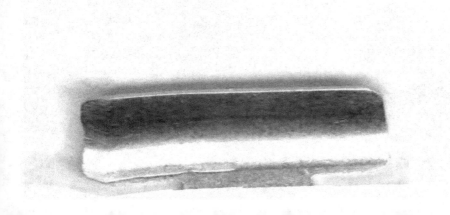

Check Out More Titles From HardPress Classics Series In this collection we are offering thousands of classic and hard to find books. This series spans a vast array of subjects – so you are bound to find something of interest to enjoy reading and learning about.

Subjects:
Architecture
Art
Biography & Autobiography
Body, Mind &Spirit
Children & Young Adult
Dramas
Education
Fiction
History
Language Arts & Disciplines
Law
Literary Collections
Music
Poetry
Psychology
Science
…and many more.

Visit us at www.hardpress.net

Im TheStory

personalised classic books

"Beautiful gift.. lovely finish,
My Niece loves it, so precious!"

Helen R Brumfieldon

★★★★★

UNIQUE
GIFT

FOR KIDS, PARTNERS
AND FRIENDS

Timeless books such as:

Kids

Alice in Wonderland · The Jungle Book · The Wonderful Wizard of Oz
Peter and Wendy · **Robin Hood** · The Prince and The Pauper
The Railway Children · Treasure Island · A Christmas Carol

Adults

Romeo and Juliet · Dracula

Highly
Customizable

Change
Books Title

Replace
Characters Names
with yours

Upload
Photo (for
inside pages)

Add
Inscriptions

Visit
Im TheStory .com
and order yours today!